OXFORD WORLD'S CLASSICS

COUSIN HENRY

ANTHONY TROLLOPE (1815–82), the son of a failing London barrister, was brought up an awkward and unhappy youth amidst debt and privation. His mother maintained the family by writing, but Anthony's own first novel did not appear until 1847, when he had at length established a successful Civil Service career in the Post Office, from which he retired in 1867. After a slow start, he achieved fame, with 47 novels and some 16 other books, and sales sometimes topping 100,000. He was acclaimed an unsurpassed portraitist of the lives of the professional and landed classes, especially in his perennially popular *Chronicles of Barsetshire* (1855–67), and his six brilliant Palliser novels (1864–80). His fascinating *Autobiography* (1883) recounts his successes with an enthusiasm which stems from memories of a miserable youth. Throughout the 1870s he developed new styles of fiction, but was losing critical favour by the time of his death.

JULIAN THOMPSON is Fellow in English at Regent's Park College, Oxford. He has also edited Trollope's *The Small House at Allington* for Penguin, and for Robinson Publishing, the *Collected Shorter Fiction* of Anthony Trollope and the *Collected Shorter Fiction* of Wilkie Collins.

OXFORD WORLD'S CLASSICS

For almost 100 years Oxford World's Classics have brought readers closer to the world's great literature. Now with over 700 titles—from the 4,000-year-old myths of Mesopotamia to the twentieth century's greatest novels—the series makes available lesser-known as well as celebrated writing.

The pocket-sized hardbacks of the early years contained introductions by Virginia Woolf, T. S. Eliot, Graham Greene, and other literary figures which enriched the experience of reading. Today the series is recognized for its fine scholarship and reliability in texts that span world literature, drama and poetry, religion, philosophy and politics. Each edition includes perceptive commentary and essential background information to meet the changing needs of readers.

OXFORD WORLD'S CLASSICS

====

ANTHONY TROLLOPE

Cousin Henry

====

Edited with an Introduction and Notes by
JULIAN THOMPSON

OXFORD
UNIVERSITY PRESS

OXFORD
UNIVERSITY PRESS

Great Clarendon Street, Oxford OX2 6DP

Oxford University Press is a department of the University of Oxford.
It furthers the University's objective of excellence in research, scholarship,
and education by publishing worldwide in

Oxford New York

Athens Auckland Bangkok Bogotá Buenos Aires Calcutta
Cape Town Chennai Dar es Salaam Delhi Florence Hong Kong Istanbul
Karachi Kuala Lumpur Madrid Melbourne Mexico City Mumbai
Nairobi Paris São Paulo Singapore Taipei Tokyo Toronto Warsaw

with associated companies in Berlin Ibadan

Oxford is a registered trade mark of Oxford University Press
in the UK and in certain other countries

Published in the United States
by Oxford University Press Inc., New York

Introduction, Note on the Text, Explanatory Notes
© Julian Thompson 1987

The moral rights of the author have been asserted

Database right Oxford University Press (maker)

First published as a World's Classics paperback 1987
Reissued as an Oxford World's Classics paperback 1999

British Library Cataloguing in Publication Data

Data available

Library of Congress Cataloging in Publication Data

Trollope, Anthony, 1815–1882.
Cousin Henry.
(Oxford world's classics)
Bibliography: p.
I. Thompson, Julian.
II. Title.
PR5684.C65 1987 823'.8 87–5749

ISBN 0–19–283846–6

1 3 5 7 9 10 8 6 4 2

Printed in Great Britain by
Cox & Wyman Ltd.
Reading, Berkshire

CONTENTS

Introduction   vii

Note on the Text   xxv

Select Bibliography   xxix

A Chronology of Anthony Trollope   xxxii

COUSIN HENRY   1

Explanatory Notes   281

ACKNOWLEDGEMENTS

I SHOULD like to thank Stephen Wall and A. O. J. Cockshut for help and advice given during the preparation of this edition.

J.T.

INTRODUCTION

THE plot of *Cousin Henry* centres on the will of Indefer Jones, the aged squire of Llanfeare in Carmarthenshire. Jones has scruples—familiar among Trollopian landed gentry—about the need to leave his property in the male line, but has more or less decided to pass it on to his favourite niece, Isabel Brodrick, whom he has as good as adopted, and whom his tenants have taken to their hearts. In his dotage, however, he reconsiders. The will is altered, and Henry Jones, a timid and unprepossessing London insurance clerk, is brought down to Llanfeare and shown round the estate. But Henry is a hard man to like, and his timid and cringing behaviour fails to impress the squire, who again alters his will, in favour of Isabel. He hides the new document in a well-thumbed volume of sermons, but dies before he can tell anybody where it is. By accident Cousin Henry, still at Llanfeare, finds the will, but keeps silent about his discovery. The previous will, in his favour, is proved, he takes possession of Llanfeare, and at this point Trollope's detailed investigation of his character and dilemma begins. Cousin Henry lacks the courage to destroy the hidden will, but is too self-seeking to produce it, so he takes to camping in his uncle's book-room, contemplating the volume in question in an agony of guilt, ambition and frustration, until everybody about him suspects he has done something underhand, and a systematic persecution begins.

It will be clear from this summary of the opening of the novel that *Cousin Henry* depends on an eccentric situation, much as *Dr Wortle's School* depends on an almost justifiable bigamy and *Mr Scarborough's Family* on the old squire's ability to make his eldest son legitimate or illegitimate at will. Trollope selects such improbable données for his later fiction not, as Hardy might, for their compelling grotesqueness, but as a means of teasing out the complexities of the characters under investigation. In a sense the characters of *Cousin Henry*—Cousin Henry himself, the old squire, Isabel Brodrick, and Mr Apjohn—are everyday people in unusual circumstances; but in a more important sense Trollope is concerned with the extraordinariness of ordinary people; and the interplay of human nature with issue and ideal in a situation deliberately convoluted in order to exhibit character in the most striking light.

This is to claim a great deal for the novel, and a great deal for Trollope as an artist. For many of Trollope's more recent critics, indeed, it is to claim far too much. Modern criticism, uneasy with an art so comprehensively based on character as Trollope's, has gone out of its way to look for thematic and structural resonance in novels where theme and structure are supportive rather than focal elements. Robert Polhemus, who wants Cousin Henry to figure as a persecuted 'Everyman' figure, is a pioneer of this school.[1] In his view, Mr Apjohn the family lawyer, Mr Cheekey the barrister, Isabel, the tenants and servants of Llanfeare, and the wider public opinion of Carmarthen are representative of the forces of corporate righteousness in mid-Victorian society that 'put upon' the defenceless individual. Nothing could be further from the truth. Cousin Henry is clearly too impotent and too easily squelched to be 'everyone's cousin'.[2] And far from presenting a united front, what Polhemus unconvincingly calls the 'tyranny of bourgeois respectability'[3] operates on Cousin Henry in the contrasted persons of an aged ditherer, an autocratic young girl, a bumptious amateur detective, and a hireling advocate. It is essential for Trollope's purpose, and for the reader's enjoyment of the novel, that the characters be recognized for what they are: so many individuals. In *Cousin Henry* Trollope is not satirizing what Mr Apjohn labels the 'litigious pugnacity of a lawyer'. He is not mounting a strenuous attack on the iniquities of awkward public opinion. Nor, any more than in *Mr Scarborough's Family*, is he bringing significantly into question the law of

---

[1] Robert M. Polhemus, '*Cousin Henry*: Trollope's Note from Underground', *Nineteenth Century Fiction* 20 (1965–6), 385–9.

[2] Ibid., p. 387.

[3] Ibid.

primogeniture. He is presenting, in detailed cross-section, the challenging imbroglio of man's social relationships, and he focuses triumphantly on character rather than issue.

Cousin Henry cannot, therefore, be read as an account of the sufferings of a representatively timid 'little man' in a hostile social environment. For one thing, no one else in Trollope's fiction is quite like Cousin Henry. A born procrastinator, he has only to destroy the will to earn himself prosperity and peace of mind, but he knows from the outset that he can never do it, and he spends much of the novel obsessively contemplating the volume in which he knows it is hidden. Poor Cousin Henry's earthly heaven is no better than having plenty of time to decide to decide later. Early in the novel he allows himself six months' grace to sort out his dilemma, and evening after evening he gives himself another 'day of life' and another untroubled night's sleep before destroying the will. The only time that he can be decisive is in a situation that comes upon him unexpectedly and doesn't give him time to think. Otherwise even his lies are so unconvincing, agonized, and premeditated that they inspire only a pitying contempt. As Mr Apjohn points out at the end of the book, 'He was like a little girl who pauses and blushes and confesses all the truth before she half murmurs her naughty fib' (p. 278).

Another of Cousin Henry's distinctive qualities

—perhaps his most distinctive—is his ability to alienate people. Although he is desperate for a friend, or at any rate a confidant, there is a dreadful logic about the way he cannot help drawing his enemies, or those who seem to be his enemies, closer to his secret. When he lies, he lies rashly and inartistically, and compounds his difficulties. When he craves company and confidence he says just enough to convince his would-be companion (such as his tenant Mr Griffith) that there is a secret to bring to light. Mr Apjohn, for all his sleuth's instinct, is really drawn into his suspicions by the perverse magnetism of Cousin Henry's inarticulate misery. Even the ubiquitous soubriquet 'Cousin Henry' suggests that the man cannot be contemplated without the hint of a sneer. And yet he is by no means despicable. 'He was a man', Trollope writes, 'with no strong affections, but also with no strong aversions' (p. 29). He has some greed and some ambition, but probably less of either than the average man. His life in London, before he comes to Llanfeare, is barely sketched in. Although sent down from Oxford 'for some offence not altogether trivial', he seems to have got his 'wild oats' out of his system (pp. 8–10). There is no evidence that he is particularly vicious, mean, or dissipated, and yet everyone at Llanfeare seems to loathe him on sight. Nobody treats him with respect. He is insulted first by Isabel and Uncle Indefer, then by the servants, the tenants, the family lawyer, and even, in the end, by an obscure 'reptile' of a lawyer's clerk. As A. O. J. Cockshut indicates, 'From one point of view the book is an exposure of the moral dangers of being repulsive to others.'[4]

The stages by which Cousin Henry's imagination is revealed are dealt with in masterly fashion. Physical objects and the outward details of human behaviour are often powerfully registered at moments of emotional heightening in Trollope's books. As with Ferdinand Lopez in *The Prime Minister*, wandering pointlessly from platform to platform at the Tenway Junction to pluck up the courage to hurl himself beneath the Inverness express, and then striding out on to the barrow-crossing with characteristic 'graceful yet un-hurried step', there is a kind of documentary accuracy about the depiction of Cousin Henry's world, a miserable domestic prison shrunk to the size of his uncle's book-room. The details of his behaviour are conceived as the visible and outward signs of a psychological state completely grasped and thoroughly personalized, and which transcends any wider considerations of sociological and even of artistic patterning. We are carried deep enough into Cousin Henry's consciousness to understand why the idea of throwing the book that contains the will into the sea suits him better than the idea of burning it,

---

[4] A. O. J. Cockshut, *Anthony Trollope: A Critical Study* (London: Collins, 1955), 34.

though the felony will be the same in each case—
he would like to sink himself into the oblivion of
the 'placid deep water', and not have to think
about the will or anything else any more. The
volume must also be 'tied with strings or cased in
paper, and leaded, that it should surely sink, *so
that the will should not by untoward chance float out of
it*' (p. 97, my italics). Time and again we are told
of the distinctive speck of dust on the book's
binding ('to him it was almost wonderful that a
stain so peculiar should not at once betray the
volume to the eyes of all' (p. 107)), or the special
arrangement of the book on the shelves, by which
means Cousin Henry satisfies himself it has not
been tampered with in his absence. Cousin
Henry, Trollope notes, is even susceptible to
qualms in the dark of his bedchamber when 'he
was not yet protected by his bed' (p. 229).

In involving us so closely with the detail of
Cousin Henry's life and thought, Trollope is
merely asking us to understand, not to pity his
central character: an unattractive, cowardly,
incompetent little man, whose 'grandiose dreams'
of 'magnanimity' in producing the will are the
fantasies of a child. Childish too is his tendency to
shape for himself fears and bugbears, such as his
vision of life at Dartmoor 'with his hair cut, and
dirty prison clothes, and hard food, and work to
do!' (p. 234), or the moment when we catch him
brooding on hellfire as he looks into a candle-
flame (p. 233). What is certain is that the reader

comes to have a strange sympathy for Cousin Henry as he wraps himself in a web of lies, obsessively spells over the libels written about him in the *Carmarthen Herald*, dines frugally because he is too timid and too guilt-ridden to ask his housekeeper for better fare, and wanders desolately about the unfamiliar landscape of his inheritance, dreaming of release in a troubled phantasmagoria:

He dreamt that he was out there in a little boat all alone, with the book hidden under the seats, and that he rowed himself out to sea till he was so far distant from the shore that no eye could see him. Then he lifted the book, and was about to rid himself for ever of his burden;—when there came by a strong man swimming. The man looked up at him so as to see exactly what he was doing, and the book was not thrown over, and the face of the swimming man was the face of that young Cantor who had been so determined in his assertion that another will had been made. (p. 113)

At moments like this, we do not pause to question what is the purpose of creating Cousin Henry or his dilemma, or whether he has some allegorical value in the sort of subversive Victorian morality drama Polhemus postulates; we merely reflect that we have been carried deep into the mind and heart of the character.

Yet, as we have seen, to concentrate one's attention too exclusively on Cousin Henry at the expense of his 'persecutors' is to do violence to Trollope's artistic intent. Trollope perhaps attempted to prevent this when he juggled with three possible titles for the book—*Cousin Henry, Getting at a Secret*, and *Uncle Indefer's Will*—and instinctively preferred *Getting at a Secret* as 'exactly apposite'. The present title was picked out of the bunch by Alexander Ireland, Trollope's serial publisher.[5] There is certainly a sense in which the old squire, who dies at the end of the fourth chapter, is as responsible for the state of things at Llanfeare as the young man he toys with making his heir. He is almost as much of a temperamental prevaricator as his unfortunate nephew, and, in failing to let his tenants know whom or what they are to expect after him, does a considerable amount of inadvertent damage, all of course for the best of motives, as the theory of male primogeniture is almost a 'religion' for him. The vignette of the vacillating old man strengthens the novel in more ways than one. Intriguing social mysteries always, in Trollope, cling to the topic of inheritance (a family's responsibility to its tenants in its choice of heir); and, given Uncle Indefer's confusion, Cousin Henry cannot be held wholly to blame for his invidious performance in a predicament which he has neither courted nor deserved. As Mr Apjohn cautions, and, in view of the oppressive fidelity of the Llanfeare tenants, his words have significant moral force: '"You will see what terrible misery may be occasioned by

---

[5] N. John Hall, ed., *The Letters of Anthony Trollope* (Stanford: Stanford University Press, 1983), ii. 805.

not allowing those who are to come after you to know what it is they are to expect'' ' (p. 279).

Equally telling in the moral structure of the book is the old squire's niece, Isabel Brodrick. Though her part in the action is fairly small, Isabel is by no means a stereotyped figure. She could easily enough have been left as an unexamined peripheral heroine, like Mary Wortle in *Dr. Wortle's School* or Mary Lowther in *The Vicar of Bullhampton*. Yet Trollope draws her into the centre of the novel and presents an unobtrusively but finely shaded portrait. Isabel's stubbornness, vigour, and freedom from self-regard have led Coral Lansbury to label her an honorary man, 'the admired young gentleman of Trollope's just society'.[6] This belittles Trollope's insight and art in the presentation of women, and is another instance of the way Trollope critics buckle down human complexity to a 'representative' role in a straightforward sociological scheme. Isabel Brodrick is an individual. She is a very headstrong girl, quite as headstrong as the hidebound Lily Dale in *The Small House at Allington* or the quasi-suicidal Emily Hotspur in *Sir Harry Hotspur of Humblethwaite*. Though her self-denial takes less vehement forms than does Emily's, the prospect of being thrown out on the streets by her parsimonious stepmother is strangely appealing to her, and for most of the novel she is resolutely

[6] Coral Lansbury, *The Reasonable Man: Trollope's Legal Fiction* (Princeton: Princeton University Press, 1981), 146.

repressing her sexuality, keeping her lover Mr Owen at bay, first because she has prospects beyond his own, then because she is a 'pauper' and will not burden him with her presence. There is nothing underpowered about her courtship of Mr Owen. Her hymn of praise to him as she turns him down is reminiscent of the language of the *Song of Songs*:

'There has never been a man whose touch has been pleasant to me;—but I could revel in yours. Kiss you? I could kiss your feet at this moment, and embrace your knees. Everything belonging to you is dear to me.' (p. 136)

There is a touch of aristocratic hauteur about Isabel for which she never makes adequate allowance, and which means that passion and personal comfort must submit to a kind of 'stubborn pride'. For much of the novel she is away from Llanfeare, which she instinctively regards as her home and portion, and plays the part of a queen keeping up her dignity in exile. Only at the end of the book, when Cousin Henry is dismissed and she is restored on her own terms to her inheritance and all the stiffly condescending dreams of her girlhood, will she propose to her lover (Mr Owen remaining characteristically passive here). In the last chapter she presents her adoring tenants with a 'grandiloquently' named heir, doing her duty like any queen of romance. Poor Cousin Henry cannot begin to compete with her. She rebuffs his dutiful proposal of marriage with a force that seems almost vindictive, and one cannot help thinking that she treats him far worse than he deserves:

> 'Pray do not trouble yourself, Cousin Henry.'
> 'Oh, certainly I shall.'
> 'Do not trouble yourself. You may be sure of this, that on no earthly consideration would I take a penny from your hands.'
> 'Why not?'
> 'We take presents from those whom we love and esteem, not from those we despise.'
> 'Why should you despise me?' he asked.
> 'I will leave that to yourself to judge of; but be sure of this, that though I were starving I would take nothing from your hands.' (p. 92)

It is hardly surprising that Llanfeare was disappointed when, expecting this feudal darling, it got Cousin Henry; nor that the sufferings of poor timorous Henry should be increased at the hands of such a forthright and purposeful girl.

Looked at in the light of the richness of Trollope's characterization, *Cousin Henry* seems a carefully ramified study in the workings of human obstinacy, vacillation, heredity, and even sexual politics rather than a wry view of the way the institutionalized status quo treads the little man down. The peccadilloes, contradictions, and often the sheer willpower of Cousin Henry's own family knock him around and impose upon him quite as much as his persecutors in Llanfeare and

Carmarthen. Of these persecutors, only the 'old family friend', Mr Apjohn, is sketched in with much vigour, and we might conclude, as Ruth apRoberts does, that he is designed to represent the ideal crusading lawyer, a Dr Grantly in forensic garb, 'charging down on quaking rogues, shaking the truth from them with a fusillade of questions, and bypassing the finer points of the law to grapple with the truth'.[7] He is nothing of the kind. His affinities in Trollope's fiction are with Frank Fenwick, Dr Wortle, and Parson Armstrong in *The Kellys and the O'Kellys*, whose breakfast-time intimidation of the craven Barry Lynch interestingly anticipates the denouement of *Cousin Henry*. Apjohn's ebullient temerity in prosecuting someone else's cause almost brings him, as theirs does them, to disaster. The stages by which he reasons himself to the exact truth as to the hiding place of the will, and his self-gratification at having done so, suggest affinities with the detective novel, which had come into vogue in the decade following the publication of Collins's *The Moonstone* in 1868. Apjohn employs the methods of Collins's hero Sergeant Cuff, but lacks Cuff's circumspection. He acts impetuously when he breaks in upon Cousin Henry and, if the latter had been sharper, might have been accused of bringing with him the will which he discovers almost at once (p. 257). Apjohn's overwhelming

[7] Ruth apRoberts, *Anthony Trollope: Artist and Moralist* (London: Chatto and Windus, 1971), 169.

vigour is of a kind common enough in Trollope and in life, but it altogether disqualifies him as a satiric embodiment of what Polhemus calls 'oppressively conformist morality'.[8] Apjohn is not like Fielding's archetypal lawyer in *Joseph Andrews*, who has 'been alive these four thousand years'; he is, like everyone else in *Cousin Henry*, an individual.

The only point in the novel at which Trollope does seem to subordinate character to social criticism is in the vignette of Mr Cheekey, the Irish barrister who is to defend the Carmarthen newspaper editor against Cousin Henry's libel suit. In the weeks before the trial, Cousin Henry suffers agonies entirely on the strength of the tales he has been told of Cheekey's barbaric prowess in dealing with witnesses, until the barrister assumes almost visionary proportions in his imagination:

He could pause in his cross-examination, look at a man, projecting his face forward by degrees as he did so, in a manner which would crush any false witness who was not armed with triple courage at his breast, —and, alas! not unfrequently a witness who was not false. (p. 192)

There are many portraits of unscrupulous 'browbeating' barristers in Trollope's earlier novels, beginning with Mr Allewinde in *The Macdermots of Ballycloran* (1847) and culminating in the literary embodiment of the type, Mr Chaffanbrass, who

8 Polhemus, op. cit., p. 387.

is presented with increasing vigour and perhaps even increasing sympathy in a succession of appearances through *The Three Clerks* (1858), *Orley Farm* (1862), and *Phineas Redux* (1874). In comparison with Chaffanbrass, 'Supercilious Jack' Cheekey remains a cipher. Nevertheless, the insight which he gives into the working of the mid-Victorian Bar is instructive, and is substantiated by contemporary accounts and the work of modern legal historians. The oratorical displays of defence counsel, particularly barristers with Old Bailey experience, such as Cheekey, were often highly organized performances. Only a few years earlier an ex-actor named John Cooper had welcomed apprentice barristers at his training-school. Two of the lights of the Victorian Bar, Charles Wilkins and Edwin James, had begun as strolling players,[9] and Herman Charles Merivale, whom Trollope put up for the Garrick in 1864 and frequently corresponded with in his later years, combined both professions, entitling his 'Autobiographical Memories' *Bar, Stage and Platform*.[10] Cheekey, a 'young-looking' man at the time of *Cousin Henry*, has ideas of chivalry and equality that were unknown to the Old Bailey barristers of an earlier generation, such as Chaffanbrass:

[9] See J. R. Lewis, *The Victorian Bar* (London: Robert Hale, 1982).
[10] Herman Charles Merivale, *Bar, Stage and Platform* (London: Chatto and Windus, 1902).

Under no circumstances would he bully a woman,—
nor would he bully a man, unless, according to his own
mode of looking at such cases, the man wanted
bullying. (p. 192)

Yet when he believes he has right on his side,
Cheekey has the teeth of a terrier. His object is the
torture and, if possible, the potential incrimina-
tion of prosecution witnesses. Trollope's cynical
comments on the process in *The Three Clerks* are
not out of place when one considers the impend-
ing ordeal of Cousin Henry at Carmarthen:

to turn a witness to good account, he must be badgered
this way and that till he is nearly mad; he must be
made a laughing-stock for the court; his very truths
must be turned into falsehoods, so that he may be
falsely shamed; he must be accused of all manner of
villainy, threatened with all manner of punishment; he
must be made to feel that he has no friend near him,
that the world is all against him; he must be
confounded till he forget his right hand from his left,
till his mind be turned into chaos, and his heart into
water; and then let him give his evidence. (*The Three
Clerks*, Ch. LX)

However, despite the documental insights into
the working of the mid-Victorian Bar which
Cheekey provides, he is fully assimilated into the
scheme of *Cousin Henry*. This contrasts with
Trollope's practice in early novels such as *The
Macdermots of Ballycloran* and *The Three Clerks*,
where the book's progress is arrested to facilitate

an essayistic aside on the evils (and, incident-
ally, the entertainment value) of the adversarial
system. The reason for the change is partly that
Trollope's art is now more efficient than it was in
the 1850s, and partly that his attitude to the
'performing' barrister has mellowed. But the
main reason for Cheekey's inclusion is clearly to
intimidate Cousin Henry, and to contribute to
the richness of Trollope's study of his central
character. Trollope may have been one of the
justest and most extensive portraitists of the mid-
Victorian lawyer among contemporary novelists,
but it must not be supposed that his novels in
general or *Cousin Henry* in particular offer a
sustained attack on the Victorian legal system.

Any approach to the novel that fails to recog-
nize that personality subserves social comment
and even moral attitude in *Cousin Henry*, and not
the other way about, inevitably does less than
justice to the book. Cousin Henry compels our
attention as a latter-day Dr Fell, not, as Polhemus
would have us believe, as a Kafkaesque scape-
goat. He does not represent the private individual
sacrificed on the altar of mid-Victorian self-
righteousness. Tenants, servants, and lawyers,
instinctively aware that they have been pandering
to base and irrational passions in knocking him,
treat him with clemency and sympathy as he bids
Llanfeare farewell. The reader's response to
Cousin Henry's departure, likewise, should not
be unequivocally critical or unequivocally

sympathetic. It should be a mixture of generosity, pity, reproof, and understanding. Mrs Griffiths, the old retainer, gets it right when she makes Cousin Henry a good broil to replace the uneaten breakfast Messrs Apjohn and Brodrick have interrupted and for the next few days endeavours 'to get him nice things to eat, trying to console him by titbits' (p. 262). The housekeeper's reparation, simple, a little comic, a little top-heavy, is a symbol of the tender, intricate, hidebound response Trollope wishes to win from his readers. 'For the man himself,' Trollope writes, 'the reader, it is hoped, will feel some compassion' (p. 262). If the reader does not feel the challenge and the qualification in Trollope's hope, then he or she will hardly get full value out of the two or three hours which it takes to peruse one of Trollope's most strikingly concentrated character-studies.

JULIAN THOMPSON

NOTE ON THE TEXT

THE 'Working Diary' for *Cousin Henry* is kept in the Bodleian Library, Oxford, under the call-mark MSS Don. c. 10. Work began on the novel on 26 October 1878, and Trollope finished the last chapter on 8 December. Since completing *Ayala's Angel* on 24 September, he had accepted a commission for a 10,000-word story for the Christmas supplement to the *Masonic Magazine*. This was 'Catherine Carmichael', and the story was delivered to the Magazine's Fleet Street office on 14 October, a mere eleven days after the negotiations with the editor had been completed (Hall, ii. 797). Trollope then prepared a paper on the morally educative effects of fiction, with special reference to the work of Dickens and Thackeray (he was to write his *Life of Thackeray* for the English Men of Letters series in the early part of 1879 (Hall, ii. 798)). *Cousin Henry* was thus composed in the midst of a familiar burst of Trollopian industry and creativity.

Gordon Ray (*HLQ* 31 (1968), Appendix B) lists the MS of *Cousin Henry* as among the holdings of Yale University. It is largely written in the hand of Trollope's amanuensis, his niece Florence Bland, but includes minor corrections in the hand of the author. Trollope saw far enough on the first morning of composition to write to his barrister friend, Charles Hall, to ask if Isabel Brodrick would be able to get her legacy out of her uncle's estate even if there were no independent funds to pay for it, a point at issue throughout the novel's first seven chapters (see Hall, ii. 799). Trollope worked solidly on *Cousin Henry* for ten days; he broke on 4 November, took a trip up to Manchester to lecture on 'The Native Races of South Africa' (Hall, ii. 800), resumed the book on 22 November, and then produced the last sixteen chapters in sixteen days, finishing on 8 December. 4 December was unproductive, and the comment 'Lewes buried' (George Henry Lewes, George Eliot's 'husband') is entered against this day in the diary.

Cousin Henry was serialized in the *Manchester Weekly Times* and the *North British Weekly Mail* from 8 March 1879 to 24 May 1879, in six numbers of four chapters, each number making its appearance an unusually short time after composition at this stage in Trollope's career (*The Duke's Children* lay on Trollope's hands for four years, and even the comparatively brief *Dr. Wortle's School* for two). This was probably because on his Manchester trip Trollope dined with Alexander Ireland, publisher and business-manager of the *Manchester Examiner and Times* (Hall, ii. 800), and 'sold' him the serial rights of the novel at that moment under his hand for £200. He refused to allow Ireland to advertise *Cousin Henry* as 'an original novel', as he did not wish to make ostentatious claims for the book's novelty; nevertheless, he seems to have been aware that he had done nothing quite like the concentrated psychological portrait of Cousin Henry elsewhere in his fiction: 'It is an original novel, but it is not for me to say so', he wrote in a letter to Ireland dated 27 February 1879 (Hall, ii. 818).

Trollope had not struck a bargain with Ireland before, and he was unimpressed when Ireland's printers took liberties with the arrangement of his dialogue. He wrote sharply, if courteously, to Ireland, stipulating that 'they should not alter my forms of expression, because they do not, and cannot, know my purpose' (Hall, ii. 820–1). He was also put out by Ireland's remissness in forwarding revise proofs. Trollope's supervision of his work through to publication, even at this late stage in his career, was thus more meticulous than has sometimes been supposed.

The more prestigious publishing houses, such as Chapman and Hall, were now refusing to take Trollope's novels in serial form, but the latter did purchase the book rights of *Cousin Henry* for £300, and published it in October 1879. There was some grumbling on the part of the reviewers about the issuing of the novel in two 'meagre' volumes at 12*s.* for the pair, as opposed to 10*s.* 6*d.* for a single-volume novel. At the height of his popularity Trollope had tried to prevent his shorter works coming out in two volumes. He refused to allow *Lotta Schmidt and Other Stories* to be 'stretched' to two volumes in 1867, and *Sir Harry Hotspur of Humblethwaite* (almost exactly the same length as *Cousin Henry*) to be so stretched in 1870. One can only suppose that any such attempt with *Cousin Henry* was abortive, or that Trollope was less able to dictate terms to his publishers late in his career.

In March 1880 W. H. Smith reissued *Cousin Henry* in a cheap edition over Chapman and Hall's imprint, and in that publisher's 'Select Library of Fiction'. The present edition is a reproduction of the first Oxford World's Classics text of 1929, which was almost certainly set from the first book edition. At least two misprints in the first edition were silently corrected by the 1929 Oxford printer: 1 Ed. 'cold-looking' became 'good-looking' on p. 15, l. 10; and 1 Ed. 'bedside' became 'beside' on p. 60, l. 3 from foot.

The book was reasonably well received, and Chapman told Trollope privately (Hall, ii. 845) that he had done very well with it. Contemporary reviews pointed out the hackneyed nature of a plot depending on a will, and stressed the commonplaceness of Trollope's materials. Yet almost all found the novel highly readable, though they were at a loss, as the *Examiner* confessed, to point out 'by what means Mr Trollope has succeeded in making a couple of hours fly so rapidly'.

SELECT BIBLIOGRAPHY

THERE is no collected edition of the works. A facsimile edition of thirty-six titles (62 vols.), *Selected Works of Anthony Trollope*, has been published by the Arno Press (1981; General Editor N. John Hall). Works by Trollope are also available in the Oxford World's Classics series; in Penguin, Dover, Alan Sutton, Encore, and Granville reprints; in the Harting Grange Library series (mostly the shorter works), published by the Caledonia Press; and in *Anthony Trollope: The Complete Short Stories* (forty-two stories in 5 vols.), ed. Betty Jane Slemp Breyer (1979–83). The standard bibliography of the works is Michael Sadleir, *Trollope: A Bibliography* (1928; reprinted 1977). *The Letters of Anthony Trollope*, 2 vols., ed. N. John Hall (1983), is now the standard edition.

There is no definitive Life. Among the more useful biographical volumes are Bradford A. Booth, *Anthony Trollope: Aspects of His Life and Work* (1958); James Pope Hennessy, *Anthony Trollope* (1971); Michael Sadleir, *Trollope: A Commentary* (1927); C. P Snow, *Trollope* (1975); and L. P. and R. P. Stebbins, *The Trollopes: The Chronicle of A Writing Family* (1945). The best sources of information about Trollope's life remain T. H. S. Escott's memoir, *Anthony Trollope: His Public Services, Private Friends and Literary Originals* (1913; reprinted 1967), and the novelist's *Autobiography* (1883). Other useful guides are W. and J. Gerould, *A Guide to Trollope* (1948), and N. John Hall, *Trollope and His Illustrators* (1980).

The best bibliographies of criticism are Rafael Helling, *A Century of Trollope Criticism* (1956), and *The Reputation of Trollope: An Annotated Bibliography 1925-75*, eds. John Charles Olmsted and Jeffrey Welch (1978); but see also Ruth apRoberts, 'Anthony Trollope' in George H. Ford, *Victorian Fiction; a Second Guide to Research* (1978), and the bibliographies published annually in *Victorian Studies*. A selection of contemporary criticism is reprinted in *Trollope: The Critical Heritage*, ed. Donald Smalley (1969), and contemporary responses are very fully discussed in David Skilton, *Anthony Trollope and his Contemporaries* (1972).

Of the many general studies of Trollope, the most useful are: Henry James, 'Anthony Trollope' in *Partial Portraits* (1888); A. O. J. Cockshut, *Anthony Trollope: A Critical Study* (1955); G. N. Ray, 'Trollope at Full Length', *Huntingdon Library Quarterly* 31 (1967-8); Ruth apRoberts, *Trollope: Artist and Moralist* (1971; *The Moral Trollope* in USA); and James R. Kincaid, *The Novels of Anthony Trollope* (1977). Cockshut includes (p. 34) a stimulating half-page discussion of *Cousin Henry*. Kincaid makes interesting points about the book in passing, seeing Trollope's art in presenting Henry as akin to dramatic monologue. A sensitive, if brief, account of the novel is provided by P. D. Edwards in *Anthony Trollope: His Art and Scope* (Harvester Press, 1978), 197-9. Robert Tracy, in *Trollope's Later Novels* (Berkeley, 1978), 253-61, discovers the aptness of the volume of Jeremy Taylor's Sermons in which the will lies hidden.

One of the few separate studies of *Cousin Henry* is that by Robert M. Polhemus (*'Cousin Henry*: Trollope's Note from Underground' in *Nineteenth-Century Fiction*, 20 (1966), 385-9; reprinted in R. M. Polhemus, *The*

Changing World of Anthony Trollope (Berkeley: University of California Press, 1968), 231–6). As well as arguing that the novel should be read as a complaint about the way in which, in Victorian England, bourgeois respectability tyrannized over 'the helpless little individual', Polhemus draws an unconvincing parallel between the universal derision surrounding Cousin Henry and Trollope's own unpopularity in his boyhood. Ruth apRoberts, in '*Cousin Henry*: Trollope's Note From Antiquity' (*Nineteenth Century Fiction*, 24 (1969), 93–8), notes a possible source for Trollope's plot in Cicero's *De Officiis*, and the idea is developed in *Trollope: Artist and Moralist* (1971).

A CHRONOLOGY
OF ANTHONY TROLLOPE

1815   Born at 6 Keppel Street, Bloomsbury,
        24 April.

1822   Sent to Harrow as a day-boy.

1825   Attends private school at Sunbury.

1827   Sent to Winchester College.

1830   Removed from Winchester and sent again to
        Harrow.

1834   Leaves Harrow, serves six weeks as classics
        teacher in a Brussels school.
        Accepts junior clerkship in General Post
        Office; settles in London.

1841   Becomes Deputy Postal Surveyor at
        Banagher, in Ireland.

1844   Marries Rose Heseltine, in June. Trans-
        ferred to Clonmel, in Ireland.

1845   Promoted to Surveyor in the Post Office and
        moves to Mallow, in Ireland.

1847   *The Macdermots of Ballycloran*, his first novel, is
        published (3 vols., T. C. Newby).

1848   *The Kellys and the O'Kellys; or Landlords and
        Tenants* (3 vols., Henry Colburn).
        Rebellion in Ireland.

1850   *La Vendée: An Historical Romance* (3 vols.,
        Henry Colburn).
        Writes *The Noble Jilt* (play; published 1923).

1851 Postal duties in western England.

1853 Returns to Ireland, settles in Belfast.

1854 Leaves Belfast and settles at Donnybrook, near Dublin.

1855 *The Warden* (1 vol., Longman).

1857 *Barchester Towers* (3 vols., Longman).
The Three Clerks (3 vols., Richard Bentley).

1858 Postal mission to Egypt; visits Palestine; postal mission to the West Indies; visits Malta, Gibraltar, and Spain.
Doctor Thorne (3 vols., Chapman & Hall).

1859 Returns to Ireland; moves to England, and settles at Waltham Cross, in Hertfordshire.
The Bertrams (3 vols., Chapman & Hall).
The West Indies and the Spanish Main (travel; 1 vol., Chapman & Hall).

1860 Visits Florence.
Tales of All Countries serialized in *Harper's New Monthly Magazine* and *Cassell's Illustrated Family Paper*, May–October.
Castle Richmond (3 vols., Chapman & Hall).

1860–1 *Framley Parsonage* serialized in the *Cornhill Magazine*, January 1860–April 1861; its huge success establishes his reputation as a novelist.

1861 *Framley Parsonage* (3 vols., Smith, Elder).
Tales of All Countries (1 vol., Chapman & Hall). Election to the Garrick Club.
Tales of All Countries: Second Series, serialized in *Public Opinion*, the *London Review*, and *The Illustrated London News*, January–December.

1861–2 *Orley Farm* published in twenty monthly

parts, March 1861–October 1862, by Chapman & Hall. Visits the United States (August 1861–May 1862). *The Struggles of Brown, Jones and Robinson: by One of the Firm*, serialized in the *Cornhill Magazine*, August 1861–March 1862.

1862　　*Orley Farm* (2 vols., Chapman & Hall).
North America (travel; 2 vols., Chapman & Hall).
The Struggles of Brown, Jones and Robinson (1 vol., New York: Harper; first English edition published 1870).
Rachel Ray (2 vols., Chapman & Hall).

1862–4　　*The Small House at Allington*, serialized in the *Cornhill Magazine*, September 1862–April 1864.

1863　　*Tales of All Countries: Second Series* (1 vol., Chapman & Hall).
Death of his mother, Frances Trollope.

1864　　Election to the Athenaeum.
The Small House at Allington (2 vols., Smith, Elder).

1864–5　　*Can You Forgive Her?* published in twenty monthly parts, January 1864–August 1865, by Chapman & Hall.

1865　　*Miss Mackenzie* (2 vols., Chapman & Hall).
Hunting Sketches (1 vol., Chapman & Hall); also serialized in the *Pall Mall Gazette*, February–March.
Travelling Sketches, serialized in the *Pall Mall Gazette*, August–September.

1865–6   *The Belton Estate*, serialized in the *Fortnightly Review*, May 1865–January 1866.
           Clergymen of the Church of England, serialized in the *Pall Mall Gazette*, November 1865–January 1866.

1866   *The Belton Estate* (3 vols., Chapman & Hall).
           Travelling Sketches (1 vol., Chapman & Hall).
           Clergymen of the Church of England (1 vol., Chapman & Hall).

1866–7   *The Claverings*, serialized in the *Cornhill Magazine*, February 1866–May 1867.
           Nina Balatka, serialized in *Blackwood's Magazine*, July 1866–January 1867.
           The Last Chronicle of Barset, published in thirty-two weekly parts, December 1866–July 1867, by Smith, Elder.

1867   *Nina Balatka* (2 vols., William Blackwood).
           The Last Chronicle of Barset (2 vols., Smith, Elder).
           The Claverings (2 vols., Smith, Elder).
           Lotta Schmidt: and Other Stories (contents published between 1861 and 1867; 1 vol., Alexander Strahan).
           Resigns from the Post Office and leaves the Civil Service.

1867–8   *Linda Tressel*, serialized in *Blackwood's Magazine*, October 1867–May 1868.

1867–9   *Phineas Finn: The Irish Member*, serialized in *St. Paul's Magazine*, October 1867–May 1869.

1867–70   Serves as Editor of *St. Paul's Magazine* (founded 1 October 1867).

1868   *Linda Tressel* (2 vols., William Blackwood).
          Visits United States to negotiate postal
          treaty.
          Stands as Liberal candidate for Beverley, in
          Yorkshire, in General Election; finishes at
          bottom of poll.

1868–9   *He Knew He Was Right*, published in thirty
          weekly parts, from October 1868–May 1869,
          by Virtue.

1869   *Phineas Finn* (2 vols., Virtue).
          He Knew He Was Right (2 vols., Alexander
          Strahan).
          Did He Steal It? A Comedy in Three Acts
          (privately printed and never performed; a
          dramatization of *The Last Chronicle of Barset*).

1869–70   *The Vicar of Bullhampton*, serialized in eleven
          monthly parts, July 1869–May 1870, by
          Bradbury & Evans.
          An Editor's Tales, serialized in *St. Paul's
          Magazine*, October 1869–May 1870.

1870   *The Vicar of Bullhampton* (1 vol., Bradbury &
          Evans).
          An Editor's Tales (1 vol., Alexander Strahan).
          The Commentaries of Caesar (1 vol., William
          Blackwood).
          Sir Harry Hotspur of Humblethwaite (1 vol.,
          Hurst & Blackett); also serialized in
          Macmillan's Magazine, May–December.

1870–1   *Ralph the Heir*, serialized in *St. Paul's
          Magazine*, January 1870–July 1871.

1871   *Ralph the Heir* (3 vols., Hurst & Blackett).
          Gives up house at Waltham Cross; visits
          Australia.

1871–2 Travelling in Australia and New Zealand.

1871–3 *The Eustace Diamonds*, serialized in the *Fortnightly Review*, July 1871–February 1873.

1872 *The Golden Lion of Granpère* (1 vol., Tinsley); also serialized in *Good Words*, January–August. Returns to England and settles at 39 Montagu Square, London.

1873 *The Eustace Diamonds* (3 vols., Chapman & Hall).
Australia and New Zealand (travel; 2 vols., Chapman & Hall).
Phineas Redux (2 vols., Chapman & Hall).
Harry Heathcote of Gangoil: A Tale of Australian Bush Life, published as the Christmas number of *The Graphic*.

1873–4 *Phineas Redux*, serialized in *The Graphic*, July 1873–January 1874.
Lady Anna, serialized in the *Fortnightly Review*, April 1873–April 1874.
Gives up London residence and settles at Harting Grange, near Petersfield.
London Tradesmen, serialized in the *Pall Mall Gazette*, July–September (published 1927).

1874 *Lady Anna* (2 vols., Chapman & Hall).
Harry Heathcote of Gangoil (1 vol., Sampson Low).

1874–5 *The Way We Live Now*, published in twenty monthly parts, February 1874–September 1875, by Chapman & Hall.

1875 *The Way We Live Now* (2 vols., Chapman & Hall). Travels to Ceylon and Australia, returns to England.

1875–6   *The Prime Minister*, published in eight monthly parts, November 1875–June 1876, by Chapman & Hall.

1876   *The Prime Minister* (4 vols., Chapman & Hall).

1876–7   *The American Senator*, serialized in *Temple Bar*, May 1876–July 1877.

1877   *The American Senator* (3 vols., Chapman & Hall). Visits South Africa, returns to England. *Christmas at Thompson Hall* (1 vol., New York: Harper).

1877–8   *Is He Popenjoy?: A Novel*, serialized in *All the Year Round*, October 1877–July 1878.

1878   *South Africa* (travel; 2 vols., Chapman & Hall). *Is He Popenjoy?* (3 vols., Chapman & Hall). Visits Iceland, returns to England. *How the 'Mastiffs' Went to Iceland* (1 vol., Virtue).

1878–9   *An Eye for An Eye*, serialized in the *Whitehall Review*, August 1878–February 1879. *John Caldigate*, serialized in *Blackwood's Magazine*, April 1878–June 1879.

1879   *An Eye for An Eye* (2 vols., Chapman & Hall). *Thackeray* (1 vol., Macmillan). *John Caldigate* (3 vols., Chapman & Hall). *Cousin Henry: A Novel* (2 vols., Chapman & Hall); also serialized, simultaneously, in the *Manchester Weekly Times* and the *North British Weekly Mail*, May–December.

1879–80   *The Duke's Children: A Novel*, serialized in *All the Year Round*, October 1879–July 1880.

1880   *The Duke's Children* (3 vols., Chapman & Hall).

The Life of Cicero (2 vols., Chapman & Hall).
Dr. Wortle's School: A Novel, serialized in *Blackwood's Magazine*, May–December.
Can You Forgive Her? (2 vols., Chapman & Hall)

1881 *Dr Wortle's School* (2 vols., Chapman & Hall).
Ayala's Angel (3 vols., Chapman & Hall).

1881–2 *The Fixed Period: A Novel*, serialized in *Blackwood's Magazine*, October 1881–March 1882.
Marion Fay: A Novel, serialized in *The Graphic*, December 1881–June 1882.

1882 Visits Ireland twice.
Why Frau Frohmann Raised Her Prices: And Other Stories (stories published 1876–8; 1 vol., William Isbister).
Lord Palmerston (1 vol., William Isbister).
Marion Fay (3 vols., Chapman & Hall).
Kept in the Dark: A Novel (2 vols., Chatto & Windus); also serialized in *Good Words*, May–December.
The Fixed Period (2 vols., William Black-wood).
Death in London, 6 December.
The Two Heroines of Plumplington, Christmas number of *Good Words* (published 1954).

1882–3 *Mr Scarborough's Family*, written 1881, serialized in *All the Year Round*, May 1882–June 1883.
The Landleaguers (unfinished), serialized in *Life*, November 1882–October 1883.

1883 *Mr Scarborough's Family* (3 vols., Chatto & Windus).

The Landleaguers (3 vols., Chatto & Windus).
An Autobiography (written 1875–6; 2 vols., William Blackwood).

1884   *An Old Man's Love* (written 1882; 2 vols., William Blackwood).

Cousin Henry

CONTENTS

I.	UNCLE INDEFER .	1
II.	ISABEL BRODRICK	12
III.	COUSIN HENRY .	24
IV.	THE SQUIRE'S DEATH .	35
V.	PREPARING FOR THE FUNERAL .	47
VI.	MR. APJOHN'S EXPLANATION .	59
VII.	LOOKING FOR THE WILL .	70
VIII.	THE READING OF THE WILL .	82
IX.	ALONE AT LLANFEARE .	92
X.	COUSIN HENRY DREAMS A DREAM .	104
XI.	ISABEL AT HEREFORD .	116
XII.	MR. OWEN .	127
XIII.	THE *CARMARTHEN HERALD* .	140
XIV.	AN ACTION FOR LIBEL .	152
XV.	COUSIN HENRY MAKES ANOTHER ATTEMPT .	164
XVI.	AGAIN AT HEREFORD .	176
XVII.	MR. CHEEKEY .	186
XVIII.	COUSIN HENRY GOES TO CARMARTHEN	199
XIX.	MR. APJOHN SENDS FOR ASSISTANCE .	211
XX.	DOUBTS .	223

XXI. MR. APJOHN'S SUCCESS . . 234

XXII. HOW COUSIN HENRY WAS LET OFF
EASILY 246

XXIII. ISABEL'S PETITION . . . 258

XXIV. CONCLUSION 270

COUSIN HENRY

CHAPTER I

UNCLE INDEFER

'I HAVE a conscience, my dear, on this matter,'* said an old gentleman to a young lady, as the two were sitting in the breakfast parlour of a country house which looked down from the cliffs over the sea on the coast of Carmarthenshire.

'And so have I, Uncle Indefer; and as my conscience is backed by my inclination, whereas yours is not—'

'You think that I shall give way?'

'I did not mean that.'

'What then?'

'If I could only make you understand how very strong is my inclination, or disinclination—how impossible to be conquered, then—'

'What next?'

'Then you would know that I could never give way, as you call it, and you would go to work with your own conscience to see whether it be imperative with you or not. You may be sure of this,—I shall never say a word to you in opposition to your conscience. If there be a word to be spoken it must come from yourself.'

There was a long pause in the conversation, a

silence for an hour, during which the girl went in
and out of the room and settled herself down at
her work. Then the old man went back abruptly
to the subject they had discussed. 'I shall obey
my conscience.'

'You ought to do so, Uncle Indefer. What
should a man obey but his conscience?'

'Though it will break my heart.'

'No; no, no!'

'And will ruin you.'

'That is a flea's bite. I can brave my ruin
easily, but not your broken heart.'

'Why should there be either, Isabel?'

'Nay, sir; have you not said but now, because
of our consciences? Not to save your heart from
breaking,—though I think your heart is dearer
to me than anything else in the world,—could
I marry my cousin Henry. We must die together, both of us, you and I, or live broken-
hearted, or what not, sooner than that. Would
I not do anything possible at your bidding?'

'I used to think so.'

'But it is impossible for a young woman with a
respect for herself such as I have to submit herself
to a man that she loathes. Do as your conscience
bids you with the old house. Shall I be less
tender to you while you live because I shall have
to leave the place when you are dead? Shall
I accuse you of injustice or unkindness in my
heart? Never! All that is only an outside circumstance to me, comparatively of little mo-

ment. But to be the wife of a man I despise!'
Then she got up and left the room.

* * * * * * *

A month passed by before the old man returned to the subject, which he did seated in the
same room, at the same hour of the day,—at
about four o'clock, when the dinner things had
been removed.

'Isabel,' he said, 'I cannot help myself.'

'As to what, Uncle Indefer?' She knew very
well what was the matter in which, as he said,
he could not help himself. Had there been anything in which his age had wanted assistance
from her youth there would have been no hesitation between them; no daughter was ever more
tender; no father was ever more trusting. But
on this subject it was necessary that he should
speak more plainly before she could reply to
him.

'As to your cousin and the property.'

'Then in God's name do not trouble yourself
further in looking for help where there is none
to be had. You mean that the estate ought to go
to a man and not to a woman?'

'It ought to go to a Jones.'

'I am not a Jones, nor likely to become a
Jones.'

'You are as near to me as he is,—and so much
dearer!'

'But not on that account a Jones. My name is
Isabel Brodrick. A woman not born to be a Jones

may have the luck to become one by marriage, but that will never be the case with me.'

'You should not laugh at that which is to me a duty.'

'Dear, dear uncle!' she said, caressing him, 'if I seemed to laugh'—and she certainly had laughed when she spoke of the luck of becoming a Jones—'it is only that you may feel how little importance I attach to it all on my own account.'

'But it is important,—terribly important!'

'Very well. Then go to work with two things in your mind fixed as fate. One is that you must leave Llanfeare to your nephew Henry Jones, and the other that I will not marry your nephew Henry Jones. When it is all settled it will be just as though the old place were entailed,* as it used to be.'

'I wish it were.'

'So do I, if it would save you trouble.'

'But it isn't the same;—it can't be the same. In getting back the land your grandfather sold I have spent the money I had saved for you.'

'It shall be all the same to me, and I will take pleasure in thinking that the old family place shall remain as you would have it. I can be proud of the family though I can never bear the name.'

'You do not care a straw for the family.'

'You should not say that, Uncle Indefer. It is not true. I care enough for the family to sympathize with you altogether in what you are doing,

but not enough for the property to sacrifice myself in order that I might have a share in it.'

'I do not know why you should think so much
evil of Henry.'

'Do you know any reason why I should think
well enough of him to become his wife? I do
not. In marrying a man a woman should be
able to love every little trick belonging to him.
The parings of his nails should be dear to her.
Every little wish of his should be a care to her.
It should be pleasant to her to serve him in
things most menial. Would it be so to me, do
you think, with Henry Jones?'

'You are always full of poetry and books.'

'I should be full of something very bad if I
were to allow myself to stand at the altar with
him. Drop it, Uncle Indefer. Get it out of your
mind as a thing quite impossible. It is the one
thing I can't and won't do, even for you. It is
the one thing that you ought not to ask me to do.
Do as you like with the property,—as you think
right.'

'It is not as I like.'

'As your conscience bids you, then; and I with
myself, which is the only little thing that I have
in the world, will do as I like, or as my conscience
bids me.'

These last words she spoke almost roughly,
and as she said them she left him, walking out
of the room with an air of offended pride. But
in this there was a purpose. If she were hard to

him, hard and obstinate in her determination, then would he be enabled to be so also to her in his determination, with less of pain to himself. She felt it to be her duty to teach him that he was justified in doing what he liked with his property, because she intended to do what she liked with herself. Not only would she not say a word towards dissuading him from this change in his old intentions, but she would make the change as little painful to him as possible by teaching him to think that it was justified by her own manner to him.

For there was a change, not only in his mind, but in his declared intentions. Llanfeare had belonged to Indefer Joneses for many generations. When the late Squire had died, now twenty years ago, there had been remaining out of ten children only one, the eldest, to whom the property now belonged. Four or five coming in succession after him had died without issue. Then there had been a Henry Jones, who had gone away and married, had become the father of the Henry Jones above mentioned, and had then also departed. The youngest, a daughter, had married an attorney named Brodrick, and she also had died, having no other child but Isabel. Mr. Brodrick had married again, and was now the father of a large family, living at Hereford, where he carried on his business. He was not very 'well-to-do' in the world. The new Mrs. Brodrick had preferred her own babies to

Isabel, and Isabel when she was fifteen years of age had gone to her bachelor uncle at Llanfeare. There she had lived for the last ten years, making occasional visits to her father at Hereford.

Mr. Indefer Jones, who was now between seventy and eighty years old, was a gentleman who through his whole life had been disturbed by reflections, fears, and hopes as to the family property on which he had been born, on which he had always lived, in possession of which he would certainly die, and as to the future disposition of which it was his lot in life to be altogether responsible. It had been entailed upon him before his birth in his grandfather's time, when his father was about to be married. But the entail had not been carried on.* There had come no time in which this Indefer Jones had been about to be married, and the former old man having been given to extravagance, and been generally in want of money, had felt it more comfortable to be without an entail. His son had occasionally been induced to join with him in raising money. Thus not only since he had himself owned the estate, but before his father's death, there had been forced upon him reflections as to the destination of Llanfeare. At fifty he had found himself unmarried, and unlikely to marry. His brother Henry was then alive; but Henry had disgraced the family,— had run away with a married woman whom he had married after a divorce, had taken to racecourses and billiard-rooms, and had been altogether odious to his brother Indefer. Nevertheless the boy which had come from this marriage, a younger Henry, had been educated at his expense, and had occasionally been received at Llanfeare. He had been popular with no one there, having been found to be a sly boy, given to lying, and, as even the servants said about the place, unlike a Jones of Llanfeare. Then had come the time in which Isabel had been brought to Llanfeare. Henry had been sent away from Oxford for some offence not altogether trivial,* and the Squire had declared to himself and others that Llanfeare should never fall into his hands.

Isabel had so endeared herself to him that before she had been two years in the house she was the young mistress of the place. Everything that she did was right in his eyes. She might have anything that she would ask, only that she would ask for nothing. At this time the cousin had been taken into an office in London, and had become,—so it was said of him,—a steady young man of business. But still, when allowed to show himself at Llanfeare, he was unpalatable to them all—unless it might be to the old Squire. It was certainly the case that in his office in London he made himself useful, and it seemed that he had abandoned that practice of running into debt and having the bills sent down to Llanfeare which he had adopted early in his career.

During all this time the old Squire was terribly troubled about the property. His will was always close at his hand. Till Isabel was twenty-one this will had always been in Henry's favour,— with a clause, however, that a certain sum of money which the Squire possessed should go to her. Then in his disgust towards his nephew he changed his purpose, and made another will in Isabel's favour. This remained in existence as his last resolution for three years; but they had been three years of misery to him. He had endured but badly the idea that the place should pass away out of what he regarded as the proper male line. To his thinking it was simply an accident that the power of disposing of the property should be in his hands. It was a religion to him that a landed estate in Britain should go from father to eldest son,* and in default of a son to the first male heir. Britain would not be ruined because Llanfeare should be allowed to go out of the proper order. But Britain would be ruined if Britons did not do their duty in that sphere of life to which it had pleased God to call them; and in this case his duty was to maintain the old order of things.

And during this time an additional trouble added itself to those existing. Having made up his mind to act in opposition to his own principles, and to indulge his own heart; having declared both to his nephew and to his niece that Isabel should be his heir, there came to him, as a consolation in his misery, the power of repurchasing a certain fragment of the property which his father, with his assistance, had sold. The loss of these acres had been always a sore wound to him, not because of his lessened income, but from a feeling that no owner of an estate should allow it to be diminished during his holding of it. He never saw those separated fields estranged from Llanfeare, but he grieved in his heart. That he might get them back again he had saved money since Llanfeare had first become his own. Then had come upon him the necessity of providing for Isabel. But when with many groans he had decided that Isabel should be the heir, the money could be allowed to go for its intended purpose. It had so gone, and then his conscience had become too strong for him, and another will was made.

It will be seen how he had endeavoured to reconcile things. When it was found that Henry Jones was working like a steady man at the London office to which he was attached, that he had sown his wild oats, then Uncle Indefer began to ask himself why all his dearest wishes should not be carried out together by a marriage between the cousins. 'I don't care a bit for his wild oats,' Isabel had said, almost playfully, when the idea had first been mooted to her. 'His oats are too tame for me rather than too wild. Why can't he look any one in the face?' Then her uncle had been angry with her, thinking that she was allowing a foolish idea to interfere with the happiness of them all.

But his anger with her was never enduring; and, indeed, before the time at which our story commenced he had begun to acknowledge to himself that he might rather be afraid of her anger than she of his. There was a courage about her which nothing could dash. She had grown up under his eyes strong, brave, sometimes almost bold, with a dash of humour, but always quite determined in her own ideas of wrong or right. He had in truth been all but afraid of her when he found himself compelled to tell her of the decision to which his conscience compelled him. But the will was made,—the third, perhaps the fourth or fifth, which had seemed to him to be necessary since his mind had been exercised in this matter. He made this will, which he assured himself should be the last, leaving Llanfeare to his nephew on condition that he should prefix the name of Indefer to that of Jones, and adding certain stipulations as to further entail. Then everything of which he might die possessed, except Llanfeare itself and the furniture in the house, he left to his niece Isabel.

'We must get rid of the horses,' he said to her about a fortnight after the conversation last recorded.

'Why that?'

'My will has been made, and there will be

so little now for you, that we must save what we can before I die.'

'Oh, bother me!' said Isabel, laughing.

'Do you suppose it is not dreadful to me to have to reflect how little I can do for you? I may, perhaps, live for two years, and we may save six or seven hundred a year. I have put a charge on the estate for four thousand pounds.* The property is only a small thing, after all;—not above fifteen hundred a year.'

'I will not hear of the horses being sold, and there is an end of it. You have been taken out about the place every day for the last twenty years, and it would crush me if I were to see a change. You have done the best you can, and now leave it all in God's hands. Pray,—pray let there be no more talking about it. If you only knew how welcome he is to it!'

CHAPTER II

ISABEL BRODRICK

WHEN Mr. Indefer Jones spoke of living for two years, he spoke more hopefully of himself than the doctor was wont to speak to Isabel. The doctor from Carmarthen visited Llanfeare twice a week, and having become intimate and confidential with Isabel, had told her that the candle had nearly burnt itself down to the socket.

There was no special disease, but he was a worn-out old man. It was well that he should allow himself to be driven out about the place every day. It was well that he should be encouraged to get up after breakfast, and to eat his dinner in the middle of the day after his old fashion. It was well to do everything around him as though he were not a confirmed invalid. But the doctor thought that he would not last long. The candle, as the doctor said, had nearly burnt itself out in the socket.

And yet there was no apparent decay in the old man's intellect. He had never been much given to literary pursuits, but that which he had always done he did still. A daily copy of whatever might be the most thoroughly Conservative paper of the day he always read carefully from the beginning to the end; and a weekly copy of the *Guardian**nearly filled up the hours which were devoted to study. On Sunday he read two sermons through, having been forbidden by the doctor to take his place in the church because of the draughts, and thinking, apparently, that it would be mean and wrong to make that an excuse for shirking an onerous duty. An hour a day was devoted by him religiously to the Bible. The rest of his time was occupied by the care of his property. Nothing gratified him so much as the coming in of one of his tenants, all of whom were so intimately known to him, that, old as he was, he never forgot the names even of their children.

The idea of raising a rent was abominable to
him. Around the house there were about two
hundred acres which he was supposed to farm.
On these some half-dozen worn-out old labourers
were maintained in such a manner that no return from the land was ever forthcoming.* On
this subject he would endure remonstrance from
no one,—not even from Isabel.

Such as he has been here described, he would
have been a happy old man during these last
half-dozen years, had not his mind been exercised
day by day, and hour by hour, by these cares as
to the property which were ever present to him.
A more loving heart than his could hardly be
found in a human bosom, and all its power of
love had been bestowed on Isabel. Nor could
any man be subject to a stronger feeling of duty
than that which pervaded him; and this feeling
of duty induced him to declare to himself that
in reference to his property he was bound to do
that which was demanded of him by the established custom of his order. In this way he had
become an unhappy man, troubled by conflict-
ing feelings, and was now, as he was approaching the hour of his final departure, tormented by
the thought that he would leave his niece without sufficient provision for her wants.

But the thing was done. The new will was
executed and tied in on the top of the bundle
which contained the other wills which he had
made. Then, naturally enough, there came back

upon him the idea, hardly amounting to a hope, that something might even yet occur to set matters right by a marriage between the cousins. Isabel had spoken to him so strongly on the subject that he did not dare to repeat his request. And yet, he thought, there was no good reason why they two should not become man and wife. Henry, as far as he could learn, had given up his bad courses. The man was not evil to the eye, a somewhat good-looking man rather than otherwise, tall with well-formed features, with light hair and blue-grey eyes, not subject to be spoken of as being unlike a gentleman, if not noticeable as being like one. That inability of his to look one in the face when he was speaking had not struck the Squire forcibly as it had done Isabel. He would not have been agreeable to the Squire had there been no bond between them,—would still have been the reverse, as he had been formerly, but for that connexion. But, as things were, there was room for an attempt at love; and if for an attempt at love on his part, why not also on Isabel's? But he did not dare to bid Isabel even to try to love this cousin.

'I think I would like to have him down again soon,' he said to his niece.

'By all means. The more the tenants know him the better it will be. I can go to Hereford at any time.'

'Why should you run away from me?'

'Not from you, Uncle Indefer, but from him.'

'And why from him?'

'Because I don't love him.'

'Must you always run away from the people you do not love?'

'Yes, when the people, or person, is a man, and when the man has been told that he ought specially to love me.'

When she said this she looked into her uncle's face, smiling indeed, but still asking a serious question. He dared to make no answer, but by his face he told the truth. He had declared his wishes to his nephew.

'Not that I mean to be in the least afraid of him,' she continued. 'Perhaps it will be better that I should see him, and if he speaks to me have it out with him. How long would he stay?'

'A month, I suppose. He can come for a month.'

'Then I'll stay for the first week. I must go to Hereford before the summer is over. Shall I write to him?' Then it was settled as she had proposed. She wrote all her uncle's letters, even to her cousin Henry, unless there was, by chance, something very special to be communicated. On the present occasion she sent the invitation as follows:—

'Llanfeare, 17th June, 187—, Monday.

'MY DEAR HENRY,—Your uncle wants you to come here on the 1st July and stay for a month. The 1st of July will be Monday. Do not travel on a Sunday as you did last time, because he does not like it. I shall be here the first part of the time, and then I shall go to Hereford. It is in the middle of the summer only that I can leave him. Your affectionate cousin,

'ISABEL BRODRICK.'

She had often felt herself compelled to sign herself to him in that way, and it had gone much against the grain with her; but to a cousin it was the ordinary thing, as it is to call any indifferent man 'My dear sir,' though he be not in the least dear. And so she had reconciled herself to the falsehood.

Another incident in Isabel's life must be told to the reader. It was her custom to go to Hereford at least once a year, and there to remain at her father's house for a month. These visits had been made annually since she had lived at Llanfeare, and in this way she had become known to many of the Hereford people. Among others who had thus become her friends there was a young clergyman, William Owen, a minor canon attached to the cathedral,* who during her last visit had asked her to be his wife. At that time she had supposed herself to be her uncle's heiress, and looking at herself as the future owner of Llanfeare had considered herself bound to regard such an offer in reference to her future duties and to the obedience which she owed to her uncle. She never told her lover, nor did she ever quite tell herself, that she would certainly accept him if bound by no such considerations;

but we may tell the reader that it was so. Had she felt herself to be altogether free, she would have given herself to the man who had offered her his love. As it was she answered him anything but hopefully, saying nothing of any passion of her own, speaking of herself as though she were altogether at the disposal of her uncle. 'He has decided now,' she said, 'that when he is gone the property is to be mine.' The minor canon, who had heard nothing of this, drew himself up as though about to declare in his pride that he had not intended to ask for the hand of the lady of Llanfeare. 'That would make no difference in me,' she continued, reading plainly the expression in the young man's face. 'My regard would be swayed neither one way nor the other by any feeling of that kind. But as he has chosen to make me his daughter, I must obey him as his daughter. It is not probable that he will consent to such a marriage.'

Then there had been nothing further between them till Isabel, on her return to Llanfeare, had written to him to say that her uncle had decided against the marriage, and that his decision was final.

Now in all this Isabel had certainly been hardly used, though her ill-usage had in part been due to her own reticence as to her own feelings. When she told the Squire that the offer had been made to her, she did so as if she herself had been almost indifferent.

'William Owen!' the Squire had said, repeating the name; 'his grandfather kept the inn at Pembroke!'*

'I believe he did,' said Isabel calmly.

'And you would wish to make him owner of Llanfeare?'

'I did not say so,' rejoined Isabel. 'I have told you what occurred, and have asked you what you thought.'

Then the Squire shook his head, and there was an end of it. The letter was written to the minor canon telling him that the Squire's decision was final.

In all this there had been no allusion to love on the part of Isabel. Had there been, her uncle could hardly have pressed upon her the claims of his nephew. But her manner in regard to the young clergyman had been so cold as to leave upon her uncle an impression that the matter was one of but little moment. To Isabel it was matter of infinite moment. And yet when she was asked again and again to arrange all the difficulties of the family by marrying her cousin, she was forced to carry on the conversation as though no such person existed as her lover at Hereford.

And yet the Squire remembered it all,—remembered that when he had thus positively objected to the grandson of the innkeeper, he had done so because he had felt it to be his duty to keep the grandson of an innkeeper out of

Llanfeare. That the grandson of old Thomas Owen, of the Pembroke Lion, should reign at Llanfeare in the place of an Indefer Jones had been abominable to him. To prevent that had certainly been within his duties. But it was very different now, when he would leave his girl poorly provided for, without a friend and without a roof of her own over her head! And yet, though her name was Brodrick, she, too, was a Jones; and her father, though an attorney, had come of a family nearly as good as his own. In no case could it be right that she should marry the grandson of old Thomas Owen. Therefore, hitherto, he had never again referred to that proposal of marriage. Should she again have spoken of it his answer might perhaps have been less decided; but neither had she again spoken of the clergyman.

All this was hard upon Isabel, who, if she said nothing, still thought of her lover. And it must be acknowledged also that though she did not speak, still she thought of her future prospects. She had laughed at the idea of being solicitous as to her inheritance. She had done so in order that she might thereby lessen the trouble of her uncle's mind; but she knew as well as did another the difference between the position which had been promised her as owner of Llanfeare, and that to which she would be reduced as the step-daughter of a stepmother who did not love her. She knew, too, that she had been cold to William

Owen, giving him no sort of encouragement, having seemed to declare to him that she had rejected him because she was her uncle's heiress. And she knew also,—or thought that she knew, —that she was not possessed of those feminine gifts which probably might make a man constant under difficulties. No more had been heard of William Owen during the last nine months. Every now and then a letter would come to her from one of her younger sisters, who now had their own anxieties and their own loves, but not a word was there in one of them of William Owen. Therefore, it may be said that that last change in her uncle's purpose had fallen upon her with peculiar hardness.

But she never uttered a complaint, or even looked one. As for utterance there was no one to whom she could have spoken it. There had never been many words between her and her own family as to the inheritance. As she had been reticent to her father so had he to her. The idea in the attorney's house at Hereford was that she was stubborn, conceited, and disdainful. It may be that in regard to her stepmother there was something of this, but, let that be as it might, there had been but little confidence between them as to matters at Llanfeare. It was, no doubt, supposed by her father that she was to be her uncle's heir.

Conceited, perhaps, she was as to certain gifts of character. She did believe herself to be strong of purpose and capable of endurance. But in some respects she was humble enough. She gave herself no credit for feminine charms such as the world loves. In appearance she was one calculated to attract attention,—somewhat tall, well set on her limbs, active, and of good figure; her brow was broad and fine, her grey eyes were bright and full of intelligence, her nose and mouth were well formed, and there was not a mean feature in her face. But there was withal a certain roughness about her, an absence of feminine softness in her complexion, which, to tell the truth of her, was more conspicuous to her own eyes than to any others. The farmers and their wives about the place would declare that Miss Isabel was the finest young woman in South Wales. With the farmers and their wives she was on excellent terms, knowing all their ways, and anxious as to all their wants. With the gentry around she concerned herself but little. Her uncle's habits were not adapted to the keeping of much company, and to her uncle's habits she had fitted herself altogether. It was on this account that neither did she know the young men around, nor did they know her. And then, because no such intimacies had grown up, she told herself that she was unlike other girls,—that she was rough, unattractive, and unpopular.

Then the day came for the arrival of Henry Jones, during the approach to which Uncle

Indefer had, from day to day, become more and more uneasy. Isabel had ceased to say a word against him. When he had been proposed to her as a lover she had declared that she had loathed him. Now that suggestion had been abandoned, or left in abeyance. Therefore she dealt with his name and with his coming as she might with that of any other guest. She looked to his room, and asked questions as to his comfort. Would it not be well to provide a separate dinner for him, seeing that three o'clock would be regarded as an awkward hour by a man from London? 'If he doesn't like it, he had better go back to London,' said the old Squire in anger. But the anger was not intended against his girl, but against the man who by the mere force of his birth was creating such a sea of troubles.*

'I have told you what my intentions are,' the Squire said to his nephew on the evening of his arrival.

'I am sure that I am very much obliged to you, my dear uncle.'

'You need not be in the least obliged to me. I have done what I conceive to be a duty. I can still change it if I find that you do not deserve it. As for Isabel, she deserves everything that can be done for her. Isabel has never given me the slightest cause for displeasure. I doubt whether there is a better creature in the world living than Isabel. She deserves everything. But as you are the male heir, I think it right that you should follow me in the property—unless you show yourself to be unworthy.'

This was certainly a greeting hard to be endured,—a speech very difficult to answer. Nevertheless it was satisfactory, if only the old Squire would not again change his mind. The young man had thought much about it, and had come to the resolution that the best way to insure the good things promised him would be to induce Isabel to be his wife.

'I'm sure she is all that you say, Uncle Indefer,' he replied.

Uncle Indefer grunted, and told him that if he wanted any supper, he had better go and get it.

CHAPTER III

COUSIN HENRY*

COUSIN HENRY found his position to be difficult and precarious. That suggestion of his uncle's,—or rather assertion,—that he could still change his mind was disagreeable. No doubt he could do so, and, as Cousin Henry thought, would be the very man to do it, if angered, thwarted, or even annoyed. He knew that more than one will had already been made and set aside. Cousin Henry had turned the whole matter very much in his mind since he had become cognizant of his uncle's character.

However imprudent he might have been in his earlier days, he was now quite alive to the importance of being Squire of Llanfeare. There was nothing that he was not ready to do to please and conciliate his uncle. Llanfeare without Isabel as a burden would no doubt be preferable, but he was quite ready to marry Isabel to-morrow, if Isabel would only accept him. The game he had to play was for Llanfeare. It was to be Llanfeare or nothing. The position offered to him was to come, not from love, but from a sense of duty on the part of the old man. If he could keep the old man firm to that idea, Llanfeare would be his own; but should he be excluded from that inheritance, there would be no lesser prize by which he might reconcile himself to the loss. His uncle would not leave him anything from love. All this he understood thoroughly, and was therefore not unnaturally nervous as to his own conduct at the present crisis.

It was only too manifest to him that his uncle did in fact dislike him. At their very first interview he was made to listen to praises of Isabel and threats against himself. He was quite prepared to put up with both, or with any other disagreeable hardship which might be inflicted upon him, if only he could do so successfully. But he believed that his best course would be to press his suit with Isabel. Should he do so successfully, he would at any rate be safe. Should she be persistent in refusing him, which he believed to be probable, then he would have shown himself desirous of carrying out his uncle's wishes. As to all this he was clear-sighted enough. But he did not quite perceive the state of his uncle's mind in regard to himself. He did not understand how painfully the old man was still vacillating between affection and duty; nor did he fathom the depth of the love which his uncle felt for Isabel. Had he been altogether wise in the matter, he would have kept out of his uncle's presence, and have devoted himself to the tenants and the land; but in lieu of this, he intruded himself as much as possible into his uncle's morning room, often to the exclusion of Isabel. Now it had come to pass that Uncle Indefer was never at his ease unless his niece were with him.

'Nobody can be more attached to another than I am to Isabel,' said the nephew to his uncle on the third morning of his arrival. Whereupon Uncle Indefer grunted. The more he saw of the man, the less he himself liked the idea of sacrificing Isabel to such a husband. 'I shall certainly do my best to carry out your wishes.'

'My wishes have reference solely to her.'

'Exactly, sir; I understand that completely. As she is not to be the heiress, the best thing possible is to be done for her.'

'You think that marrying you would be the best thing possible!' This the uncle said in a tone of scorn which must have been very hard to bear. And it was unjust too, as the unfortunate nephew had certainly not intended to speak of himself personally as being the best thing possible for Isabel.

But this too had to be borne. 'I meant, sir, that if she would accept my hand, she would have pretty nearly as great an interest in the property as I myself.'

'She would have much more,' said Uncle Indefer angrily. 'She knows every man, woman, and child about the place. There is not one of them who does not love her. And so they ought, for she has been their best friend. As far as they are concerned it is almost cruel that they should not be left in her hands.'

'So it will be, sir, if she will consent to do as you and I wish.'

'Wish! Pshaw!' Then he repeated his grunts, turning his shoulder round against his nephew, and affecting to read the newspaper which he had held in his hand during the conversation. It must be acknowledged that the part to be played by the intended heir was very difficult. He could perceive that his uncle hated him, but he could not understand that he might best lessen that hatred by relieving his uncle of his presence. There he sat looking at the empty grate, and pretending now and again to read an old newspaper which was lying on the table, while his uncle fumed and grunted. During every moment that was so passed Uncle Indefer was asking himself whether that British custom as to male heirs was absolutely essential to the welfare of the country. Here were two persons suggested to his mind, one of whom was to be his future successor. One of them was undoubtedly the sweetest human being that had ever crossed his path; the other,—as he was inclined to think at the present moment,—was the least sweet. And as they were to him, would they not be to the tenants whose welfare was to depend so much on the future owner of the property? The longer that he endured the presence of the man the more desirous did he feel of turning to the drawer which was close at hand, and destroying the topmost of those documents which lay there tied in a bundle together.

But he did not allow himself to be at once driven to a step so unreasonable. The young man had done nothing which ought to offend him,—had, indeed, only obeyed him in coming down to South Wales. That custom of the country was good and valid and wise. If he believed in anything of the world worldly,* he believed in primogeniture in respect of land. Though Isabel was ever so sweet, duty was duty. Who was he that he should dare to say to himself that he could break through what he believed to be a law on his conscience without a sin? If he might permit himself to make a special exemption for himself in the indulgence of his own affection, then why might not another, and another, and so on? Did he not know that it would have been better that the whole thing should have been settled for him by an entail? And, if so, how could it be right that he should act in opposition to the spirit of such an entail, merely because he had the power to do so? Thus he argued with himself again and again; but these arguments would never become strong till his nephew had relieved him of his presence.

While he was so arguing, Cousin Henry was trying his hand with Isabel. There had been but a week for him to do it, and three days had already passed away. At the end of the week Isabel was to go to Hereford, and Henry, as far as he knew, was still expected by his uncle to make an offer to his cousin. And, as regarded himself, he was well enough disposed to do so. He was a man with no strong affections, but also with no strong aversions,—except that at present he had a strong affection for Llanfeare, and a strong aversion to the monotonous office in which he was wont to earn his daily bread up in London. And he, too, was desirous of doing his duty,—as long as the doing of his duty might tend to the desired possession of Llanfeare. He was full of the idea that a great deal was due to Isabel. A great deal was certainly due to Isabel, if only, by admitting so much, his possession of Llanfeare was to be ensured.

'So you are going away in two or three days?' he said to her.

'In four days. I am to start on Monday.'

'That is very soon. I am so sorry that you are to leave us! But I suppose it is best that dear Uncle Indefer should not be left alone.'

'I should have gone at this time in any case,' said Isabel, who would not allow it to be supposed that he could fill her place near their uncle.

'Nevertheless I am sorry that you should not have remained while I am here. Of course it cannot be helped.' Then he paused, but she had not a word further to say. She could see by the anxiety displayed in his face, and by a more than usually unnatural tone in his voice, that he was about to make his proposition. She was quite prepared for it, and remained silent, fixed, and attentive. 'Isabel,' he said, 'I suppose Uncle Indefer has told you what he intends?'

'I should say so. I think he always tells me what he intends.'

'About the property, I mean.'

'Yes; about the property. I believe he has made a will leaving it to you. I believe he has done this, not because he loves you the best, but because he thinks it ought to go to the male heir. I quite agree with him that these things should not be governed by affection. He is so good that he will certainly do what he believes to be his duty.'

'Nevertheless the effect is the same.'

'Oh yes; as regards you, the effect will be the same. You will have the property, whether it comes from love or duty.'

'And you will lose it.'

'I cannot lose what never was mine,' she said, smiling.

'But why should we not both have it,—one as well as the other?'

'No; we can't do that.'

'Yes, we can; if you will do what I wish, and what he wishes also. I love you with all my heart.'

She opened her eyes as though driven to do so by surprise. She knew that she should not have expressed herself in that way, but she could not avoid the temptation.

'I do, indeed, with all my heart. Why should we not—marry, you know? Then the property would belong to both of us.'

'Yes; then it would.'

'Why should we not; eh, Isabel?' Then he approached her as though about to make some ordinary symptom of a lover's passion.

'Sit down there, Henry, and I will tell you why we cannot do that. I do not love you in the least.'

'You might learn to love me.'

'Never; never! That lesson would be impossible to me. Now let there be an end of it. Uncle Indefer has, I dare say, asked you to make this proposition.'

'He wrote a letter, just saying that he would like it.'

'Exactly so. You have found yourself compelled to do his bidding, and you have done it.

Then let there be an end of it. I would not marry an angel even to oblige him or to get Llanfeare; and you are not an angel,—to my way of thinking.'

'I don't know about angels,' he said, trying still to be good-humoured.

'No, no. That was my nonsense. There is no question of angels. But not for all Llanfeare, not even to oblige him, would I undertake to marry a man, even if I were near to loving him. I should have to love him entirely, without reference to Llanfeare. I am not at all near to loving you.'

'Why not, Isabel?' he asked foolishly.

'Because,—because,—because you are odious to me!'

'Isabel!'

'I beg your pardon. I should not have said so. It was very wrong; but, then, why did you ask so foolish a question? Did I not tell you to let there be an end of it? And now will you let me give you one little bit of advice?'

'What is it?' he asked angrily. He was beginning to hate her, though he was anxious to repress his hatred, lest by indulging it he should injure his prospects.

'Do not say a word about me to my uncle. It will be better for you not to tell him that there has been between us any such interview as this. If he did once wish that you and I should become man and wife, I do not think that he wishes it now. Let the thing slide, as they say. He has quite made up his mind in your favour, because it is his duty. Unless you do something to displease him very greatly, he will make no further change. Do not trouble him more than you can help by talking to him on things that are distasteful. Anything in regard to me, coming from you, will be distasteful to him. You had better go about among the farms, and see the tenants, and learn the condition of everything. And then talk to him about that. Whatever you do, never suggest that the money coming from it all is less than it ought to be. That is my advice. And now, if you please, you and I need not talk about it any more.' Then she got up and left the room without waiting for a reply.

When he was alone he resolved upon complying with her advice, at any rate in one respect. He would not rencw his offer of marriage; nor would he hold any further special conversation with her. Of course, she was hateful to him, having declared so plainly to him her own opinion regarding himself. He had made the offer, and had thereby done his duty. He had made the offer, and had escaped.

But he did not at all believe in the sincerity of her advice as to their uncle. His heart was throbbing with the desire to secure the inheritance to himself,—and so he thought, no doubt, was hers as to herself. It might be that the old man's intention would depend upon his obedience, and if so, it was certainly necessary that the old man should know that he had been obedient. Of course, he would tell the old man what he had done.

But he said not a word till Isabel had gone. He did take her advice about the land and the tenants, but hardly to much effect. If there were a falling roof here or a half-hung door there, he displayed his zeal by telling the Squire of these defaults. But the Squire hated to hear of such defaults. It must be acknowledged that it would have required a man of very great parts to have given satisfaction in the position in which this young man was placed.

But as soon as Isabel was gone he declared his obedience.

'I have asked her, sir, and she has refused me,' he said in a melancholy, low, and sententious voice.

'What did you expect?'

'At any rate, I did as you would have me.'

'Was she to jump down your throat when you asked her?'

'She was very decided,—very. Of course, I spoke of your wishes.'

'I have not any wishes.'

'I thought that you desired it.'

'So I did, but I have changed my mind. It would not do at all. I almost wonder how you could have had the courage to ask her. I don't suppose that you have the insight to see that she is different from other girls.'

'Oh, yes; I perceived that.'

'And yet you would go and ask her to be your wife off-hand, just as though you were going to buy a horse! I suppose you told her that it would be a good thing because of the estate?'

'I did mention it,' said the young man, altogether astounded and put beyond himself by his uncle's manner and words.

'Yes; just as if it were a bargain! If you will consent to put up with me as a husband, why, then you can go shares with me in the property. That was the kind of thing, wasn't it? And then you come and tell me that you have done your duty by making the offer!'

The heir expectant was then convinced that it would have been better for him to have followed the advice which Isabel had given him, but yet he could not bring himself to believe that the advice had been disinterested. Why should Isabel have given him disinterested advice in opposition to her own prospects? Must not Isabel's feeling about the property be the same as his own?

CHAPTER IV

THE SQUIRE'S DEATH

WITH a sore heart Isabel went her way to Hereford,—troubled because she saw nothing but sorrow and vexation in store for her uncle.

'I know that I am getting weaker every day,'

he said. And yet it was not long since he had spoken of living for two years.

'Shall I stay?' asked Isabel.

'No; that would be wrong. You ought to go to your father. I suppose that I shall live till you come back.'

'Oh, Uncle Indefer!'

'What if I did die? It is not that that troubles me.' Then she kissed him and left him. She knew how vain it was to ask any further questions, understanding thoroughly the nature of his sorrow. The idea that this nephew must be the master of Llanfeare was so bitter to him that he could hardly endure it; and then, added to this, was the vexation of the nephew's presence. That three weeks should be passed alone with the man, —three weeks of the little that was left to him of life, seemed to be a cruel addition to the greater sorrow! But Isabel went, and the uncle and nephew were left to do the best they could with each other's company.

Isabel had not seen Mr. Owen or heard from him since the writing of that letter in which she had told him of her uncle's decision. Now it would be necessary that she should meet him, and she looked forward to doing so almost with fear and trembling. On one point she had made up her mind, or thought that she had made up her mind. As she had refused him when supposed to be heiress of Llanfeare, she certainly would not accept him, should he feel himself constrained by a sense of honour to renew his offer to her now that her position was so different. She had not accused him in her own heart of having come to her because of her supposed wealth. Thinking well of him in other matters, she thought well of him also in that. But still there was the fact that she had refused him when supposed to be an heiress; and not even to secure her happiness would she allow him to think that she accepted him because of her altered circumstances. And yet she was in love with him, and had now acknowledged to herself that it was so. Her position in this as in all things seemed to be so cruel! Had she been the heiress of Llanfeare she could not have married him, because it would then have been her duty to comply with the wishes of her uncle. No such duty would now be imposed upon her, at any rate after her uncle's death. As simple Isabel Brodrick she might marry whom she would without bringing discredit upon the Indefer Joneses. But that which she had been constrained to do before her uncle had changed his purpose now tied her hands.

It did seem to her cruel; but she told herself that it was peculiarly her duty to bear such cruelty without complaint. Of her uncle's intense love to her she was fully aware, and, loving him as warmly, was prepared to bear everything on his account. His vacillation had been unfortunate for her, but in everything he had done the best according to his lights. Perhaps there was present to her mind something of the pride of a martyr. Perhaps she gloried a little in the hardship of her position. But she was determined to have her glory and her martyrdom all to herself. No human being should ever hear from her lips a word of complaint against her Uncle Indefer.

The day after her arrival her father asked her a few questions as to her uncle's intentions in reference to the property.

'I think it is all settled,' she said. 'I think it has been left to my Cousin Henry.'

'Then he has changed his mind,' said her father angrily. 'He did mean to make you his heiress?'

'Henry is at Llanfeare now, and Henry will be his heir.'

'Why has he changed? Nothing can be more unjust than to make a promise in such a matter and then to break it.'

'Who says that he made a promise? You have never heard anything of the kind from me. Papa, I would so much rather not talk about Llanfeare. Ever since I have known him, Uncle Indefer has been all love to me. I would not allow a thought of mine to be polluted by ingratitude towards him. Whatever he has done, he has done because he has thought it to be the best. Perhaps I ought to tell you that he has made some charge on the property on my behalf, which will prevent my being a burden upon you.'

A week or ten days after this, when she had been nearly a fortnight at Hereford, she was told that William Owen was coming in to drink tea. This communication was made to her by her stepmother, in that serious tone which is always intended to convey a matter of importance. Had any other minor canon or any other gentleman been coming to tea, the fact would have been announced in a different manner.

'I shall be delighted to see him,' said Isabel, suppressing with her usual fortitude any slightest symptom of emotion.

'I hope you will, my dear. I am sure he is very anxious to see you.'

Then Mr. Owen came and drank his tea in the midst of the family. Isabel could perceive that he was somewhat confused,—not quite able to talk in his usual tone, and that he was especially anxious as to his manner towards her. She took her part in the conversation as though there were nothing peculiar in the meeting. She spoke of Llanfeare, of her uncle's failing health, and of her cousin's visit, taking care to indicate by some apparently chance word, that Henry was received there as the heir. She played her part well, evincing no sign of special feeling; but her ear was awake to the slightest tone in his voice after he had received the information she had given him. She knew that his voice was altered, but she did not read the alteration altogether aright.

'I shall call in the morning,' he said, as he gave her his hand at parting. There was no pressure of the hand, but still he had addressed himself especially to her.

Why should he come in the morning? She had made up her mind, at the spur of the moment, that the news which he had heard had settled that matter for ever. But if so, why should he come in the morning? Then she felt, as she sat alone in her room, that she had done him a foul injustice in that spur of the moment. It must be that she had done him an injustice, or he would not have said that he would come. But if he could be generous, so could she. She had refused him when she believed herself to be the heiress of Llanfeare, and she certainly would not accept him now.

On the next morning about eleven o'clock he came. She had become aware that it was the intention of all the family that she should see him alone, and she made no struggle against that intention. As such intention existed, the interview must of course take place, and as well now as later. There was no confidence on the matter between herself and her stepmother,— no special confidence between even herself and her half-sisters. But she was aware that they all supposed that Mr. Owen was to come there on that morning for the sake of renewing his offer to her. It was soon done when he had come.

'Isabel,' he said, 'I have brought with me that

letter which you wrote to me. Will you take it back again?' And he held it out in his hand.

'Nay; why should I take back my own letter?' she answered, smiling.

'Because I hope,—I do not say I trust,— but I hope that I may receive an altered answer.'

'Why should you hope so?' she asked, foolishly enough.

'Because I love you so dearly. Let me say something very plainly. If it be a long story, forgive me because of its importance to myself. I did think that you were,—well, inclined to like me.'

'Like you! I always liked you. I do like you.'

'I hoped more. Perhaps I thought more. Nay, Isabel, do not interrupt me. When they told me that you were to be your uncle's heir, I knew that you ought not to marry me.'

'Why not?'

'Well, I knew that it should not be so. I knew that your uncle would think so.'

'Yes, he thought so.'

'I knew that he would, and I accepted your answer as conveying his decision. I had not intended to ask the heiress of Llanfeare to be my wife.'

'Why not? Why not?'

'I had not intended to ask the heiress of Llanfeare to be my wife,' he said, repeating the words. 'I learned last night that it was not to be so.'

'No; it is not to be so.'

'Then why should not Isabel Brodrick be the wife of William Owen, if she likes him,—if only she can bring herself to like him well enough?'

She could not say that she did not like him well enough. She could not force herself to tell such a lie! And yet there was her settled purpose still strong in her mind. Having refused him when she believed herself to be rich, she could not bring herself to take him now that she was poor. She only shook her head mournfully.

'You cannot like me well enough for that?'

'It must not be so.'

'Must not? Why must not?'

'It cannot be so.'

'Then, Isabel, you must say that you do not love me.'

'I need say nothing, Mr. Owen.' Again she smiled as she spoke to him. 'It is enough for me to say that it cannot be so. If I ask you not to press me further, I am sure that you will not do so.'

'I shall press you further,' he said, as he left her; 'but I will leave you a week to think of it.'

She took the week to think of it, and from day to day her mind would change as she thought of it. Why should she not marry him, if thus they might both be happy? Why should she cling to a resolution made by her when she was in error as to the truth? She knew now, she was now quite certain, that when he had first come to her he had known nothing of her promised inheritance. He had come then simply because he loved her, and for that reason, and for that reason only, he had now come again. And yet, —and yet, there was her resolution! And there was the ground on which she had founded it! Though he might not remember it now, would he not remember hereafter that she had refused him when she was rich and accepted him when she was poor? Where then would be her martyrdom, where her glory, where her pride? Were she to do so, she would only do as would any other girl. Though she would not have been mean, she would seem to have been mean, and would so seem to his eyes. When the week was over she had told herself that she must be true to her resolution.

There had been something said about him in the family, but very little. The stepmother was indeed afraid of Isabel, though she had endeavoured to conquer her own fear by using authority; and her half-sisters, though they loved her, held her in awe. There was so little that was weak about her, so little that was self-indulgent, so little that was like the other girls around them! It was known that Mr. Owen was to come again on a certain day at a certain hour, and it was known also for what purpose he was to come; but no one had dared to ask a direct question as to the result of his coming.

He came, and on this occasion her firmness

almost deserted her. When he entered the room he seemed to her to be bigger than before, and more like her master. As the idea that he was so fell upon her, she became aware that she loved him better than ever. She began to know that with such a look as he now wore he would be sure to conquer. She did not tell herself that she would yield, but thoughts flitted across her as to what might be the best manner of yielding.

'Isabel,' he said, taking her by the hand, ' Isabel, I have come again, as I told you that I would.'

She could not take her hand from him, nor could she say a word to him in her accustomed manner. As he looked down upon her, she felt that she had already yielded, when suddenly the door was opened, and one of the girls hurried into the room.

'Isabel,' said her sister, 'here is a telegram for you, just come from Carmarthen.'

Of course she opened it instantly with perturbed haste and quivering fingers. The telegram was as follows:—'Your uncle is very ill, very ill indeed, and wishes you to come back quite immediately.' The telegram was not from her Cousin Henry, but from the doctor.

There was no time then either for giving love or for refusing it. The paper was handed to her lover to read, and then she rushed out of the room as though the train which was to carry her would start instantly.

'You will let me write to you by-and-by?' said Mr. Owen as she left him; but she made no answer to him as she rushed out of the room; nor would she make any answer to any of the others as they expressed either hope or consolation. When was the next train? When should she reach Carmarthen? When would she once more be at the old man's bedside? In the course of the afternoon she did leave Hereford,* and at about ten o'clock that night she was at Carmarthen. Some one concerned had looked into this matter of the trains, and there at the station was a fly ready to take her to Llanfeare.* Before eleven her uncle's hand was in hers, as she stood by his bedside.

Her Cousin Henry was in the room, and so was the housekeeper who had been with him constantly almost ever since she had left him. She had seen at once by the manner of the old servants as she entered the house, from the woeful face of the butler, and from the presence of the cook, who had lived in the family for the last twenty years, that something terrible was expected. It was not thus that she would have been received had not the danger been imminent.

'Dr. Powell says, Miss Isabel, that you are to be told that he will be here quite early in the morning.'

This coming from the cook, told her that her uncle was expected to live that night, but that no more was expected.

'Uncle Indefer,' she said, 'how is it with you?

Uncle Indefer, speak to me!' He moved his head a little upon the pillow; he turned his face somewhat towards hers; there was some slight return to the grasp of her hand; there was a gleam of loving brightness left in his eye; but he could not then speak a word. When, after an hour, she left his room for a few minutes to get rid of her travelling clothes, and to prepare herself for watching by him through the night, the housekeeper, whom Isabel had known ever since she had been at Llanfeare, declared that in her opinion her uncle would never speak again.

'The doctor, Miss Isabel, thought so, when he left us.'

She hurried down, and at once occupied the place which the old woman had filled for the last three days and nights. Before long she had banished the woman, so that to her might belong the luxury of doing anything, if aught could be done. That her cousin should be there was altogether unnecessary. If the old man could know any one at his deathbed, he certainly would not wish to see the heir whom he had chosen.

'You must go—you must indeed,' said Isabel. Then the cousin went, and so at last, with some persuasion, did the housekeeper.

She sat there hour after hour, with her hand lying gently upon his. When she would move it for a moment, though it was to moisten his lips, he would give some sign of impatience. For hours he lay in that way, till the early dawn of the summer morning broke into the room through the chink of the shutters. Then there came from him some sign of a stronger life, and at last, with a low muttered voice, indistinct, but not so indistinct but that the sounds were caught, he whispered a word or two.

'It is all right. It is done.'

Soon afterwards she rang the bell violently, and when the nurse entered the room she declared that her old master was no more. When the doctor arrived at seven, having ridden out from Carmarthen, there was nothing for him further to do but to give a certificate as to the manner of death of Indefer Jones, Esq., late of Llanfeare, in the county of Carmarthen.

CHAPTER V

PREPARING FOR THE FUNERAL

ISABEL, when she was left alone, felt that a terrible weight of duty was imposed on her. She seemed to be immediately encompassed by a double world of circumstances. There was that world of grief which was so natural, but which would yet be easy, could she only be allowed to sit down and weep. But it was explained to her that until after the funeral, and till the will should have been read, everything about Llanfeare must be done by her and in obedience to her orders. This necessity of action, —of action which in her present condition of mind did not seem clear to·her,—was not at all easy.

The doctor was good to her, and gave her some instruction before he left her. 'Shall I give the keys to my cousin?' she said to him. But even as she said this there was the doubt on her mind what those last words of her uncle had been intended to mean. Though her grief was very bitter, though her sorrow was quite sincere, she could not keep herself from thinking of those words. It was not that she was anxious to get the estate for herself. It was hardly in that way that the matter in these moments presented itself to her. Did the meaning of those words impose on her any duty? Would it be right that she should speak of them, or be silent? Ought she to suppose that they had any meaning, and if so, that they referred to the will?

'I think that you should keep the keys till after the will has been read,' said the doctor.

'Even though he should ask for them?'

'Even though he should ask for them,' said the doctor. 'He will not press such a request if you tell him that I say it ought to be so. If there be any difficulty, send for Mr. Apjohn.'

Mr. Apjohn was the lawyer; but there had been quite lately some disagreement between her uncle and Mr. Apjohn, and this advice was not palatable to her.

'But,' continued Dr. Powell, 'you will not find any difficulty of that kind. The funeral had better be on Monday. And the will, I suppose, can be read afterwards. Mr. Apjohn will come out and read it. There can be no difficulty about that. I know that Mr. Apjohn's feelings are of the kindest towards your uncle and yourself.'

Mr. Apjohn had taken upon himself to 'scold' her uncle because of the altered will,—the will that had been altered in favour of Cousin Henry. So much the old man had said to Isabel himself. 'If I think it proper, he has no right to scold me,' the old man had said. The 'scolding' had probably been in the guise of that advice which a lawyer so often feels himself justified in giving.

Isabel thought that she had better keep those words to herself, at any rate for the present. She almost resolved that she would keep those words altogether to herself, unless other facts should come out which would explain their meaning and testify to their truth. She would say nothing of them in a way that would seem to imply that she had been led by them to conceive that she expected the property. She did certainly think that they alluded to the property. 'It is all right. It is done.' When her uncle had uttered these words, using the last effort of his mortal strength for the purpose, he no doubt was thinking of the property. He had meant to imply that he had done something to make his last decision 'right' in her favour. She was, she thought, sure of so

much. But then she bore in mind the condition
of the old man's failing mind,—those wandering
thoughts which would so naturally endeavour to
fix themselves upon her and upon the property
in combination with each other. How probable
was it that he would dream of something that he
would fain do, and then dream that he had done
it! And she knew, too, as well as the lawyer
would know himself, that the words would go
for nothing, though they had been spoken before
a dozen witnesses. If a later will was there, the
later will would speak for itself. If no later will
was there, the words were empty breath.

But above all was she anxious that no one
should think that she was desirous of the property,—that no one should suppose that she
would be hurt by not having it. She was not
desirous, and was not hurt. The matter was so
important, and had so seriously burdened her
uncle's mind, that she could not but feel the
weight herself; but as to her own desires, they
were limited to a wish that her uncle's will, whatever it might be, should be carried out. Not to
have Llanfeare, not to have even a shilling from
her uncle's estate, would hurt her but little,—
would hurt her heart not at all. But to know that
it was thought by others that she was disappointed,
—that would be a grievous burden to her! Therefore she spoke to Dr. Powell, and even to her
cousin, as though the estate were doubtless now
the property of the latter.

Henry Jones at this time,—during the days immediately following his uncle's death,—seemed to be so much awe-struck by his position, as to be incapable of action. To his Cousin Isabel he was almost servile in his obedience. With bated breath he did suggest that the keys should be surrendered to him, making his proposition simply on the ground that she would thus be saved from trouble; but when she told him that it was her duty to keep them till after the funeral, and that it would be her duty to act as mistress in the house till after that ceremony, he was cringing in his compliance.

'Whatever you think best, Isabel, shall be done. I would not interfere for a moment.'

Then some time afterwards, on the following day, he assured her that whatever might be the nature of the will, she was to regard Llanfeare as her home as long as it would suit her to remain there.

'I shall go back to papa very soon,' she had said, 'as soon, indeed, as I can have my things packed up after the funeral. I have already written to papa to say so.'

'Everything shall be just as you please,' he replied; 'only, pray, believe that if I can do anything for your accommodation it shall be done.'

To this she made some formal answer of courtesy, not, it may be feared, very graciously. She did not believe in his civility; she did not think he was kind to her in heart, and she could not bring herself to make her manner false to her feelings. After that, during the days that remained before the funeral, very little was said between them. Her dislike to him grew in bitterness, though she failed to explain even to herself the cause of her dislike. She did know that her uncle had been in truth as little disposed to love him as herself, and that knowledge seemed to justify her. Those last words had assured her at any rate of that, and though she was quite sure of her own conscience in regard to Llanfeare, though she was certain that she did not covet the possession of the domain, still she was unhappy to think that it should become his. If only for the tenants' sake and the servants, and the old house itself, there were a thousand pities in that. And then the belief would intrude itself upon her that her uncle in the last expression of his wishes had not intended his nephew to be his heir.

Then, in these days reports reached her which seemed to confirm her own belief. It had not been the habit of her life to talk intimately with the servants, even though at Llanfeare there had been no other woman with whom she could talk intimately. There had been about her a sense of personal dignity which had made such freedom distasteful to herself, and had repressed it in them. But now the housekeeper had come to her with a story to which Isabel had found it impossible not to listen. It was reported about the place that the Squire had certainly executed another will a few days after Isabel had left Llanfeare.

'If so,' said Isabel sternly, ' it will be found when Mr. Apjohn comes to open the papers.'

But the housekeeper did not seem satisfied with this. Though she believed that some document had been written, Mr. Apjohn had not been sent for, as had always been done on former similar occasions. The making of the Squire's will had been a thing always known and well understood at Llanfeare. Mr. Apjohn had been sent for on such occasions, and had returned after a day or two, accompanied by two clerks. It was quite understood that the clerks were there to witness the will. The old butler, who would bring in the sherry and biscuits after the operation, was well acquainted with all the testamentary circumstances of the occasions. Nothing of that kind had occurred now; but old Joseph Cantor, who had been a tenant on the property for the last thirty years, and his son, Joseph Cantor the younger, had been called in, and it was supposed that they had performed the duty of witnessing the document. The housekeeper seemed to think that they, when interrogated, had declined to give any information on the subject. She herself had not seen them, but she had seen others of the tenants, and she was certain, she said, that Llanfeare generally believed that the old Squire had executed a will during the absence of his niece.

In answer to all this Isabel simply said that if a new will, which should turn out to be the real will, had actually been made, it would be found among her uncle's papers. She knew well the manner in which those other wills had been tied and deposited in one of the drawers of her uncle's tables. She had been invited to read them all, and had understood from a thousand assurances that he had wished that nothing should be kept secret from her. The key of the very drawer was at this moment in her possession. There was nothing to hinder her from searching, should she wish to search. But she never touched the drawer. The key which locked it she placed in an envelope, and put it apart under another lock and key. Though she listened, though she could not but listen, to the old woman's narrative, yet she rebuked the narrator. 'There should be no talking about such things,' she said. It had been, she said, her uncle's intention to make his nephew the owner of Llanfeare, and she believed that he had done so. It was better that there should be no conversation on the matter until the will had been read.

During these days she did not go beyond the precincts of the garden, and was careful not to encounter any of the tenants, even when they called at the house. Mr. Apjohn she did not see, nor Dr. Powell again, till the day of the funeral. The lawyer had written to her more than once, and had explained to her exactly the manner in which he intended to proceed. He, with Dr. Powell, would be at the house at eleven o'clock; the funeral would be over at half-past twelve; they would lunch at one, and immediately afterwards the will should be 'looked for' and read. The words 'looked for' were underscored in his letter, but no special explanation of the underscoring was given. He went on to say that the tenants would, as a matter of course, attend the funeral, and that he had taken upon himself to invite some few of those who had known the Squire most intimately, to be present at the reading of the will. These he named, and among them were Joseph Cantor the elder, and Joseph Cantor the younger. It immediately occurred to Isabel that the son was not himself a tenant, and that no one else who was not a tenant was included in the list. From this she was sure that Mr. Apjohn had heard the story which the housekeeper had told her. During these days there was little or no intercourse between Isabel and her cousin. At dinner they met, but only at dinner, and even then almost nothing was said between them. What he did with himself during the day she did not even know. At Llanfeare there was a so-called book-room, a small apartment, placed between the drawing-room and the parlour, in which were kept the few hundred volumes which constituted the library of Llanfeare. It had not been much used by the late

Squire, except that from time to time he would
enter it for the sake of taking down with his own
hands some volume of sermons from the shelves.
He himself had for years been accustomed to sit
in the parlour, in which he ate his meals, and
had hated the ceremony of moving even into the
drawing-room. Isabel herself had a sitting-room
of her own upstairs, and she, too, had never used
the book-room. But here Cousin Henry had
now placed himself, and here he remained
through the whole day, though it was not believed
of him that he was given to much reading. For
his breakfast and his supper he went to the
parlour alone. At dinner time Isabel came down.
But through all the long hours of the day he remained among the books, never once leaving
the house till the moment came for receiving
Mr. Apjohn and Dr. Powell before the funeral.
The housekeeper would say little words about
him, wondering what he was doing in the
book-room. To this Isabel would apparently
pay no attention, simply remarking that it was
natural that at such a time he should remain in
seclusion.

'But he does get so very pale, Miss Isabel,'
said the housekeeper. 'He wasn't white, not like
that, when he come first to Llanfeare.' To this
Isabel made no reply; but she, too, had remarked
how wan, how pallid, and how spiritless he had
become.

On the Monday morning, when the men up-

stairs were at work on their ghastly duty, before
the coming of the doctor and the lawyer, she
went down to him, to tell him something of the
programme for the day. Hitherto he had simply
been informed that on that morning the body
would be buried under the walls of the old parish
church, and that after the funeral the will would
be read. Entering the room somewhat suddenly
she found him seated, vacant, in a chair, with
an open book indeed on the table near him, but
so placed that she was sure that he had not been
occupied with it. There he was, looking apparently at the book-shelves, and when she entered
the room he jumped up to greet her with an air
of evident surprise.

'Mr. Apjohn and Dr. Powell will be here at
eleven,' she said.

'Oh, ah; yes,' he replied.

'I thought I would tell you, that you might
be ready.'

'Yes; that is very kind. But I am ready. The
men came in just now, and put the band on my
hat, and laid my gloves there. You will not go,
of course?'

'Yes; I shall follow the body. I do not see why
I should not go as well as you. A woman may
be strong enough at any rate for that. Then
they will come back to lunch.'

'Oh, indeed; I did not know that there would
be a lunch.'

'Yes; Dr. Powell says that it will be proper.

I shall not be there, but you, of course, will be present to take the head of the table.'

'If you wish it.'

'Of course; it would be proper. There must be some one to seem at any rate to entertain them. When that is over Mr. Apjohn will find the will, and will read it. Richard will lay the lunch here, so that you may go at once into the parlour, where the will will be read. They tell me that I am to be there. I shall do as they bid me, though it will be a sore trouble to me. Dr. Powell will be there, and some of the tenants. Mr. Apjohn has thought it right to ask them, and therefore I tell you. Those who will be present are as follows;—John Griffith, of Coed; William Griffith, who has the home farm; Mr. Mortimer Green, of Kidwelly; Samuel Jones, of Llanfeare Grange; and the two Cantors, Joseph Cantor the father, and Joseph the son. I don't know whether you know them by appearance as yet.'

'Yes,' said he, 'I know them.' His face was almost sepulchral as he answered her, and as she looked at him she perceived that a slight quiver came upon his lips as she pronounced with peculiar clearness the two last names on the list.

'I thought it best to tell you all this,' she added. 'If I find it possible, I shall go to Hereford on Wednesday. Most of my things are already packed. It may be that something may occur to stop me, but if it is possible I shall go on Wednesday.'

CHAPTER VI

MR. APJOHN'S EXPLANATION

THE reader need not be detained with any elaborate account of the funeral. Every tenant and every labourer about the place was there; as also were many of the people from Carmarthen. Llanfeare Church, which stands on a point of a little river just as it runs into a creek of the sea, is not more than four miles distant from the town; but such was the respect in which the old squire was held that a large crowd was present as the body was lowered into the vault. Then the lunch followed, just as Isabel had said. There was Cousin Henry, and there were the doctor and the lawyer, and there were the tenants who had been specially honoured by invitation, and there was Joseph Cantor the younger. The viands were eaten freely, though the occasion was not a happy one. Appetites are good even amidst grief, and the farmers of Llanfeare took their victuals and their wine in funereal silence, but not without enjoyment. Mr. Apjohn and Dr. Powell also were hungry, and being accustomed, perhaps, to such entertainments, did not allow the good things prepared to go to waste. But Cousin Henry, though he made an attempt, could not swallow a morsel. He took a glass of wine, and then a second, helping himself from the bottle as it stood near at hand; but he ate nothing, and spoke hardly a word. At first he made some attempt, but his voice seemed to fail him. Not one of the farmers addressed a syllable to him. He had before the funeral taken each of them by the hand, but even then they had not spoken to him. They were rough of manner, little able to conceal their feelings; and he understood well from their bearing that he was odious to them. Now as he sat at table with them, he determined that as soon as this matter should be settled he would take himself away from Llanfeare, even though Llanfeare should belong to him. While they were at the table both the lawyer and the doctor said a word to him, making a struggle to be courteous, but after the first struggle the attempt ceased also with them. The silence of the man, and even the pallor of his face, might be supposed to be excused by the nature of the occasion.

'Now,' said Mr. Apjohn, rising from the table when the eating and drinking had ceased, 'I think we might as well go into the next room. Miss Brodrick, who has consented to be present, will probably be waiting for us.'

Then they passed through the hall into the parlour in a long string, Mr. Apjohn leading the way, followed by Cousin Henry. There they found Isabel sitting with the housekeeper beside her. She shook hands in silence with the attorney, the doctor, and all the tenants, and then, as she took her seat, she spoke a word to Mr. Apjohn. 'As I have felt it hard to be alone, I have asked Mrs. Griffith to remain with me. I hope it is not improper?'

'There can be no reason on earth,' said Mr. Apjohn, 'why Mrs. Griffith should not hear the will of her master, who respected her so thoroughly.' Mrs. Griffith bobbed a curtsey in return for this civility, and then sat down, intently interested in the coming ceremony.

Mr. Apjohn took from his pocket the envelope containing the key, and, opening the little packet very slowly, very slowly opened the drawer, and took out from it a bundle of papers tied with red tape. This he undid, and then, sitting with the bundle loosened before him, he examined the document lying at the top. Then, slowly spreading them out, as though pausing over every operation with premeditated delay, he held in his hand that which he had at first taken; but he was in truth thinking of the words which he would have to use at the present moment. He had expected, but had expected with some doubt, that another document would have been found there. Close at his right hand sat Dr. Powell. Round the room, in distant chairs, were ranged the six farmers, each with his hat in hand between his knees. On a sofa opposite were Isabel and the housekeeper. Cousin Henry sat alone, not very far from the end of the sofa, almost in the middle of the room. As the operation went on, one of his hands quivered so much that he endeavoured to hold it with the other to keep it from shaking. It was impossible that any one there should not observe his trepidation and too evident discomfort.

The document lying at the top of the bundle was opened out very slowly by the attorney, who smoothed it down with his hand preparatory to reading it. Then he looked at the date to assure himself that it was the last will which he himself had drawn. He knew it well, and was cognizant with its every legal quiddity. He could judiciously have explained every clause of it without reading a word, and might probably have to do so before the occasion was over; but he delayed, looking down upon it and still smoothing it, evidently taking another minute or two to collect his thoughts. This will now under his hand was very objectionable to him, having been made altogether in opposition to his own advice, and having thus created that 'scolding' of which the Squire had complained to Isabel. This will bequeathed the whole of the property to Cousin Henry. It did also affect to leave a certain sum of money to Isabel, but the sum of money had been left simply as a sum of money, and not as a charge on the property. Now, within the last few days, Mr. Apjohn had learnt that there were no funds remaining for the payment of such a legacy. The will, therefore, was to him thoroughly distasteful. Should that will in truth be found to be the last will and testament of the old Squire, then it would be his duty to declare that the estate and everything upon it belonged to Cousin Henry, and that there would be, as he feared, no source from which any considerable part of the money nominally left to Miss Brodrick could be defraycd. To his thinking nothing could be more cruel, nothing more unjust, than this.

He had heard tidings which would make it his duty to question the authenticity of this will which was now under his hand; and now had come the moment in which he must explain all this.

'The document which I hold here,' he said, 'purports to be the last will of our old friend. Every will does that as a matter of course. But then there may always be another and a later will.' Here he paused, and looked round the room at the faces of the farmers.

'So there be,' said Joseph Cantor the younger.

'Hold your tongue, Joe, till you be asked,' said the father.

At this little interruption all the other farmers turned their hats in their hands. Cousin Henry gazed round at them, but said never a word. The lawyer looked into the heir's face, and saw the great beads of sweat standing on his brow.

'You hear what young Mr. Cantor has said,' continued the lawyer. 'I am glad that he interrupted me, because it will make my task easier.'

'There now, feyther!' said the young man triumphantly.

'You hold your tongue, Joe, till you be asked, or I'll lend ye a cuff.'

'Now I must explain,' continued Mr. Apjohn, 'what passed between me and my dear old friend when I received instructions from him in this room as to this document which is now before me. You will excuse me, Mr. Jones,'—this he said addressing himself especially to Cousin Henry— 'if I say that I did not like this new purpose on the Squire's part. He was proposing an altogether new arrangement as to the disposition of his property; and though there could be no doubt, not a shadow of doubt, as to the sufficiency of his mental powers for the object in view, still I did not think it well that an old man in feeble health should change a purpose to which he had come in his maturer years, after very long deliberation, and on a matter of such vital moment. I expressed my opinion strongly, and he explained his reasons. He told me that he thought it right to keep the property in the direct line of his family. I endeavoured to explain to him that this might be sufficiently done though the property were left to a lady, if the lady were required to take the name, and to confer the name on her husband, should she afterwards marry. You will probably all understand the circumstances.'

'We understand them all,' said John Griffith, of Coed, who was supposed to be the tenant of most importance on the property.

'Well, then, I urged my ideas perhaps too strongly. I am bound to say that I felt them very strongly. Mr. Indefer Jones remarked that it was not my business to lecture him on a matter in which his conscience was concerned. In this he was undoubtedly right; but still I thought I had done no more than my duty, and could only be sorry that he was angry with me. I can assure you that I never for a moment entertained a feeling of anger against him. He was altogether in his right, and was actuated simply by a sense of duty.'

'We be quite sure of that,' said Samuel Jones, from 'The Grange', an old farmer, who was supposed to be a far-away cousin of the family.

'I have said all this,' continued the lawyer, 'to explain why it might be probable that Mr. Jones should not have sent for me, if, in his last days, he felt himself called on by duty to alter yet once again the decision to which he had come. You can understand that if he determined in his illness to make yet another will—'

'Which he did,' said the younger Cantor, interrupting him.

'Exactly; we will come to that directly.'

'Joe, ye shall be made to sit out in the kitchen; ye shall,' said Cantor the father.

'You can understand, I say, that he might not like to see me again upon the subject. In such case he would have come back to the opinion which I had advocated; and, though no man in his strong health would have been more ready to acknowledge an error than Indefer Jones, of Llanfeare, we all know that with failing strength comes failing courage. I think that it must have been so with him, and that for this reason he did not avail himself of my services. If there be such another will—'

'There be!' said the irrepressible Joe Cantor the younger. Upon this his father only looked at him. 'Our names is to it,' continued Joe.

'We cannot say that for certain, Mr. Cantor,' said the lawyer. 'The old Squire may have made another will, as you say, and may have destroyed it. We must have the will before we can use it. If he left such a will, it will be found among his papers. I have turned over nothing as yet; but as it was here in this drawer and tied in this bundle that Mr. Jones was accustomed to keep his will,—as the last will which I made is here, as I expected to find it, together with those which he had made before and which he seems never to have wished to destroy, I have had to explain all this to you. It is, I suppose, true, Mr. Cantor, that you and your son were called upon by the Squire to witness his signature to a document which he purported to be a will on Monday the 15th of July?'

Then Joseph Cantor the father told all the circumstances as they had occurred. When Mr. Henry Jones had been about a fortnight at Llanfeare, and when Miss Isabel had been gone a

week, he, Cantor, had happened to come up to
see the Squire, as it was his custom to do at least
once a week. Then the Squire had told him that
his services and those also of his son were needed
for the witnessing of a deed. Mr. Jones had gone
on to explain that this deed was to be his last
will. The old farmer, it seemed, had suggested
to his landlord that Mr. Apjohn should be employed. The Squire then declared that this
would be unnecessary; that he himself had copied
a former will exactly, and compared it word for
word, and reproduced it with no other alteration than that of the date. All that was wanted
would be his signature, efficiently witnessed by
two persons who should both be present together with the testator. Then the document
had been signed by the Squire, and after that by
the farmer and his son. It had been written,
said Joseph Cantor, not on long, broad paper
such as that which had been used for the will
now lying on the table before the lawyer, but
on a sheet of square paper such as was now found
in the Squire's desk. He, Cantor, had not read
a word of what had there been set down, but he
had been enabled to see that it was written in
that peculiarly accurate and laborious hand-
writing which the Squire was known to use, but
not more frequently than he could help.

Thus the story was told,—at least, all that
there was to tell as yet. The drawer was opened
and ransacked, as were also the other drawers

belonging to the table. Then a regular search was made by the attorney, accompanied by the doctor, the butler, and the housemaid, and continued through the whole afternoon,—in vain. The farmers were dismissed as soon as the explanation had been given as above described. During the remainder of the day Cousin Henry occupied a chair in the parlour, looking on as the search was continued. He offered no help, which was natural enough; nor did he make any remark as to the work in hand, which was, perhaps, also natural. The matter was to him one of such preponderating moment that he could hardly be expected to speak of it. Was he to have Llanfeare and all that belonged to it, or was he to have nothing? And then, though no accusation was made against him, though no one had insinuated that he had been to blame in the matter, still there was apparent among them all a strong feeling against him. Who had made away with this will, as to the existence of which at one time there was no doubt? Of course the idea was present to his mind that they must think that he had done so. In such circumstances it was not singular that he should say nothing and do nothing.

Late in the evening Mr. Apjohn, just before he left the house, asked Cousin Henry a question, and received an answer.

'Mrs. Griffiths tells me, Mr. Jones, that you were closeted with your uncle for about an hour immediately after the Cantors had left him on that Monday;—just after the signatures had been written. Was it so?'

Again the drops of sweat came out and stood thick upon his forehead. But this Mr. Apjohn could understand without making an accusation against the man, even in his heart. The unexpressed suspicion was so heavy that a man might well sweat under the burden of it! He paused a moment, and tried to look as though he were thinking. 'Yes,' said he; 'I think I was with my uncle on that morning.'

'And you knew that the Cantors had been with him?'

'Not that I remember. I think I did know that somebody had been there. Yes, I did know it. I had seen their hats in the hall.'

'Did he say anything about them?'

'Not that I remember.'

'Of what was he talking? Can you tell me? I rather fancy that he did not talk much to you.'

'I think it was then that he told me the names of all the tenants. He used to scold me because I did not understand the nature of their leases.'

'Did he scold you then?'

'I think so. He always scolded me. He did not like me. I used to think that I would go away and leave him. I wish that I had never come to Llanfeare. I do;—I do.'

There seemed to be a touch of truth about this which almost softened Mr. Apjohn's heart to the poor wretch. 'Would you mind answering one more question, Mr. Jones?' he said. 'Did he tell you that he had made another will?'

'No.'

'Nor that he intended to do so?'

'No.'

'He never spoke to you about another will,—a further will, that should again bestow the estate on your cousin?'

'No,' said Cousin Henry, with the perspiration still on his brow.

Now it seemed to Mr. Apjohn certain that, had the old man made such a change in his purpose, he would have informed his nephew of the fact.

CHAPTER VII

LOOKING FOR THE WILL

THE search was carried on up to nine o'clock that evening, and then Mr. Apjohn returned to Carmarthen, explaining that he would send out two men to continue the work on the Tuesday, and that he would come out again on the Wednesday to read whatever might then be regarded as the old Squire's will,—the last prepared document if it could be found, and the former one should the search have been unsuccessful. 'Of course,' said he, in the presence of the two cousins, ' my reading the document will give it no force. Of those found, the last in date will be good—until one later be found. It will be well, however, that some steps should be taken, and nothing can be done till the will has been read.' Then he took his leave and went back to Carmarthen.

Isabel had not shown herself during the whole of the afternoon. When Mr. Apjohn's explanation had been given, and the search commenced, she retired and went to her own room. It was impossible for her to take a part in the work that was being done, and almost equally impossible for her to remain without seeming to take too lively an interest in the proceeding. Every point of the affair was clear to her imagination. It could not now be doubted by her that her uncle, doubly actuated by the presence of the man he disliked and the absence of her whom he so dearly loved, had found himself driven to revoke the decision to which he had been brought. As she put it to herself, his love had got the better of his conscience during the weakness of his latter days. It was a pity,—a pity that it should have been so! It was to be regretted that there should have been no one near him to comfort him in the misery which had produced such a lamentable result. A will, she thought, should be the outcome of a man's strength, and not of his weakness. Having obeyed his conscience, he should have clung to his conscience. But all that could not affect what had been done. It seemed to be certain to her that this other will had been made and executed. Even though it should have been irregularly executed so as to be null and void, still it must for a time at least have had an existence. Where was it now? Having these thoughts in her mind, it was impossible for her to go about the house among those who were searching. It was impossible for her to encounter the tremulous misery of her cousin. That he should shiver and shake and be covered with beads of perspiration during a period of such intense perturbation did not seem to her to be unnatural. It was not his fault that he had not been endowed with especial manliness. She disliked him in his cowardice almost more than before; but she would not on that account allow herself to suspect him of a crime.

Mr. Apjohn, just before he went, had an interview with her in her own room.

'I cannot go without a word,' he said, 'but its only purport will be to tell you that I cannot as yet express any decided opinion in this matter.'

'Do not suppose, Mr. Apjohn, that I am anxious for another will,' she said.

'I am;—but that has nothing to do with it. That he did make a will, and have it witnessed by these two Cantors, is, I think, certain. That he should afterwards have destroyed the will without telling the witnesses, who would be sure hereafter to think and talk of what they had done, seems to be most unlike the thoughtful consideration of your uncle. But his weakness increased upon him very quickly just at that time. Dr. Powell thinks that he was certainly competent on that day to make a will, but he thinks also he may have destroyed it a day or two afterwards when his mind was hardly strong enough to enable him to judge of what he was doing. If, at last, this new will shall not be forthcoming, I think we must be bound to interpret the matter in that way. I tell you this before I go in order that it may assist you perhaps a little in forming your own opinion.' Then he went.

It was impossible but that she should bethink herself at that moment that she knew more than either Dr. Powell or Mr. Apjohn. The last expression of the old man's thoughts upon that or upon any matter had been made to herself. The last words that he had uttered had been whispered into her ears; 'It is all right. It is done.' Let the light of his failing intellect have been ever so dim, let his strength have faded from him ever so completely, he would not have whispered these words had he himself destroyed that last document. Mr. Apjohn had spoken of the opinion which she was to form, and she felt how impossible to her it would be not to have an opinion in the matter. She could not keep her mind vacant even if she would. Mr. Apjohn had said that, if the will were not found, he should think that the Squire had in his weakness again changed his mind and destroyed it. She was sure that this was not so. She, and she alone, had heard those last words. Was it or was it not her duty to tell Mr. Apjohn that such words had been uttered? Had they referred to the interest of any one but herself, of course it would have been her duty. But now,—now she doubted. She did not choose to seem even to put forth a claim on her own account. And of what use would be any revelation as to the uttering of those words? They would be accepted in no court of law as evidence in one direction or another. Upon the whole, she thought she would keep her peace regarding them, even to Mr. Apjohn. If it was to be that her cousin should live there as squire and owner of Llanfeare, why should she seek to damage his character by calling in question the will under which he would inherit the property? Thus she determined that she would speak of her uncle's last words to no one.

But what must be her opinion as to the whole transaction? At the present moment she felt herself bound to think that this missing document would be found. That to her seemed to be the only solution which would not be terrible to contemplate. That other solution,—of the destruction of the will by her uncle's own hands, —she altogether repudiated. If it were not found, then——! What then? Would it not then be evident that some fraud was being perpetrated?

And if so, by whom? As these thoughts forced themselves upon her mind, she could not but think of that pallid face, those shaking hands, and the great drops of sweat which from time to time had forced themselves on to the man's brow. It was natural that he should suffer. It was natural that he should be perturbed under the consciousness of the hostile feeling of all those around him. But yet there had hardly been occasion for all those signs of fear which she had found it impossible not to notice as she had sat there in the parlour while Mr. Apjohn was explaining the circumstances of the two wills. Would an innocent man have trembled like that because the circumstances around him were difficult? Could anything but guilt have betrayed itself by such emotions? And then, had the will in truth been made away with by human hands, what other hands could have done it? Who else was interested? Who else was there at Llanfeare not interested in the preservation of a will which would have left the property to her? She did not begrudge him the estate. She had acknowledged the strength of the reasons which had induced the Squire to name him as heir; but she declared to herself that, if that latter document were not found, a deed of hideous darkness would have been perpetrated by him. With these thoughts disturbing her breast she lay awake during the long hours of the night.

When Mr. Apjohn had taken his departure,

and the servants had gone to their beds, the butler having barred and double-barred the door after his usual manner, Cousin Henry still sat alone in the book-room. After answering those questions from Mr. Apjohn, he had spoken to no one, but still sat alone with a single candle burning on the table by his elbow. The butler had gone to him twice, asking him whether he wanted anything, and suggesting to him that he had better go to his bed. But the heir, if he was the heir, had only resented the intrusion, desiring that he might be left alone. Then he was left alone, and there he sat.

His mind at this moment was tormented grievously within him. There was a something which he might do, and a something which he might not do, if he could only make up his mind. 'Honesty is the best policy!' 'Honesty is the best policy!' He repeated the well-known words to himself a thousand times, without, however, moving his lips or forming a sound. There he sat, thinking it all out, trying to think it out. There he sat, still trembling, still in an agony, for hour after hour. At one time he had fully resolved to do that by which he would have proved to himself his conviction that honesty is the best policy, and then he sat doubting again —declaring to himself that honesty itself did not require him to do this meditated deed. 'Let them find it,' he said to himself at last, aloud. 'Let them find it. It is their business: not mine.'

But still he sat looking up at the row of books opposite to him.

When it was considerably after midnight, he got up from his chair and began to walk the room. As he did so, he wiped his brow continually as though he were hot with the exertion, but keeping his eye still fixed upon the books. He was urging himself, pressing upon himself the expression of that honesty. Then at last he rushed at one of the shelves, and, picking out a volume of Jeremy Taylor's works,*threw it upon the table. It was the volume on which the old Squire had been engaged when he read the last sermon which was to prepare him for a flight to a better world. He opened the book, and there between the leaves was the last will and testament which his uncle had executed.

At that moment he heard a step in the hall and a hand on the door, and as he did so with quick eager motion he hid the document under the book.

'It is near two o'clock, Mr. Henry,' said the butler. 'What are you doing up so late?'

'I am only reading,' said the heir.

'It is very late to be reading. You had better go to bed. He never liked people to be a-reading at these contrairy hours. He liked folk to be all a-bed.'

The use of a dead man's authority, employed against him by one who was, so to say, his own servant, struck even him as absurd and improper.

He felt that he must assert himself unless he meant to sink lower and lower in the estimation of all those around him. 'I shall stay just as late as I please,' he said. 'Go away, and do not disturb me any more.'

'His will ought to be obeyed, and he not twenty-four hours under the ground,' said the butler.

'I should have stayed up just as long as I had pleased even had he been here,' said Cousin Henry. Then the man with a murmur took his departure and closed the door after him.

For some minutes Cousin Henry sat perfectly motionless, and then he got up very softly, very silently, and tried the door. It was closed, and it was the only door leading into the room. And the windows were barred with shutters. He looked round and satisfied himself that certainly no other eye was there but his own. Then he took the document up from its hiding-place, placed it again exactly between the leaves which had before enclosed it, and carefully restored the book to its place on the shelf.

He had not hidden the will. He had not thus kept it away from the eyes of all those concerned. He had opened no drawer. He had extracted nothing, had concealed nothing. He had merely carried the book from his uncle's table where he had found it, and, in restoring it to its place on the shelves, had found the paper which it contained. So he told himself now, and so he had told himself a thousand times. Was it his duty

to produce the evidence of a gross injustice
against himself? Who could doubt the injustice
who knew that he had been summoned thither
from London to take his place at Llanfeare as
heir to the property? Would not the ill done
against him be much greater than any he would
do were he to leave the paper there where he had
chanced to find it?

In no moment had it seemed to him that he
himself had sinned in the matter, till Mr. Apjohn
had asked him whether his uncle had told him
of this new will. Then he had lied. His uncle
had told him of his intention before the will
was executed, and had told him again, when the
Cantors had gone, that the thing was done. The
old man had expressed a thousand regrets, but
the young one had remained impassive, sullen,
crushed with a feeling of the injury done to
him, but still silent. He had not dared to re-
monstrate, and had found himself unable to
complain of the injustice.

There it was in his power. He was quite
awake to the strength of his own position,—but
also to its weakness. Should he resolve to leave
the document enclosed within the cover of the
book, no one could accuse him of dishonesty.
He had not placed it there. He had not hidden
it. He had done nothing. The confusion occasioned by the absence of the will would have
been due to the carelessness of a worn-out old
man who had reached the time of life in which

he was unfit to execute such a deed. It seemed to him that all justice, all honesty, all sense of right and wrong, would be best served by the everlasting concealment of such a document. Why should he tell of its hiding-place? Let them who wanted it search for it, and find it if they could. Was he not doing much in the cause of honesty in that he did not destroy it, as would be so easy for him?

But, if left there, would it not certainly be found? Though it should remain week after week, month after month,—even should it remain year after year, would it not certainly be found at last, and brought out to prove that Llanfeare was not his own? Of what use to him would be the property,—of what service;—how would it contribute to his happiness or his welfare, knowing, as he would know, that a casual accident, almost sure to happen sooner or later, might rob him of it for ever? His imagination was strong enough to depict the misery to him which such a state of things would produce. How he would quiver when any stray visitor might enter the room! How terrified he would be at the chance assiduity of a housemaid! How should he act if the religious instincts of some future wife should teach her to follow out that reading which his uncle had cultivated?

He had more than once resolved that he would be mad were he to leave the document where he found it. He must make it known to those who

were searching for it,—or he must destroy it.
His common sense told him that one alternative
or the other must be chosen. He could certainly
destroy it, and no one would be the wiser. He
could reduce it, in the solitude of his chamber,
into almost impalpable ashes, and then swallow
them. He felt that, let suspicion come as it
might into the minds of men, let Apjohn, and
Powell, and the farmers,—let Isabel herself,—
think what they might, no one would dare to
accuse him of such a deed. Let them accuse
him as they might, there would be no tittle of
evidence against him.

But he could not do it. The more he thought
of it, the more he had to acknowledge that he
was incapable of executing such a deed. To
burn the morsel of paper;—oh, how easy! But
yet he knew that his hands would refuse to
employ themselves on such a work. He had
already given it up in despair; and, having told
himself that it was impossible, had resolved to
extricate the document and, calling Isabel up
from her bed in the middle of the night, to hand
it over to her at once. It would have been easy
to say he had opened one book after another,
and it would, he thought, be a deed grand to do.
Then he had been interrupted, and insulted by
the butler, and in his anger he had determined
that the paper should rest there yet another day.

CHAPTER VIII

ON the whole of the next day the search was continued. In spite of his late watches, Cousin Henry rose up early, not looking at anything that was being done while the search was continued in other rooms, but still sitting, as he had heretofore sat, among the books. The two men whom Mr. Apjohn had sent from his office, together with the butler and Mrs. Griffith, began their work in the old man's bed-room, and then carried it on in the parlour. When they came to the book-room, as being the next in turn, Cousin Henry took his hat and went out into the garden. There, as he made short turns upon the gravel path, he endeavoured to force himself away from the close vicinity of the window; but he could not do it. He could not go where he would have been unable to see what was being done. He feared,—he trembled in his fear,—lest they should come upon the guilty volume. And yet he assured himself again and again that he wished that they might find it. Would it not in every way be better for him that they should find it? He could not bring himself to destroy it, and surely, sooner or later, it would be found.

Every book was taken from its shelf, apparently with the object of looking into the vacant spaces behind them. Through the window he could see all that was done. As it happened, the compartment in which was the fatal shelf,—on which was the fatal volume,—was the last that they reached. No attempt was made to open the books one by one; but then this volume, with so thick an enclosure to betray it, would certainly open of itself. He himself had gone to the place so often that certainly the enclosure would betray itself. Well, let it betray itself! No one could say that he had had guilty cognizance of its whereabouts! But yet he knew that he would have been unable to speak, would have gasped, and would surely have declared himself to be guilty by his awestruck silence.

Three by three the books came down, and then were replaced. And now they were at the shelf! Why could he not go away? Why must he stand there fixed at the window? He had done nothing,—nothing, nothing; and yet he stood there trembling, immovable, with the perspiration running off his face, unable to keep his eyes for a moment from what they were doing! At last the very three came down, in the centre of which was the volume containing the will. There was a tree against which he leaned, unable to support himself, as he looked into the room. The vacant place was searched, and then the three books were replaced! No attempt was made to examine the volumes. The men who did the work clearly did not know that these very volumes had been in constant use with the old Squire. They were replaced, and then the search, as far as that room was concerned, was over. When they were gone, Cousin Henry returned again to the room, and there he remained during the rest of the day. The search as it was carried on elsewhere had no interest for him.

Whatever harm might be done to others, whoever else might be injured, certainly no one was ill-treated as he had been ill-treated. It was thus he thought of it. Even should the will never be found, how cruel would be the injustice done to him! He had not asked to be made heir to the property! It was not his doing. He had been invited to come in order that he might be received as the heir, and since he had come, every one about the place had misused him. The tenants had treated him with disdain; the very servants had been insolent; his Cousin Isabel, when he had offered to share everything with her, had declared that he was hateful to her; and his uncle himself had heaped insult upon injury, and had aggravated injustice with scorn.

'Yes; I had intended that you should be my heir, and have called you hither for that purpose. Now I find you to be so poor a creature that I have changed my mind.' That in truth was what his uncle had said to him and had done for him. Who, after that, would expect him to go out of his way in search of special magnanimity? Let them find the will if they wanted it!

Even though he should resolve himself to have nothing to do with the property, even though he should repudiate any will in his own favour, still he would not tell them where this will might be found. Why should he help them in their difficulty?

Every carpet was taken up, every piece of furniture was moved, every trunk and box in the house was examined, but it occurred to no one that every book should be opened. It was still July, and the day was very long. From six in the morning till nine at night they were at work, and when the night came they declared that every spot about the place had been searched.

'I think, Miss, that the old Squire did destroy it. He was a little wandering at last.' It was thus that Mrs. Griffith had expressed her opinion to Isabel.

Isabel was sure that it was not so, but said nothing in reply.

If she could only get away from Llanfeare and have done with it, she would be satisfied. Llanfeare had become odious to her and terrible! She would get away, and wash her hands of it. And yet she was aware how sad would be her condition. Mr. Apjohn had already explained to her that the Squire had so managed his affairs as to have left no funds from which could be paid the legacy which had nominally been left to her. She had told her father when at Hereford that her uncle had taken such care of her that she would not become a burden upon him. Now it seemed that she would have to return home without a shilling of her own. For one so utterly penniless to think of marrying a man who had little but his moderate professional income would, she felt, be mean as well as wrong. There must be an end to everything between her and Mr. Owen. If her father could not support her, she must become a governess or, failing that, a housemaid. But even the poor-house would be better than Llanfeare, if Llanfeare were to be the property of Cousin Henry.

Mr. Apjohn had told her that she could not now leave the place on the Wednesday as she had intended. On the Wednesday he again came to Llanfeare, and then she saw him before he proceeded to his business. It was his intention now to read the last will which had been found, and to explain to those who heard it that he proposed, as joint executor with Dr. Powell, to act upon that as the last will;—but still with a proviso that another will might possibly be forthcoming. Though he had in a measure quarrelled with the Squire over the making of that will, nevertheless, he had been appointed in it as the executor, such having been the case in the wills previously made. All this he explained to her up in her room, assenting to her objection to be again present when the will should be read.

'I could not do it,' she said; 'and of what use

could it be, as I know everything that is in it? It would be too painful.'

He, remembering the futile legacy which it contained for herself, and the necessity which would be incumbent upon him to explain that there were no funds for paying it, did not again ask her to be present.

'I shall go to-morrow,' she said.

Then he asked her whether she could not remain until the beginning of next week, urging objections to this final surrender of Llanfeare; but she was not to be turned from her purpose. 'Llanfeare will have been surrendered,' she said; 'the house will be his to turn me out of if he pleases.'

'He would not do that.'

'He shall not have the chance. I could not hide it from you if I would. He and I do not love each other. Since he has been here I have kept away from him with disgust. He cannot but hate me, and I will not be a guest in his house. Besides, what can I do?'

'The will will not have been proved, you know.'

'What difference will there be in that? It will be proved at once. Of course he will have the keys, and will be master of everything. There are the keys.' As she said this she handed over to him various bunches. 'You had better give them to him yourself when you have read the will, so that I need have nothing to say to him.

There are some books of mine which my uncle gave me. Mrs. Griffith will pack them, and send them to me at Hereford,—unless he objects. Everything else belonging to me I can take with me. Perhaps you will tell them to send a fly out for me in time for the early train.'

And so it was settled.

Then that will was read,—that will which we know not to have been the last will,—in the presence of Cousin Henry, of Dr. Powell, who had again come out with Mr. Apjohn, and of the farmers, who were collected as before.

It was a long, tedious document, in which the testator set forth at length his reasons for the disposition which he made of the property. Having much considered the matter, he had thought the estate should descend to the male heir, even in default of a regular deed of entail. Therefore, although his love for his dearest niece, Isabel Brodrick, was undiminished, and his confidence in her as perfect as ever, still he had thought it right to leave the old family property to his nephew, Henry Jones. Then, with all due circumstances of description, the legacy was made in favour of his nephew. There were other legacies; a small sum of money to Mr. Apjohn himself, for the trouble imposed upon him as executor, a year's wages to each of his servants, and other matters of the kind. There was also left to Isabel that sum of four thousand pounds of which mention has been made. When the lawyer had completed the reading of the document, he declared that to the best of his knowledge no such money was in existence. The testator had no doubt thought that legacies so made would be paid out of the property, whereas the property could be made subject to no such demand unless it had, by proper instrument to that effect, been charged with the amount.

'But,' he said, 'Mr. Henry Jones, when he comes into possession of the estate, will probably feel himself called upon to set that matter right, and to carry out his uncle's wishes.'

Upon this Cousin Henry, who had not as yet spoken a word throughout the ceremony, was profuse in his promises. Should the estate become his, he would certainly see that his uncle's wishes were carried out in regard to his dear cousin. To this Mr. Apjohn listened, and then went on to explain what remained to be said. Though this will, which he had now read, would be acted upon as though it were the last will and testament of the deceased,—though, in default of that for which futile search had been made, it certainly was what it purported to be,—still there existed in full force all those reasons which he had stated on the Monday for supposing that the late Squire had executed another. Here Joseph Cantor, junior, gave very strong symptoms of his inclination to reopen that controversy, but was stopped by the joint efforts of his father and the lawyer. If such a document should ever be found, then that would be the actual will, and not the one which he had now read. After that, when all due formalities had been performed, he took his leave, and went back to Carmarthen.

The keys were given up to Cousin Henry, and he found himself to be, in fact, the lord and master of the house, and the owner of everything within it. The butler, Mrs. Griffith, and the gardener gave him notice to quit. They would stay, if he wished it, for three months, but they did not think that they could be happy in the house now that the old Squire was dead, and that Miss Isabel was going away. There certainly did not come to him at the present moment any of the pleasures of ownership. He would have been willing,—he thought that he would have been willing,—to abandon Llanfeare altogether, if only it could have been abandoned without any of the occurrences of the last month. He would have been pleased that there should have been no Llanfeare.

But as it was, he must make up his mind to something. He must hide the paper in some deeper hiding-place, or he must destroy it, or he must reveal it. He thought that he could have dropped the book containing the will into the sea, though he could not bring himself to burn the will itself. The book was now his own, and he might do what he liked with it. But it would be madness to leave the paper there!

Then again there came to him the idea that

it would be best for him, and for Isabel too, to divide the property. In one way it was his,—having become his without any fraudulent doing on his part. So he declared to himself. In another way it was hers,—though it could not become hers without some more than magnanimous interference on his part. To divide it would certainly be best. But there was no other way of dividing it but by a marriage. For any other division, such as separating the land or the rents, no excuse could be made, nor would any such separation touch the fatal paper which lay between the leaves of the book. Were she to consent to marry him, then he thought he might find courage to destroy the paper.

It was necessary that he should see her on that afternoon, if only that he might bid her adieu, and tell her that she should certainly have the money that had been left her. If it were possible he would say a word also about that other matter.

'You did not hear the will read,' he said to her.

'No,' she answered abruptly.

'But you have been told its contents?'

'I believe so.'

'About the four thousand pounds?'

'There need be no question about the four thousand pounds. There is not a word to be said about it,—at any rate between you and me.'

'I have come to tell you,' said he,—not understanding her feeling in the least, and evidently showing by the altered tone of his voice that he thought that his communication would be received with favour,—'I have come to tell you that the legacy shall be paid in full. I will see to that myself as soon as I am able to raise a penny on the property.'

'Pray do not trouble yourself, Cousin Henry.'

'Oh, certainly I shall.'

'Do not trouble yourself. You may be sure of this, that on no earthly consideration would I take a penny from your hands.'

'Why not?'

'We take presents from those whom we love and esteem, not from those we despise.'

'Why should you despise me?' he asked.

'I will leave that to yourself to judge of; but be sure of this, that though I were starving I would take nothing from your hands.'

Then she got up, and, retiring into the inner room, left him alone. It was clear to him then that he could not divide the property with her in the manner that he had suggested to himself.

CHAPTER IX

ALONE AT LLANFEARE

ON the day after the reading of the will, Henry Indefer Jones, Esq., of Llanfeare, as he was now to be called, was left alone in his house, his cousin Isabel having taken her departure from the place in the manner proposed

by her. And the lawyer was gone, and the
doctor, and the tenants did not come near him,
and the butler and the housekeeper kept out
of his way, and there was probably no man
in [all South Wales more lonely and desolate
than the new Squire of Llanfeare on that
morning.

The cruelty of it, the injustice of it, the un-
precedented hardness of it all! Such were the
ideas which presented themselves to him as hour
after hour he sat in the book-room with his eyes
fixed on the volume of Jeremy Taylor's sermons.
He had done nothing wrong,—so he told himself,—had not even coveted anything that did
not belong to him. It was in accordance with his
uncle's expressed desire that he had come to
Llanfeare, and been introduced to the tenants as
their future landlord, and had taken upon himself the place of the heir. Then the old man had
announced to him his change of mind; but had
not announced it to others, had not declared his
altered purpose to the world at Llanfeare, and
had not at once sent him back to his London
office. Had he done so, that would have been
better. There would have been a gross injustice,
but that would have been the end of it, and he
would have gone back to his London work unhappy indeed, but with some possibility of life
before him. Now it seemed as though any mode
of living would be impossible to him. While that
fatal paper remained hidden in the fatal volume

he could do nothing but sit there and guard it in solitude.

He knew well enough that it behoved him as a man to go out about the estate and the neighbourhood, and to show himself, and to take some part in the life around him, even though he might be miserable and a prey to terror whilst he was doing so. But he could not move from his seat till his mind had been made up as to his future action. He was still in fearful doubt. Through the whole of that first day he declared to himself that his resolution had not yet been made,—that he had not yet determined what it would be best that he should do. It was still open to him to say that at any moment he had just found the will. If he could bring himself to do so he might rush off to Carmarthen with the document in his pocket, and still appear before the lawyer as a man triumphant in his own honesty, who at the first moment that it was possible had surrendered all that which was not legally his own, in spite of the foul usage to which he had been subjected. He might still assume the grand air of injured innocence, give back the property to the young woman who had insulted him, and return to his desk in London, leaving behind him in Carmarthenshire a character for magnanimity and honour. Such a line of conduct had charms in his eyes. He was quite alive to the delight of heaping coals of fire on his cousin's head. She had declared that she would receive nothing at his hands, because she despised him. After that there would be a sweetness, the savour of which was not lost upon his imagination, in forcing her to take all from his hands. And it would become known to all men that it was he who had found the will,—he who might have destroyed it without the slightest danger of discovery,—he who without peril might thus have made himself owner of Llanfeare. There would be a delight to him in the character which he would thus achieve. But then she had scorned him! No bitterer scorn had ever fallen from the lips or flashed from the eyes of a woman. 'We take presents from those we love, not from those we despise!' He had not resented the words at the moment; he had not dared to do so; but not the less had they entered upon his very soul,— not the less had he hated the woman who had dared so to reply to the generous offer which he had made her.

And then there was an idea present to him through it all that abstract justice, if abstract justice could be reached, would declare that the property should be his. The old man had made his will with all the due paraphernalia of will-making. There had been the lawyer and the witnesses brought by the lawyer; and, above all, there had been the declared reason of the will and its understood purpose. He had been sent for, and all Carmarthenshire had been made to understand why it was to be so. Then, in his sickness, the old man had changed his mind through some fantastic feeling, and almost on his death-bed, with failing powers, in a condition probably altogether unfit for such a duty, had executed a document which the law might respect, but which true justice, if true justice could be invoked, would certainly repudiate. Could the will be abolished, no more than justice would be done. But, though the will were in his own power, it could not be abolished by his own hands.

As to that abolishing he was perfectly conscious of his own weakness. He could not take the will from its hiding-place and with his own hand thrust it into the flames. He had never as yet even suggested to himself that he would do so. His hair stood on end as he thought of the horrors attendant on such a deed as that. To be made to stand in the dock and be gazed at by the angry eyes of all the court, to be written of as the noted criminal of the day, to hear the verdict of guilty, and then the sentence, and to be aware that he was to be shut up and secluded from all comforts throughout his life! And then, and then, the dread hereafter! For such a deed as that would there not be assured damnation? Although he told himself that justice demanded the destruction of the will, justice could not be achieved by his own hand after such fashion as that.

No; he could not himself destroy the document, though it should remain there for years to make his life a burden to him. As to that he had made up his mind, if to nothing else. Though there might be no peril as to this world,—though he might certainly do the deed without a chance of detection from human eyes,—though there would in truth be no prospect of that angry judge and ready jury and crushing sentence, yet he could not do it. There was something of a conscience within him. Were he to commit a felony, from the moment of the doing of the deed the fear of eternal punishment would be heavy on his soul, only to be removed by confession and retribution,—and then by that trial with the judge, and the jury, and the sentence! He could not destroy the document. But if the book could get itself destroyed, what a blessing it would be! The book was his own, or would be in a few days, when the will should have been properly proved. But if he were to take away the book and sink it in a well, or throw it into the sea, or bury it deep beneath the earth, then it would surely reappear by one of those ever-recurring accidents which are always bringing deeds of darkness to the light. Were he to cast the book into the sea, tied with strings or cased in paper, and leaded, that it should surely sink, so that the will should not by untoward chance float out of it, the book tied and bound and leaded would certainly come up in evidence against him. Were he to move the book, the vacant space would lead to suspicion. He would be safe only by leaving the book where it was, by giving no trace that he had ever been conscious of the contents of the book.

And yet, if the document were left there, the book would certainly divulge its dread secret at last. The day would come, might come, ah! so quickly, on which the document would be found, and he would be thrust out, penniless as far as any right to Llanfeare was concerned. Some maid-servant might find it; some religious inmate of his house who might come there in search of godly teaching! If he could only bring himself to do something at once,—to declare that it was there, so that he might avoid all these future miseries! But why had she told him that she despised him, and why had the old man treated him with such unexampled cruelty? So it went on with him for three or four days, during which he still kept his place among the books.

There would be great delight in possessing Llanfeare, if he could in very truth possess it. He would not live there. No; certainly not that. Every tenant about the place had shown him that he was despised. Their manner to him before the old Squire's death, their faces as they had sat there during the ceremonies of the will, and the fact that no one had been near him since the reading of the will, had shown him that. He had not dared to go to church during the Sunday; and though no one had spoken to him of his daily life, he felt that tales were being told of him. He was sure that Mrs. Griffiths had whispered about the place the fact of his constant residence in one room, and that those who heard it would begin to say among themselves that a practice so strange must be connected with the missing will. No, he would not willingly live at Llanfeare. But if he could let Llanfeare, were it but for a song, and enjoy the rents up in London, how pleasant would that be! But then, had ever any man such a sword of Damocles*to hang over his head by a single hair, as would be then hanging over his head were he to let Llanfeare or even to leave the house, while that book with its enclosure was there upon the shelves? It did seem to him, as he thought of it, that life would be impossible to him in any room but that as long as the will remained among the leaves of the volume.

Since the moment in which he had discovered the will he had felt the necessity of dealing with the officials of the office in London at which he had been employed. This was an establishment called the Sick and Healthy Life Assurance Company, in which he held some shares, and at which he was employed as a clerk. It would of course be necessary that he should either resign his place or go back to his duties. That the Squire of Llanfeare should be a clerk at the Sick and Healthy would be an anomaly. Could he really be in possession of his rents, the Sick and Healthy would of course see no more of him; but were he to throw up his position and then to lose Llanfeare, how sad, how terrible, how cruel would be his fate! But yet something must be done. In these circumstances he wrote a letter to the manager, detailing all the circumstances with a near approach to the truth, keeping back only the one little circumstance that he himself was acquainted with the whereabouts of the missing will.

'It may turn up at any moment,' he explained to the manager, 'so that my position as owner of the property is altogether insecure. I feel this so thoroughly that were I forced at the present to choose between the two I should keep my clerk-ship in the office; but as the condition of things is so extraordinary, perhaps the directors will allow me six months in which to come to a decision, during which I may hold my place, without, of course, drawing any salary.'

Surely, he thought, he could decide on something before the six months should be over. Either he would have destroyed the will, or have sunk the book beneath the waves, or have resolved to do that magnanimous deed which it was still within his power to achieve. The only one thing not possible would be for him to leave Llanfeare and take himself up to the delights of London while the document was yet hidden within the volume.

'I suppose, sir, you don't know yet as to what your plans are going to be?' This was said by Mrs. Griffiths as soon as she made her way into the book-room after a somewhat imperious knock-ing at the door. Hitherto there had been but little communication between Cousin Henry and his servants since the death of the old Squire. Mrs. Griffiths had given him warning that she would leave his service, and he had somewhat angrily told her that she might go as soon as it pleased her. Since that she had come to him once daily for his orders, and those orders had certainly been very simple. He had revelled in no luxuries of the table or the cellar since the keys of the house had been committed to his charge. She had been told to provide him with simple food, and with food she had provided him. The condition of his mind had been such that no appetite for the glories of a rich man's table had yet come to him. That accursed book on the opposite shelf had destroyed all his taste for both wine and meat.

'What do you want to know for?' he asked.

'Well, sir; it is customary for the housekeeper to know something, and if there is no mistress she can only go to the master. We always were very quiet here, but Miss Isabel used to tell me something of what was expected.'

'I don't expect anything,' said Cousin Henry.

'Is there anybody to come in my place?' she asked.

'What can that be to you? You can go when you please.'

'The other servants want to go, too. Sally won't stay, nor yet Mrs. Bridgeman.' Mrs. Bridgeman was the cook. 'They say they don't like to live with a gentleman who never goes out of one room.'

'What is it to them what room I live in? I suppose I may live in what room I please in my own house.' This he said with an affectation of anger, feeling that he was bound to be indignant at such inquiries from his own servant, but with more of fear than wrath in his mind. So they had in truth already begun to inquire why it was that he sat there watching the books!

'Just so, Mr. Jones. Of course you can live anywhere you like,—in your own house.'

There was an emphasis on the last words which was no doubt intended to be impertinent. Every one around was impertinent to him.

'But so can they, sir,—not in their own house. They can look for situations, and I thought it my duty just to tell you, because you wouldn't like to find yourself all alone here, by yourself like.'

'Why is it that everybody turns against me?' he asked suddenly, almost bursting into tears.

At this her woman's heart was a little softened, though she did despise him thoroughly. 'I don't know about turning, Mr. Jones, but they have been used to such different ways.'

'Don't they get enough to eat?'

'Yes, sir; there's enough to eat, no doubt. I don't know as you have interfered about that; not but what as master you might. It isn't the victuals.'

'What is it, Mrs. Griffiths? Why do they want to go away?'

'Well, it is chiefly because of your sitting here alone,—never moving, never having your hat on your head, sir. Of course a gentleman can do as he pleases in his own house. There is nothing to make him go out, not even to see his own tenants, nor his own farm, nor nothing else. He's his own master, sir, in course;—but it is mysterious. There is nothing goes against them sort of people,'—meaning the servants inferior to herself,—'like mysteries.'

Then they already felt that there was a mystery! Oh! what a fool he had been to shut himself up and eat his food there! Of course they would know that this mystery must have some reference to the will. Thus they would so far have traced the truth as to have learnt that the will had a mystery, and that the mystery was located in that room!

There is a pleasant game, requiring much sagacity, in which, by a few answers, one is led closer and closer to a hidden word, till one is enabled to touch it.* And as with such a word, so it was with his secret. He must be careful that no eye should once see that his face was turned towards the shelf. At this very moment he shifted his position so as not to look at the shelf, and then thought that she would have observed the movement, and divined the cause.

'Anyways, they begs to say respectful that

they wishes you to take a month's warning. As for me, I wouldn't go to inconvenience my old master's heir. I'll stay till you suits yourself, Mr. Jones; but the old place isn't to me now what it was.'

'Very well, Mrs. Griffiths,' said Cousin Henry, trying to fix his eyes upon an open book in his hands.

CHAPTER X

COUSIN HENRY DREAMS A DREAM

FROM what had passed with Mrs. Griffiths, it was clear to Cousin Henry that he must go out of the house and be seen about the place. The woman had been right in saying that his seclusion was mysterious. It was peculiarly imperative upon him to avoid all appearance of mystery. He ought to have been aware of this before. He ought to have thought of it, and not to have required to be reminded by a rebuke from the housekeeper. He could now only amend the fault for the future, and endeavour to live down the mystery which had been created. Almost as soon as Mrs. Griffiths had left him, he prepared to move. But then he bethought himself that he must not seem to have obeyed, quite at the moment, the injunctions of his own servant; so he re-seated himself, resolved to postpone for a day or two his intention of calling

upon one of the tenants. He re-seated himself,
but turned his back to the shelf, lest the aspect
of his countenance should be watched through
the window.

On the following morning he was relieved
from his immediate difficulty by the arrival of
a letter from Mr. Apjohn. It was necessary that
a declaration as to the will should be made before
a certain functionary at Carmarthen, and as the
papers necessary for the occasion had been prepared in the lawyer's office, he was summoned
into Carmarthen for the purpose. Immediately
after that he would be put into full possession of
the property. Mr. Apjohn also informed him
that the deed had been prepared for charging
the estate with four thousand pounds on behalf
of his Cousin Isabel. By this he would bind himself to pay her two hundred a year for the next
two years, and at the end of that period to hand
over to her the entire sum. Here was an excuse
provided for him to leave the house and travel
as far as Carmarthen. There were the horses
and the carriage with which his uncle had been
accustomed to be taken about the estate, and
there was still the old coachman, who had been
in the service for the last twenty years. So he
gave his orders, and directed that the carriage
should be ready soon after two, in order that he
might keep the appointment made by the lawyer
at three. The order was sent out to the stable
through the butler, and as he gave it he felt how

unable he was to assume the natural tone of a master to his servants.

'The carriage, sir!' said the butler, as though surprised. Then the owner of Llanfeare found himself compelled to explain to his own man that it was necessary that he should see the lawyer in Carmarthen.

Should he or should he not take the book with him as he went? It was a large volume, and could not well be concealed in his pocket. He might no doubt take a book,—any book,—with him for his own recreation in the carriage; but, were he to do so, the special book which he had selected would be marked to the eyes of the servants. It required but little thought to tell him that the book must certainly be left in its place. He could have taken the will and kept it safe, and certainly unseen, in the pocket of his coat. But then, to take the will from its hiding-place, and to have it on his person, unless he did so for the purpose of instant and public revelation, would, as he thought, be in itself a felony. There would be the doing of a deed in the very act of abstracting the document; and his safety lay in the abstaining from any deed. What if a fit should come upon him, or he should fall and hurt himself and the paper be found in his possession? Then there would at once be the intervention of the police, and the cell, and the angry voices of the crowd, and the scowling of the judge, and the quick sentence, and that dwelling among thieves and felons for the entire period of his accursed life! Then would that great command, 'Thou shalt not steal,' be sounding always in his ear! Then would self-condemnation be heavy upon him! Not to tell of the document, not to touch it, not to be responsible in any way for its position there on the shelf, —that was not to steal it. Hitherto the word 'felon' had not come home to his soul. But were he to have it in his pocket, unless with that purpose of magnanimity of which he thought so often, then he would be a felon.

Soon after two he left the room, and at the moment was unable not to turn a rapid glance upon the book. There it was, safe in its place. How well he knew the appearance of the volume! On the back near the bottom was a small speck, a spot on the binding, which had been so far disfigured by some accident in use. This seemed to his eyes to make it marked and separate among a thousand. To him it was almost wonderful that a stain so peculiar should not at once betray the volume to the eyes of all. But there it was, such as it was, and he left it amidst its perils. Should they pounce upon it the moment that he had left the room, they could not say that he was guilty because it contained the will.

He went to Carmarthen, and there his courage was subjected to a terrible trial. He was called upon to declare before the official that to the best of his belief the will, which was about to be proved, was the last will and testament of Indefer Jones. Had this been explained to him by the lawyer in his letter, he might probably have abstained from so damning a falsehood There would have been time then for some resolution. Had Mr. Apjohn told him what it was that he was about to be called upon to perform, even then, before the necessity of performance was presented to him, there would have been a moment for consideration, and he might have doubted. Had he hesitated in the presence of the lawyer, all would have been made known. But he was carried before the official not knowing that the lie was to be submitted to him, and before he could collect his thoughts the false declaration had been made!

'You understand, Mr. Jones,' said the lawyer in the presence of the official, 'that we still think that a further will may eventually be found?'

'I understand that,' croaked the poor wretch.

'It is well that you should bear it in mind,' said Mr. Apjohn severely;—'for your own sake, I mean.'

There was nothing further spoken on the subject, and he was given to understand that Llanfeare was now in truth his own;—his own, whatever chance there might be that it should be wrested from him hereafter.

Then followed the business as to the charge upon the property which was to be made on behalf of Isabel. The deeds were prepared, and only required the signature of the new Squire.

'But she has refused to take a penny from me,' said the Squire, hesitating with a pen in his hand. Let us give him his due by declaring that, much as he hated his cousin, he did not doubt as to bestowing the money upon her. As far as he was concerned, she was welcome to the four thousand pounds.

But the lawyer misinterpreted his client's manner. 'I should think, Mr. Jones,' he said, with still increased severity, 'that you would have felt that under the peculiar circumstances you were bound to restore to your cousin money which was expended by your uncle under a misconception in purchasing land which will now be yours.'

'What can I do if she will not take it?'

'Not take it? That is an absurdity. In a matter of such importance as this she will of course be guided by her father. It is not a matter requiring gratitude on her part. The money ought to be regarded as her own, and you will only be restoring to her what is in truth her own.'

'I am quite willing. I have made no difficulty, Mr. Apjohn. I don't understand why you should speak to me in that way about it, as though I had hesitated about the money.' Nevertheless, the lawyer maintained the severe look, and there was still the severe tone as the poor wretch left the office. In all this there was so great an aggravation of his misery! It was only too manifest that every one suspected him of something. Here he was ready to give away,—absolutely anxious to give away out of his own pocket,—a very large sum of money to his cousin who had mis-used and insulted him, by signing the document without a moment's hesitation as soon as it was presented to him, and yet he was rebuked for his demeanour as he did it. Oh, that accursed will! Why had his uncle summoned him away from the comparative comfort of his old London life?

When he returned to the book-room, he made himself sure that the volume had not been moved. There was a slight variation in the positions of that and the two neighbouring books, the centre one having been pushed a quarter of an inch further in; and all this he had marked so ac-curately that he could not but know whether any hand had been at the shelf. He did not go near to the shelf, but could see the variation as he stood at the table. His eye had become minutely exact as to the book and its position. Then he resolved that he would not look at the book again, would not turn a glance on it unless it might be when he had made up his mind to reveal its contents. His neck became absolutely stiff with the efforts necessary not to look at the book.

That night he wrote a letter to his cousin, which was as follows;—

'MY DEAR ISABEL,

'I have been into Carmarthen to-day, and

I have signed a document in the presence of Mr. Apjohn, by which four thousand pounds is made over to you as a charge upon the property. He stated that you had what might be called a right to that money, and I perfectly agreed with him. I have never doubted about the money since my uncle's will was read. The agent who receives the rents will remit to you one hundred pounds half yearly for the next two years. By that time I shall have been able to raise the money, and you shall then be paid in full.

'I don't want you to take this as any favour from me. I quite understood what you said to me. I think that it was undeserved, and, after all that I have suffered in this matter, cruel on your part. It was not my fault that my uncle changed his mind backwards and forwards. I never asked him for the estate. I came to Llanfeare only because he bade me. I have taken possession of the property only when told to do so by Mr. Apjohn. If I could not make myself pleasant to you, it was not my fault. I think you ought to be ashamed of what you said to me,—so soon after the old man's death!

'But all that has nothing to do with the money, which, of course, you must take. As for myself, I do not think I shall continue to live here. My uncle has made the place a nest of hornets for me, and all through no fault of my own. Should you like to come and live here as owner, you are welcome to do so on paying me a certain sum out of the rents. I am quite in earnest, and you had better think of it.

'Yours truly,
'HENRY JONES.'

His resolution as to the first portion of the above letter was taken as he returned in the carriage from Carmarthen; but it was not until the pen was in his hand, and the angry paragraph had been written in which he complained of her cruelty, that he thought of making that offer to her as to the residence. The idea flashed across his mind, and then was carried out instantly. Let her come and live there, and let her find the will herself if she pleased. If her mind was given to godly reading, this might be her reward. Such conduct would, at any rate, show them all that he was afraid of nothing. He would, he thought, if this could be arranged, still remain at his office; would give up that empty title of Squire of Llanfeare, and live in such comfort as might come to him from the remittances which would be made to him on account of the rents, till—that paper had been found. Such was his last plan, and the letter proposing it was duly sent to the post office.

On the following day he again acknowledged the necessity of going about the place,—so that the feeling of mystery might, if possible, be gradually dissipated,—and he went out for a walk. He roamed down towards the cliffs, and there sat in solitude, looking out upon the waters.

His mind was still intent upon the book. Oh, if the book could be buried there below the sea,— be drowned and no hand of his be necessary for the drowning! As he sat there, feeling himself constrained to remain away from the house for a certain period, he fell asleep by degrees and dreamed. He dreamt that he was out there in a little boat all alone, with the book hidden under the seats, and that he rowed himself out to sea till he was so far distant from the shore that no eye could see him. Then he lifted the book, and was about to rid himself for ever of his burden;— when there came by a strong man swimming. The man looked up at him so as to see exactly what he was doing, and the book was not thrown over, and the face of the swimming man was the face of that young Cantor who had been so determined in his assertion that another will had been made.

The dream was still vivid as a reality to his intellect when he was awakened suddenly, whether by a touch or a sound he did not know. He looked up, and there was the young man whom he had seen swimming to him across the sea. The land he was on was a portion of old Cantor's farm, and the presence of the son need not have surprised him had he thought of it; but it was to him as though the comer had read every thought of his mind, and had understood clearly the purport of the dream.

'Be that you, Squire?' said the young man.

'Yes, it is I,' said Cousin Henry, as he lay trembling on the grass.

'I didn't know you was here, sir. I didn't know you ever com'd here. Good morning, sir.' Then the young man passed on, not caring to have any further conversation with a landlord so little to his taste.

After this he returned home almost cowed. But on the following morning he determined to make a still further effort, so that he might, if possible, return to the ways of the world, which were already becoming strange to him from the desolation of the life which he had been leading. He went out, and, taking the road by the church, up the creek, he came at about a distance of two miles from his own house to Coed, the farmstead of John Griffiths, the farmer who held the largest number of acres on the property. At the garden gate he found his tenant, whom he was inclined to think somewhat more civil,—a little, perhaps, more courteous,—than others who had met him.

'Yes, sir,' said John Griffiths, 'it's a fine day, and the crops are doing well enough. Would you like to come in and see the missus? She'll take it civil.'

Cousin Henry entered the house and said a few words to the farmer's wife, who was not, however, specially gracious in her demeanour. He had not the gift of saying much to such persons, and was himself aware of his own deficiency. But still he had done something,—had shown that he was not afraid to enter a tenant's house. As he was leaving, the farmer followed him to the gate, and began to offer him some advice, apparently in kindness.

'You ought to be doing something, sir, with those paddocks between the shrubberies and the road.'

'I suppose so, Mr. Griffiths; but I am no farmer.'

'Then let them, sir. William Griffiths will be glad enough to have them and pay you rent. The old Squire didn't like that the land he had held himself should go into other hands. But he never did much good with them lately, and it's different now.'

'Yes, it's different now. I don't think I shall live here, Mr. Griffiths.'

'Not live at Llanfeare?'

'I think not. I'm not quite fitted to the place. It isn't my doing, but among you all, I fear, you don't like me.' As he said this he tried to carry it off with a laugh.

'You'd live down that, Squire, if you did your duty, and was good to the people;—and took no more than was your own. But perhaps you don't like a country life.'

'I don't like being where I ain't liked; that's the truth of it, Mr. Griffiths.'

'Who'll come in your place, if I may be so bold as to ask?'

'Miss Brodrick shall,—if she will. It was not I who asked my uncle to bring me here.'

'But she is not to have the property?'

'Not the property;—at least I suppose not. But she shall have the house and the grounds, and the land adjacent. And she shall manage it all, dividing the rents with me, or something of that kind. I have offered it to her, but I do not say that she will agree. In the meantime, if you will come up and see me sometimes, I will take it as a kindness. I do not know that I have done any harm, so as to be shunned.'

Then Farmer Griffiths readily said that he would go up occasionally and see his landlord.

CHAPTER XI

ISABEL AT HEREFORD

ISABEL had not been many hours at home at Hereford before, as was natural, her father discussed with her the affairs of the property and her own peculiar interest in the will which had at last been accepted. It has to be acknowledged that Isabel was received somewhat as an interloper in the house. She was not wanted there, at any rate by her stepmother,—hardly by her brothers and sisters,—and was, perhaps, not cordially desired even by her father. She and her stepmother had never been warm friends.

Isabel herself was clever and high-minded; but high-spirited also, imperious, and sometimes hard. It may be said of her that she was at all points a gentlewoman. So much could hardly be boasted of the present Mrs. Brodrick; and, as was the mother, so were that mother's children. The father was a gentleman, born and bred as such; but in his second marriage he had fallen a little below his station, and, having done so, had accommodated himself to his position. Then there had come many children, and the family had increased quicker than the income. So it had come to pass that the attorney was not a wealthy man. This was the home which Isabel had been invited to leave when, now many years since, she had gone to Llanfeare to become her uncle's darling. There her life had been very different from that of the family at Hereford. She had seen but little of society, but had been made much of, and almost worshipped, by those who were around her. She was to be,—was to have been,—the Lady of Llanfeare. By every tenant about the place she had been loved and esteemed. With the servants she had been supreme. Even at Carmarthen, when she was seen there, she was regarded as the great lady, the acknowledged heiress, who was to have, at some not very distant time, all Llanfeare in her own hands. It was said of her, and said truly, that she was possessed of many virtues. She was charitable, careful for others, in no way self-indulgent, sedulous in every duty, and, above all things, affectionately attentive to her uncle. But she had become imperious, and inclined to domineer, if not in action, yet in spirit. She had lived much among books, had delighted to sit gazing over the sea with a volume of poetry in her hand, truly enjoying the intellectual gifts which had been given her. But she had, perhaps, learnt too thoroughly her own superiority, and was somewhat apt to look down upon the less refined pleasure of other people. And now her altered position in regard to wealth rather increased than diminished her foibles. Now, in her abject poverty,—for she was determined that it should be abject,—she would be forced to sustain her superiority solely by her personal gifts. She determined that, should she find herself compelled to live in her father's house, she would do her duty thoroughly by her stepmother and her sisters. She would serve them as far as it might be within her power; but she could not giggle with the girls, nor could she talk little gossip with Mrs. Brodrick. While there was work to be done, she would do it, though it should be hard, menial, and revolting; but when her work was done, there would be her books.

It will be understood that, such being her mood and such her character, she would hardly make herself happy in her father's house,—or make others happy. And then, added to all this, there was the terrible question of money! When last at Hereford, she had told her father that, though her uncle had revoked his grand intention in her favour, still there would be coming to her enough to prevent her from being a burden on the resources of her family. Now that was all changed. She was determined that it should be changed. If her father should be unable or unwilling to support her, she would undergo any hardship, any privation; but would certainly not accept bounty from the hands of her cousin. Some deed had been done, she felt assured,—some wicked deed, and Cousin Henry had been the doer of it. She and she alone had heard the last words which her uncle had spoken, and she had watched the man's face narrowly when her uncle's will had been discussed in the presence of the tenants. She was quite sure. Let her father say what he might, let her stepmother look at her ever so angrily with her greedy, hungry eyes, she would take no shilling from her Cousin Henry. Though she might have to die in the streets, she would take no bread from her Cousin Henry's hand.

She herself began the question of the money on the day after her arrival. 'Papa,' she said, 'there is to be nothing for me after all.'

Now Mr. Apjohn, the lawyer, like a cautious family solicitor as he was, had written to Mr. Brodrick, giving him a full account of the whole affair, telling him of the legacy of four thousand pounds, explaining that there was no fund from which payment could be legally exacted, but stating also that the circumstances of the case were of such a nature as to make it almost impossible that the new heir should refuse to render himself liable for the amount. Then had come another letter saying that the new heir had assented to do so.

'Oh, yes, there will, Isabel,' said the father.

Then she felt that the fighting of the battle was incumbent upon her, and she was determined to fight it. 'No, papa, no; not a shilling.'

'Yes, my dear, yes,' he said, smiling. 'I have heard from Mr. Apjohn, and understand all about it. The money, no doubt, is not there; but your cousin is quite prepared to charge the estate with the amount. Indeed, it would be almost impossible for him to refuse to do so. No one would speak to him were he to be so base as that. I do not think much of your Cousin Henry, but even Cousin Henry could not be so mean. He has not the courage for such villany.'

'I have the courage,' said she.

'What do you mean?'

'Oh, papa, do not be angry with me! Nothing, —nothing shall induce me to take my Cousin Henry's money.'

'It will be your money,—your money by your uncle's will. It is the very sum which he himself has named as intended for you.'

'Yes, papa; but Uncle Indefer had not got the

money to give. Neither you nor I should be angry with him; because he intended the best.'

'I am angry with him,' said the attorney in wrath, 'because he deceived you and deceived me about the property.'

'Never; he deceived no one. Uncle Indefer and deceit never went together.'

'There is no question of that now,' said the father. 'He made some slight restitution, and there can, of course, be no question as to your taking it.'

'There is a question, and there must be a question, papa. I will not have it. If my being here would be an expense too great for you, I will go away.'

'Where will you go?'

'I care not where I go. I will earn my bread. If I cannot do that, I would rather live in the poor-house than accept my cousin's money.'

'What has he done?'

'I do not know.'

'As Mr. Apjohn very well puts it, there is no question whatsoever as to gratitude, or even of acceptance. It is a matter of course. He would be inexpressibly vile were he not to do this.'

'He is inexpressibly vile.'

'Not in this respect. He is quite willing. You will have nothing to do but to sign a receipt once every half-year till the whole sum shall have been placed to your credit.'

'I will sign nothing on that account; nor will I take anything.'

'But why not? What has he done?'

'I do not know. I do not say that he has done anything. I do not care to speak of him. Pray do not think, papa, that I covet the estate, or that I am unhappy about that. Had he been pleasant to my uncle and good to the tenants, had he seemed even to be like a man, I could have made him heartily welcome to Llanfeare. I think my uncle was right in choosing to have a male heir. I should have done so myself,—in his place.'

'He was wrong, wickedly wrong, after his promises.'

'There were no promises made to me: nothing but a suggestion, which he was, of course, at liberty to alter if he pleased. We need not, however, go back to that, papa. There he is, owner of Llanfeare, and from him, as owner of Llanfeare, I will accept nothing. Were I starving in the street I would not take a crust of bread from his fingers.'

Over and over again the conversation was renewed, but always with the same result. Then there was a correspondence between the two attorneys, and Mr. Apjohn undertook to ask permission from the Squire to pay the money to the father's receipt without asking any acknowledgment from the daughter. On hearing this, Isabel declared that if this were done she would certainly leave her father's house. She would go out of it, even though she should not know

whither she was going. Circumstances should
not be made so to prevail upon her as to force
her to eat meat purchased by her cousin's
money.

Thus it came to pass that Isabel's new home
was not made comfortable to her on her first
arrival. Her stepmother would hardly speak to
her, and the girls knew that she was in disgrace.
There was Mr. Owen, willing enough, as the
stepmother knew, to take Isabel away, and
relieve them all from this burden, and with
the 4000*l.* Mr. Owen would, no doubt, be able
at once to provide a home for her. But Mr.
Owen could hardly do this without some help.
And even though Mr. Owen should be so generous,—and thus justify the name of 'softie' which
Mrs. Brodrick would sometimes give him in
discussing his character with her own daughters,
—how preferable would it be to have a relation
well-provided! To Mrs. Brodrick the girl's objection was altogether unintelligible. The more of
a Philistine*Cousin Henry was, the more satisfaction should there be in fleecing him. To refuse
a legacy because it was not formal was, to her
thinking, an act of insanity. To have the payment of one refused to her because of informality
would have been heart-breaking. But the making
of such a difficulty as this she could not stomach.
Could she have had her will, she would have
been well pleased to whip the girl! Therefore
Isabel's new home was not pleasant to her.

At this time Mr. Owen was away, having gone for his holiday to the Continent. To all the Brodricks it was a matter of course that he would marry Isabel as soon as he came back. There was no doubt that he was a 'softie'. But then how great is the difference between having a brother-in-law well off, and a relation tightly constrained by closely limited means! To refuse, —even to make a show of refusing,—those good things was a crime against the husband who was to have them. Such was the light in which Mrs. Brodrick looked at it. To Mr. Brodrick himself there was an obstinacy in it which was sickening to him. But to Isabel's thinking the matter was very different. She was as firmly resolved that she would not marry Mr. Owen as that she would not take her cousin's money;—almost as firmly resolved.

Then there came the angry letter from Cousin Henry, containing two points which had to be considered. There was the offer to her to come to Llanfeare, and live there as though she was herself the owner. That, indeed, did not require much consideration. It was altogether out of the question, and only dwelt in her thoughts as showing how quickly the man had contrived to make himself odious to every one about the place. His uncle, he said, had made the place a nest of hornets to him. Isabel declared that she knew why the place was a nest of hornets. There was no one about Llanfeare to whom so unmanly, so cringing, so dishonest a creature would not be odious. She could understand all that.

But then there was the other point, and on that her mind rested long.

'I think you ought to be ashamed of what you said to me,—so soon after the old man's death.'

She sat long in silence thinking of it, meditating whether he had been true in that,—whether it did behove her to repent her harshness to the man. She remembered well her words;—'We take presents from those we love, not from those we despise.'

They had been hard words—quite unjustifiable unless he had made himself guilty of something worse than conduct that was simply despicable. Not because he had been a poor creature, not because he had tormented the old man's last days by an absence of all generous feeling, not because he had been altogether unlike what, to her thinking, a Squire of Llanfeare should be, had she answered him with those crushing words. It was because at the moment she had believed him to be something infinitely worse than that.

Grounding her aversion on such evidence as she had,—on such evidence as she thought she had,—she had brought against him her heavy accusation. She could not tell him to his face that he had stolen the will, she could not accuse him of felony, but she had used such quick mode of expression as had come to her for assuring him that he stood as low in her esteem as a felon might stand. And this she had done when he was endeavouring to perform to her that which had been described to him as a duty! And now he had turned upon her and rebuked her,—rebuked her as he was again endeavouring to perform the same duty,—rebuked her as it was so natural that a man should do who had been subjected to so gross an affront!

She hated him, despised him, and in her heart condemned him. She still believed him to have been guilty. Had he not been guilty, the beads of perspiration would not have stood upon his brow; he would not have become now red, now pale, by sudden starts; he would not have quivered beneath her gaze when she looked into his face. He could not have been utterly mean as he was, had he not been guilty. But yet,—and now she saw it with her clear-seeing intellect, now that her passion was in abeyance,—she had not been entitled to accuse him to his face. If he were guilty, it was for others to find it out, and for others to accuse him. It had been for her as a lady, and as her uncle's niece, to accept him in her uncle's house as her uncle's heir. No duty could have compelled her to love him, no duty would have required her to accept even his friendship. But she was aware that she had misbehaved herself in insulting him. She was ashamed of herself in that she had not been able to hide her feelings within her own high heart, but had allowed him to suppose that she had been angered because she had been deprived of her uncle's wealth. Having so resolved, she wrote to him as follows;—

'MY DEAR HENRY,

'Do not take any further steps about the money, as I am quite determined not to accept it. I hope it will not be sent, as there would only be the trouble of repaying it. I do not think that it would do for me to live at Llanfeare, as I should have no means of supporting myself, let alone the servants. The thing is of course out of the question. You tell me that I ought to be ashamed of myself for certain words that I spoke to you. They should not have been spoken. I am ashamed of myself, and I now send you my apology.

'Yours truly,
'ISABEL BRODRICK.'

The reader may perhaps understand that these words were written by her with extreme anguish; but of that her Cousin Henry understood nothing.

CHAPTER XII

MR. OWEN

IN this way Isabel spent four very uncomfortable weeks in her new home before Mr. Owen returned to Hereford. Nor was her discomfort much relieved by the prospect of his return. She knew all the details of his circumstances, and told herself that the man would be wrong to marry without any other means than those he at present possessed. Nor did she think of herself that she was well qualified to be the wife of a poor gentleman. She believed that she could starve if it were required of her, and support her sufferings with fortitude. She believed that she could work,—work from morning till night, from week to week, from month to month, without complaining; but she did not think that she could make herself sweet as a wife should be sweet to a husband with a threadbare coat, or that she could be tender as a mother should be tender while dividing limited bread among her children. To go and die and have done with it, if that might be possible, was the panacea of her present troubles most commonly present to her mind. Therefore, there was no comfort to her in that promised coming of her lover of which the girls chattered to her continually. She had refused her lover when she held the proud position of the heiress of Llanfeare,—refused him, no doubt, in obedience to her uncle's word, and not in accordance with her own feelings; but still she had refused him. Afterwards, when she had believed that there would be a sum of money coming to her from her uncle's will, there had been room for possible doubt. Should the money have proved sufficient to cause her to be a relief rather than a burden to the husband, it might have been her duty to marry him, seeing that she loved him with all her heart,—seeing that she was sure of his love. There would have been much against it even then, because she had refused him when she had been a grand lady; but, had the money been forthcoming, there might have been a doubt. Now there could be no doubt. Should she who had denied him her hand because she was her uncle's heiress,—on that avowed ground alone,—should she, now that she was a pauper, burden him with her presence? He, no doubt, would be generous enough to renew his offer. She was well aware of his nobility. But she, too, could be generous, and, as she thought, noble. Thus it was that her spirit spoke within her, bidding her subject all the sweet affections of her heart to a stubborn pride.

The promised return, therefore, of Mr. Owen did not make her very happy.

'He will be here to-morrow,' said her step-mother to her. 'Mrs. Richards expects him by the late train to-night. I looked in there yesterday and she told me.' Mrs. Richards was the respectable lady with whom Mr. Owen lodged.

'I dare say he will,' said Isabel wearily—sorry, too, that Mr. Owen's goings and comings should have been investigated.

'Now, Isabel, let me advise you. You cannot be so unjust to Mr. Owen as to make him fancy for a moment that you will refuse your uncle's money. Think of his position,—about two hundred and fifty a year in all! With your two hundred added it would be positive comfort; without it you would be frightfully poor.'

'Do you think I have not thought of it?'

'I suppose you must. But then you are so odd and so hard, so unlike any other girl I ever saw. I don't see how you could have the face to refuse the money, and then to eat his bread.'

This was an unfortunate speech as coming from Mrs. Brodrick, because it fortified Isabel in the reply she was bound to make. Hitherto the stepmother had thought it certain that the marriage would take place in spite of such maiden denials as the girl had made; but now the denial had to be repeated with more than maiden vigour.

'I have thought of it,' said Isabel,—'thought of it very often, till I have told myself that conduct such as that would be inexpressibly base. What! to eat his bread after refusing him mine when it was believed to be so plentiful! I certainly have not face enough to do that,—neither face nor courage for that. There are ignoble things which require audacity altogether beyond my reach.'

'Then you must accept the money from your cousin.'

'Certainly not,' said Isabel; 'neither that nor yet the position which Mr. Owen will perhaps offer me again.'

'Of course he will offer it to you.'

'Then he must be told that on no consideration can his offer be accepted.'

'That is nonsense. You are both dying for each other.'

'Then we must die. But as for that, I think that neither men nor young women die for love now-a-days. If we love each other, we must do without each other, as people have to learn to do without most of the things that they desire.'

'I never heard of such nonsense, such wickedness! There is the money. Why should you not take it?'

'I can explain to you, mother,' she said sternly, it being her wont to give the appellation but very seldom to her stepmother, 'why I should not take Mr. Owen, but I cannot tell you why I cannot take my cousin's money. I can only simply assure you that I will not do so, and that I most certainly shall never marry any man who would accept it.'

'I consider that to be actual wickedness,— wickedness against your own father.'

'I have told papa. He knows I will not have the money.'

'Do you mean to say that you will come here into this house as an additional burden, as a weight upon your poor father's shoulder, when you have it in your power to relieve him altogether? Do you not know how pressed he is, and that there are your brothers to be educated?' Isabel, as she listened to this, sat silent, looking upon the ground, and her stepmother went on, understanding nothing of the nature of the mind of her whom she was addressing. 'He had reason to expect, ample reason, that you would never cost him a shilling. He had been told a hundred times that you would be provided for by your uncle. Do you not know that it was so?'

'I do. I told him so myself when I was last here before Uncle Indefer's death.'

'And yet you will do nothing to relieve him? You will refuse this money, though it is your own, when you could be married to Mr. Owen to-morrow?' Then she paused, waiting to find what might be the effect of her eloquence.

'I do not acknowledge papa's right or yours to press me to marry any man.'

'But I suppose you acknowledge your right to be as good as your word? Here is the money; you have only got to take it.'

'What you mean is that I ought to acknowledge my obligation to be as good as my word. I do. I told my father that I would not be a burden to him, and I am bound to keep to that. He will have understood that at the present moment I am breaking my promise through a mistake of Uncle Indefer's which I could not have anticipated.'

'You are breaking your promise because you will not accept money that is your own.'

'I am breaking my promise, and that is sufficient. I will go out of the house and will cease to be a burden. If I only knew where I could go, I would begin to-morrow.'

'That is all nonsense,' said Mrs. Brodrick, getting up and bursting out of the room in anger. 'There is the man ready to marry you, and there is the money. Anybody can see with half an eye what is your duty.'

Isabel, with all the eyes that she had, could not see what was her duty. That it could not be her duty to take a present of money from the man whom she believed to be robbing her of the estate she felt quite sure. It could not be her duty to bring poverty on a man whom she loved, —especially not as she had refused to confer wealth upon him. It was, she thought, clearly her duty not to be a burden upon her father, as she had told him that no such burden should fall upon him. It was her duty, she thought, to earn her own bread, or else to eat none at all. In her present frame of mind she would have gone out of the house on the moment if any one would have accepted her even as a kitchenmaid. But there was no one to accept her. She had questioned her father on the matter, and he had ridiculed her idea of earning her bread. When she had spoken of service, he had become angry with her. It was not thus that he could be relieved. He did not want to see his girl a maidservant or even a governess. It was not thus that she could relieve him. He simply wanted to drive her into his views, so that she might accept the comfortable income which was at her disposal, and become the wife of a gentleman whom every one esteemed. But she, in her present frame of mind, cared little for any disgrace she might bring on others by menial service. She was told that she was a burden, and she desired to cease to be burdensome.

Thinking it over all that night, she resolved that she would consult Mr. Owen himself. It would, she thought, be easy,—or if not easy at any rate feasible,—to make him understand that there could be no marriage. With him she would be on her own ground. He, at least, had no authority over her, and she knew herself well enough to be confident of her own strength. Her father had a certain right to insist. Even her stepmother had a deputed right. But her lover had none. He should be made to understand that she would not marry him,—and then he could advise her as to that project of being governess, housemaid, schoolmistress, or whatnot.

On the following morning he came, and was soon closeted with her. When he arrived, Isabel was sitting with Mrs. Brodrick and her sisters, but they soon packed up their hemmings and sewings, and took themselves off, showing that it was an understood thing that Isabel and Mr. Owen were to be left together. The door was no sooner closed than he came up to her, as though to embrace her, as though to put his arm round her waist before she had a moment to retreat, preparing to kiss her as though she were already his own. She saw it all in a moment. It was as though, since her last remembered interview, there had been some other meeting which she had forgotten,—some meeting at which she had consented to be his wife. She could not be angry with him. How can a girl be angry with a man whose love is so good, so true? He would not have dreamed of kissing her had she stood there before him the declared heiress of Llanfeare. She felt more than this. She was sure by his manner that he knew that she had determined not to take her cousin's money. She was altogether unaware that there had already been some talking that morning between him and her father; but she was sure that he knew. How could she be angry with him?

But she escaped. 'No, not that,' she said. 'It must not be so, Mr. Owen;—it must not. It cannot be so.'

'Tell me one thing, Isabel, before we go any further, and tell me truly. Do you love me?'

She was standing about six feet from him,*and she looked hard into his face, determined not to blush before his eyes for a moment. But she could hardly make up her mind as to what would be the fitting answer to his demand.

'I know', said he, 'that you are too proud to tell me a falsehood.'

'I will not tell you a falsehood.'

'Do you love me?' There was still a pause. 'Do you love me as a woman should love the man she means to marry?'

'I do love you!'

'Then, in God's name, why should we not kiss? You are my love and I am yours. Your father and mother are satisfied that it should be so. Seeing that we are so, is it a disgrace to kiss? Having won your heart, may I not have the delight of thinking that you would wish me to be near you?'

'You must know it all,' she said, 'though it may be unwomanly to tell so much.'

'Know what?'

'There has never been a man whose touch has been pleasant to me;—but I could revel in yours. Kiss you? I could kiss your feet at this moment, and embrace your knees. Everything belonging to you is dear to me. The things you have touched have been made sacred to me. The Prayer-Book tells the young wife that she should love her husband till death shall part them.* I think my love will go further than that.'

'Isabel! Isabel!'

'Keep away from me: I will not even give you my hand to shake till you have promised to be of one mind with me. I will not become your wife.'

'You shall become my wife!'

'Never! Never! I have thought it out, and I know that I am right. Things have been hard with me.'

'Not to me! They will not have been hard to me when I shall have carried my point with you.'

'I was forced to appear before your eyes as the heiress of my uncle.'

'Has that made any difference with me?'

'And I was forced to refuse you in obedience to him who had adopted me.'

'I understand all that very completely.'

'Then he made a new will, and left me some money.'

'Of all that I know, I think, every particular.'

'But the money is not there.' At this he nodded his head as though smiling at her absurdity in going back over circumstances which were so well understood by both of them. 'The money is offered to me by my cousin, but I will not take it.'

'As to that I have nothing to say. It is the one point on which, when we are married, I shall decline to give you any advice.'

'Mr. Owen,' and now she came close to him, but still ready to spring back should it be necessary, 'Mr. Owen, I will tell you what I have told no one else.'

'Why me?'

'Because I trust you as I trust no one else.'

'Then tell me.'

'There is another will. There was another will rather, and he has destroyed it.'

'Why do you say that? You should not say that. You cannot know it.'

'And, therefore, I say it only to you, as I would to my own heart. The old man told me so—in his last moments. And then there is the look of the man. If you could have seen how his craven spirit cowered beneath my eyes!'

'One should not judge by such indications. One cannot but see them and notice them; but one should not judge.'

'You would have judged had you seen. You could not have helped judging. Nothing, however, can come of it, except this,—that not for all the world would I take his money.'

'It may be right, Isabel, that all that should be discussed between you and me,—right if you wish it. It will be my delight to think that there shall be no secret between us. But, believe me, dearest, it can have no reference to the question between us.'

'Not that I should be absolutely penniless?'

'Not in the least.'

'But it will, Mr. Owen. In that even my father agrees with me.' In this she was no doubt wrong. Her father had simply impressed upon her the necessity of taking the money because of her lover's needs. 'I will not be a burden at any rate to you; and as I cannot go to you without being a burden, I will not go at all. What does it matter whether there be a little more suffering or a little less? What does it matter?'

'It matters a great deal to me.'

'A man gets over that quickly, I think.'

'So does a woman,—if she be the proper sort of woman for getting over her difficulties of that kind. I don't think you are.'

'I will try.'

'I won't.' This he said, looking full into her face. 'My philosophy teaches me to despise the grapes which hang too high, but to make the most of those which come within my reach. Now, I look upon you as being within my reach.'

'I am not within your reach.'

'Yes; pardon me for my confidence, but you are. You have confessed that you love me.'

'I do.'

'Then you will not be so wicked as to deny to me that which I have a right to demand? If you love me as a woman should love the man who is to become her husband, you have no right to refuse me. I have made good my claim, unless there be other reasons.'

'There is a reason.'

'None but such as I have to judge of. Had your father objected, that would have been a reason; or when your uncle disapproved because of the property, that was a reason. As to the money, I will never ask you to take it, unless you can plead that you yourself are afraid of the poverty—.' Then he paused, looking at her as though he defied her to say so much on her own behalf. She could not say that, but sat there panting, frightened by his energy.

'Nor am I,' he continued very gently, 'the least in the world. Think of it, and you will find that I am right; and then, when next I come,

then, perhaps, you will not refuse to kiss me.'
And so he went.

Oh, how she loved him! How sweet would it
be to submit her pride, her independence, her
maiden reticences to such a man as that! How
worthy was he of all worship, of all confidence,
of all service! How infinitely better was he than
any other being that had ever crossed her path!
But yet she was quite sure that she would not
marry him.

CHAPTER XIII

THE *CARMARTHEN HERALD*

THERE was a great deal said at Carmarthen
about the old Squire's will. Such scenes as
that which had taken place in the house, first
when the will was produced, then when the
search was made, and afterwards when the will
was read, do not pass without comment. There
had been many present, and some of them had
been much moved by the circumstances. The
feeling that the Squire had executed a will subsequent to that which had now been proved was
very strong, and the idea suggested by Mr.
Apjohn that the Squire himself had, in the
weakness of his latter moments, destroyed this
document, was not generally accepted. Had he
done so, something of it would have been known.
The ashes of the paper or the tattered fragments

would have been seen. Whether Mr. Apjohn
himself did or did not believe that it had been so,
others would not think it. Among the tenants
and the servants at Llanfeare there was a general
feeling that something wrong had been done.
They who were most inclined to be charitable in
their judgment, such as John Griffith of Coed,
thought that the document was still hidden, and
that it might not improbably be brought to light
at last. Others were convinced that it had fallen
into the hands of the present possessor of the
property, and that it had been feloniously but
successfully destroyed. No guess at the real truth
was made by any one. How should a man have
guessed that the false heir should have sat there
with the will, as it were, before his eyes, close at
his hand, and neither have destroyed nor revealed
its existence?

Among those who believed the worst as to
Cousin Henry were the two Cantors. When a
man has seen a thing done himself he is prone to
believe in it,—and the more so when he has had
a hand in the doing. They had been selected for
the important operation of witnessing the will,
and did not in the least doubt that the will had
been in existence when the old Squire died. It
might have been destroyed since. They believed
that it had been destroyed. But they could not
be brought to understand that so great an injustice should be allowed to remain on the face
of the earth without a remedy or without punish-

ment. Would it not be enough for a judge to know that they, two respectable men, had witnessed a new will, and that this new will had certainly been in opposition to the one which had been so fraudulently proved? The younger Cantor especially was loud upon the subject, and got many ears in Carmarthen to listen to him.

The *Carmarthen Herald*,* a newspaper bearing a high character throughout South Wales, took the matter up very strongly, so that it became a question whether the new Squire would not be driven to defend himself by an action for libel. It was not that the writer declared that Cousin Henry had destroyed the will, but that he published minute accounts of all that had been done at Llanfeare, putting forward in every paper as it came out the reason which existed for supposing that a wrong had been done. That theory that old Indefer Jones had himself destroyed his last will without saying a word of his purpose to any one was torn to tatters. The doctor had been with him from day to day, and must almost certainly have known it had such an intention been in his mind. The housekeeper would have known it. Henry Jones himself must have known it. The nephew and professed heir had said not a word to any one of what had passed between himself and his uncle. Could they who had known old Indefer Jones for so many years, and were aware that he had been governed by the highest sense of honour through

his entire life, could they bring themselves to
believe that he should have altered the will made
in his nephew's favour, and then realtered it,
going back to his intentions in that nephew's
favour, without saying a word to his nephew on
the subject? But Henry Jones had given no account of any such word. Henry Jones had been
silent as to all that occurred during those last
weeks. Henry Jones had not only been silent
when the will was being read, when the search
was being made, but had sat there still in continued silence. 'We do not say', continued the
writer in the paper, 'that Henry Jones since he
became owner of Llanfeare has been afraid to
mingle with his brother men. We have no right
to say so. But we consider it to be our duty to
declare that such has been the fact. Circumstances will from time to time occur in which it
becomes necessary on public grounds to inquire
into the privacy of individuals, and we think that
the circumstances now as to this property are of
this nature.' As will be the case in such matters,
these expressions became gradually stronger, till
it was conceived to be the object of those concerned in making them to drive Henry Jones to
seek for legal redress,—so that he might be subjected to cross-examination as to the transactions
and words of that last fortnight before his uncle's
death. It was the opinion of many that if he
could be forced into a witness-box, he would be
made to confess if there were anything to confess.

The cowardice of the man became known,—or was rather exaggerated in the minds of those around him. It was told of him how he lived in the one room, how rarely he left the house, how totally he was without occupation. More than the truth was repeated as to his habits, till all Carmarthenshire believed that he was so trammelled by some mysterious consciousness of crime as to be unable to perform any of the duties of life. When men spoke to him he trembled; when men looked at him he turned away.

All his habits were inquired into. It was said of him that the *Carmarthen Herald* was the only paper that he saw, and declared of him that he spent hour after hour in spelling the terrible accusations which, if not absolutely made against him, were insinuated. It became clear to lawyers, to Mr. Apjohn himself, that the man, if honest, should, on behalf of the old family and long-respected name, vindicate himself by prosecuting the owner of the paper for libel. If he were honest in the matter, altogether honest, there could be no reason why he should fear to encounter a hostile lawyer. There were at last two letters from young Joseph Cantor printed in the paper which were undoubtedly libellous,—letters which young Cantor himself certainly could not have written,—letters which all Carmarthen knew to have been written by some one connected with the newspaper, though signed by the young farmer,—in which it was positively declared that the old Squire had left a later will behind him. When it was discussed whether or no he could get a verdict, it was clearly shown that the getting of a verdict should not be the main object of the prosecution. 'He has to show', said Mr. Apjohn, 'that he is not afraid to face a court of justice.'

But he was afraid. When we last parted with him after his visit to Coed he had not seen the beginning of these attacks. On the next day the first paper reached him, and they who were concerned in it did not spare to send him the copies as they were issued. Having read the first, he was not able to refuse to read what followed. In each issue they were carried on, and, as was told of him in Carmarthen, he lingered over every agonizing detail of the venom which was entering into his soul. It was in vain that he tried to hide the paper, or to pretend to be indifferent to its coming. Mrs. Griffith knew very well where the paper was, and knew also that every word had been perused. The month's notice which had been accepted from her and the butler in lieu of the three months first offered had now expired. The man had gone, but she remained, as did the two other women. Nothing was said as to the cause of their remaining; but they remained. As for Cousin Henry himself, he was too weak, too frightened, too completely absorbed by the horrors of his situation to ask them why they stayed, or to have asked them why they went.

He understood every word that was written of

him with sharp, minute intelligence. Though
his spirit was cowed, his mind was still alive to
all the dangers of his position. Things were being
said of him, charges were insinuated, which he
declared to himself to be false. He had not
destroyed the will. He had not even hidden it. He
had only put a book into its own place, carrying
out as he did so his innocent intention when he
had first lifted the book. When these searchers
had come, doing their work so idly, with such
incurious futility, he had not concealed the book.
He had left it there on its shelf beneath their
hands. Who could say that he had been guilty?
If the will were found now, who could reasonably suggest that there had been guilt on his
part? If all were known,—except that chance
glance of his eye which never could be known,—
no one could say that he was other than innocent!
And yet he knew of himself that he would lack
strength to stand up in court and endure the
sharp questions and angry glances of a keen
lawyer. His very knees would fail to carry him
through the court. The words would stick in his
jaws. He would shake and shiver and faint before the assembled eyes. It would be easier for
him to throw himself from the rocks on which
he had lain dreaming into the sea than to go into
a court of law and there tell his own story as to
the will. They could not force him to go. He
thought he could perceive as much as that. The
action, if action there were to be, must originate

with him. There was no evidence on which they could bring a charge of felony or even of fraud against him. They could not drag him into the court. But he knew that all the world would say that if he were an honest man, he himself would appear there, denounce his defamers, and vindicate his own name. As day by day he failed to do so, he would be declaring his own guilt. Yet he knew that he could not do it.

Was there no escape? He was quite sure now that the price at which he held the property was infinitely above its value. Its value! It had no value in his eyes. It was simply a curse of which he would rid himself with the utmost alacrity if only he could rid himself of all that had befallen him in achieving it. But how should he escape? Were he now himself to disclose the document and carry it into Carmarthen, prepared to deliver up the property to his cousin, was there one who would not think that it had been in his possession from before his uncle's death, and that he had now been driven by his fears to surrender it? Was there one who would not believe that he had hidden it with his own hands? How now could he personate that magnanimity which would have been so easy had he brought forth the book and handed it with its enclosure to Mr. Apjohn when the lawyer came to read the will?

He looked back with dismay at his folly at having missed an opportunity so glorious. But now there seemed to be no escape. Though he left the room daily, no one found the will. They were welcome to find it if they would, but they did not. That base newspaper lied of him,—as he told himself bitterly as he read it,—in saying that he did not leave his room. Daily did he roam about the place for an hour or two,—speaking, indeed, to no one, looking at no one. There the newspaper had been true enough. But that charge against him of self-imprisonment had been false as far as it referred to days subsequent to the rebuke which his housekeeper had given him. But no one laid a hand upon the book. He almost believed that, were the paper left open on the table, no eye would examine its contents. There it lay still hidden within the folds of the sermon, that weight upon his heart, that incubus on his bosom,* that nightmare which robbed him of all his slumbers, and he could not rid himself of its presence. Property, indeed! Oh! if he were only back in London, and his cousin reigning at Llanfeare!

John Griffith, from Coed, had promised to call upon him; but when three weeks had passed by, he had not as yet made his appearance. Now, on one morning he came and found his landlord alone in the book-room. 'This is kind of you, Mr. Griffith,' said Cousin Henry, struggling hard to assume the manner of a man with a light heart.

'I have come, Mr. Jones,' said the farmer very seriously, 'to say a few words which I think ought to be said.'

'What are they, Mr. Griffith?'

'Now, Mr. Jones, I am not a man as is given to interfering,—especially not with my betters.'

'I am sure you are not.'

'And, above all, not with my own landlord.' Then he paused; but as Cousin Henry could not find an appropriate word either for rebuke or encouragement, he was driven to go on with his story. 'I have been obliged to look at all those things in the *Carmarthen Herald*.' Then Cousin Henry turned deadly pale. 'We have all been driven to look at them. I have taken the paper these twenty years, but it is sent now to every tenant on the estate, whether they pay or whether they don't. Mrs. Griffith, there, in the kitchen has it. I suppose they sent it to you, sir?'

'Yes; it does come,' said Cousin Henry, with the faintest attempt at a smile.

'And you have read what they say?'

'Yes, the most of it.'

'It has been very hard, sir.' At this Cousin Henry could only affect a ghastly smile. 'Very hard,' continued the farmer. 'It has made my flesh creep as I read it. Do you know what it all means, Mr. Jones?'

'I suppose I know.'

'It means,—that you have stolen,—the estates, —from your cousin,—Miss Brodrick!' This the man said very solemnly, bringing out each single word by itself. 'I am not saying so, Mr. Jones.'

'No, no, no,' gasped the miserable wretch.

'No, indeed. If I thought so, I should not be here to tell you what I thought. It is because I believe that you are injured that I am here.'

'I am injured; I am injured!'

'I think so. I believe so. I cannot tell what the mystery is, if mystery there be; but I do not believe that you have robbed that young lady, your own cousin, by destroying such a deed as your uncle's will.'

'No, no, no.'

'Is there any secret that you can tell?'

Awed, appalled, stricken with utter dismay, Cousin Henry sat silent before his questioner.

'If there be, sir, had you not better confide it to some one? Your uncle knew me well for more than forty years, and trusted me thoroughly, and I would fain, if I could, do something for his nephew. If there be anything to tell, tell it like a man.'

Still Cousin Henry sat silent. He was unable to summon courage at the instant sufficient to deny the existence of the secret, nor could he resolve to take down the book and show the document. He doubted, when the appearance of a doubt was in itself evidence of guilt in the eyes of the man who was watching him. 'Oh, Mr. Griffith,' he exclaimed after a while, 'will you be my friend?'

'I will indeed, Mr. Jones, if I can,—honestly.'

'I have been cruelly used.'

'It has been hard to bear,' said Mr. Griffith.

'Terrible, terrible! Cruel, cruel!' Then again he paused, trying to make up his mind, endeavouring to see by what means he could escape from this hell upon earth. If there were any means, he might perhaps achieve it by aid of this man. The man sat silent, watching him, but the way of escape did not appear to him.

'There is no mystery,' he gasped at last.

'None?' said the farmer severely.

'No mystery. What mystery should there be? There was the will. I have destroyed nothing. I have hidden nothing. I have done nothing. Because the old man changed his mind so often, am I to be blamed?'

'Then, Mr. Jones, why do you not say all that in a court of law,—on your oath?'

'How can I do that?'

'Go to Mr. Apjohn, and speak to him like a man. Bid him bring an action in your name for libel against the newspaper. Then there will be an inquiry. Then you will be put into a witness-box, and be able to tell your own story on your oath.'

Cousin Henry, groaning, pale and affrighted, murmured out something signifying that he would think of it. Then Mr. Griffith left him. The farmer, when he entered the room, had believed his landlord to be innocent, but that belief had vanished when he took his leave.

CHAPTER XIV

AN ACTION FOR LIBEL

WHEN the man had asked him that question, —Is there any secret you can tell?—Cousin Henry did, for half a minute, make up his mind to tell the whole story, and reveal everything as it had occurred. Then he remembered the lie which he had told, the lie to which he had signed his name when he had been called upon to prove the will in Carmarthen. Had he not by the unconsidered act of that moment committed some crime for which he could be prosecuted and sent to gaol? Had it not been perjury? From the very beginning he had determined that he would support his possession of the property by no criminal deed. He had not hidden the will in the book. He had not interfered in the search. He had done nothing incompatible with innocence. So it had been with him till he had been called upon, without a moment having been allowed to him for thinking, to sign his name to that declaration. The remembrance of this came to him as he almost made up his mind to rise from his seat and pull the book down from the shelf. And then another thought occurred to him. Could he not tell Mr. Griffith that he had discovered the document since he had made that declaration,—that he had discovered it only on that morning? But he had felt that a story such as that would receive no belief, and he had feared to estrange his only friend by a palpable lie. He had therefore said that there was no secret,—had said so after a pause which had assured Mr. Griffith of the existence of a mystery, —had said so with a face which of itself had declared the truth.

When the farmer left him he knew well enough that the man doubted him,—nay, that the man was assured of his guilt. It had come to be so with all whom he had encountered since he had first reached Llanfeare. His uncle who had sent for him had turned from him; his cousin had scorned him; the tenants had refused to accept him when there certainly had been no cause for their rejection. Mr. Apjohn from the first had looked at him with accusing eyes; his servants were spies upon his actions; this newspaper was rending his very vitals; and now this one last friend had deserted him. He thought that if only he could summon courage for the deed, it would be best for him to throw himself from the rocks.

But there was no such courage in him. The one idea remaining to him was to save himself from the horrors of a criminal prosecution. If he did not himself touch the document, or give any sign of his consciousness of its presence, they could not prove that he had known of its where-abouts. If they would only find it and let him go! But they did not find it, and he could not put them on its trace. As to these wicked libels, Mr. Griffith had asked him why he did not have recourse to a court of law, and refute them by the courage of his presence. He understood the proposition in all its force. Why did he not show himself able to bear any questions which the ingenuity of a lawyer could put to him? Simply because he was unable to bear them. The truth would be extracted from him in the process. Though he should have fortified himself with strongest resolves, he would be unable to hide his guilty knowledge. He knew that of himself. He would be sure to give testimony against himself, on the strength of which he would be dragged from the witness-box to the dock.

He declared to himself that, let the newspaper say what it would, he would not of his own motion throw himself among the lion's teeth which were prepared for him. But in so resolving he did not know what further external force might be applied to him. When the old tenant had sternly told him that he should go like a man into the witness-box and tell his own story on his oath, that had been hard to bear. But there came worse than that,—a power more difficult to resist. On the following morning Mr. Apjohn arrived at Llanfeare, having driven himself over from Carmarthen, and was at once shown into the book-room. The lawyer was a man who, by his friends and by his clients in

general, was considered to be a pleasant fellow
as well as a cautious man of business. He was
good at a dinner-table, serviceable with a gun,
and always happy on horseback. He could catch
a fish, and was known to be partial to a rubber
at whist. He certainly was not regarded as a
hard or cruel man. But Cousin Henry, in looking at him, had always seen a sternness in his
eye, some curve of a frown upon his brow, which
had been uncomfortable to him. From the
beginning of their intercourse he had been afraid
of the lawyer. He had felt that he was looked
into and scrutinized, and found to be wanting.
Mr. Apjohn had, of course, been on Isabel's side.
All Carmarthenshire knew that he had done his
best to induce the old squire to maintain Isabel
as his heiress. Cousin Henry was well aware of
that. But still why had this attorney always
looked at him with accusing eyes? When he had
signed that declaration at Carmarthen, the attorney had shown by his face that he believed
the declaration to be false. And now this man
was there, and there was nothing for him but to
endure his questions.

'Mr. Jones,' said the lawyer, 'I have thought
it my duty to call upon you in respect to these
articles in the *Carmarthen Herald*.'

'I cannot help what the *Carmarthen Herald*
may say.'

'But you can, Mr. Jones. That is just it.
There are laws which enable a man to stop

libels and to punish them if it be worth his while to do so.' He paused a moment, but Cousin Henry was silent, and he continued, 'For many years I was your uncle's lawyer, as was my father before me. I have never been commissioned by you to regard myself as your lawyer, but as cir-cumstances are at present, I am obliged to occupy the place until you put your business into other hands. In such a position I feel it to be my duty to call upon you in reference to these articles. No doubt they are libellous.'

'They are very cruel; I know that,' said Cousin Henry, whining.

'All such accusations are cruel, if they be false.'

'These are false; damnably false.'

'I take that for granted; and therefore I have come to you to tell you that it is your duty to repudiate with all the strength of your own words the terrible charges which are brought against you.'

'Must I go and be a witness about myself?'

'Yes; it is exactly that. You must go and be a witness about yourself. Who else can tell the truth as to all the matters in question as well as yourself? You should understand, Mr. Jones, that you should not take this step with the view of punishing the newspaper.'

'Why, then?'

'In order that you may show yourself willing to place yourself there to be questioned. "Here I am," you would say. "If there be any point

in which you wish me to be examined as to this property and this will, here I am to answer you."
It is that you may show that you are not afraid of investigation.' But it was exactly this of which Cousin Henry was afraid. 'You cannot but be aware of what is going on in Carmarthen.'

'I know about the newspaper.'

'It is my duty not to blink the matter. Every one, not only in the town but throughout the country, is expressing an opinion that right has not been done.'

'What do they want? I cannot help it if my uncle did not make a will according to their liking.'

'They think that he did make a will according to their liking, and that there has been foul play.'

'Do they accuse me?'

'Practically they do. These articles in the paper are only an echo of the public voice. And that voice is becoming stronger and stronger every day because you take no steps to silence it. Have you seen yesterday's paper?'

'Yes; I saw it,' said Cousin Henry, gasping for breath.

Then Mr. Apjohn brought a copy of the newspaper out of his pocket, and began to read a list of questions which the editor was supposed to ask the public generally. Each question was an insult, and Cousin Henry, had he dared, would have bade the reader desist, and have turned him out of the room for his insolence in reading them.

'Has Mr. Henry Jones expressed an opinion of his own as to what became of the will which the Messrs. Cantor witnessed?'

'Has Mr. Henry Jones consulted any friend, legal or otherwise, as to his tenure of the Llanfeare estate?'

'Has Mr. Henry Jones any friend to whom he can speak in Carmarthenshire?'

'Has Mr. Henry Jones inquired into the cause of his own isolation?'

'Has Mr. Henry Jones any idea why we persecute him in every fresh issue of our newspaper?'

'Has Mr. Henry Jones thought of what may possibly be the end of all this?'

'Has Mr. Henry Jones any thought of prosecuting us for libel?'

'Has Mr. Henry Jones heard of any other case in which an heir has been made so little welcome to his property?'

So the questions went on, an almost endless list, and the lawyer read them one after another, in a low, plain voice, slowly, but with clear accentuation, so that every point intended by the questioner might be understood. Such a martyrdom surely no man was ever doomed to bear before. In every line he was described as a thief. Yet he bore it; and when the lawyer came to an end of the abominable questions, he sat silent, trying to smile. What was he to say?

'Do you mean to put up with that?' asked

Mr. Apjohn, with that curve of his eyebrow of which Cousin Henry was so much afraid.

'What am I to do?'

'Do! Do anything rather than sit in silence and bear such injurious insult as that. Were there nothing else to do, I would tear the man's tongue from his mouth,—or at least his pen from his grasp.'

'How am I to find him? I never did do anything of that rough kind.'

'It is not necessary. I only say what a man would do if there were nothing else to be done. But the step to be taken is easy. Instruct me to go before the magistrates at Carmarthen, and indict the paper for libel. That is what you must do.'

There was an imperiousness in the lawyer's tone which was almost irresistible. Nevertheless Cousin Henry made a faint effort at resisting. 'I should be dragged into a lawsuit.'

'A lawsuit! Of course you would. What lawsuit would not be preferable to that? You must do as I bid you, or you must consent to have it said and have it thought by all the country that you have been guilty of some felony, and have filched your cousin's property.'

'I have committed nothing,' said the poor wretch, as the tears ran down his face.

'Then go and say so before the world,' said the attorney, dashing his fist down violently upon the table. 'Go and say so, and let men hear you, instead of sitting here whining like a woman.

Like a woman! What honest woman would ever bear such insult? If you do not, you will convince all the world, you will convince me and every neighbour you have, that you have done something to make away with that will. In that case we will not leave a stone unturned to discover the truth. The editor of that paper is laying himself open purposely to an action in order that he may force you to undergo the cross-questioning of a barrister, and everybody who hears of it says that he is right. You can prove that he is wrong only by accepting the challenge. If you refuse the challenge, as I put it to you now, you will acknowledge that—that you have done this deed of darkness!'

Was there any torment ever so cruel, ever so unjustifiable as this! He was asked to put himself, by his own act, into the thumbscrew, on the rack, in order that the executioner might twist his limbs and tear out his vitals! He was to walk into a court of his own accord that he might be worried like a rat by a terrier, that he might be torn by the practised skill of a professional tormentor, that he might be forced to give up the very secrets of his soul in his impotence;—or else to live amidst the obloquy of all men. He asked himself whether he had deserved it, and in that moment of time he assured himself that he had not deserved such punishment as this. If not altogether innocent, if not white as snow, he had done nothing worthy of such cruel usage.

'Well,' said Mr. Apjohn, as though demanding a final answer to his proposition.

'I will think of it,' gasped Cousin Henry.

'There must be no more thinking. The time has gone by for thinking. If you will give me your instructions to commence proceedings against the *Carmarthen Herald*, I will act as your lawyer. If not, I shall make it known to the town that I have made this proposition to you; and I shall also make known the way in which it has been accepted. There has been more than delay enough.'

He sobbed, and gasped, and struggled with himself as the lawyer sat and looked at him. The one thing on which he had been intent was the avoiding of a court of law. And to this he was now to bring himself by his own act.

'When would it have to be?' he asked.

'I should go before the magistrates to-morrow. Your presence would not be wanted then. No delay would be made by the other side. They would be ready enough to come to trial. The assizes begin here at Carmarthen on the 29th of next month. You might probably be examined on that day, which will be a Friday, or on the Saturday following. You will be called as a witness on your own side to prove the libel. But the questions asked by your counsel would amount to nothing.'

'Nothing!' exclaimed Cousin Henry.

'You would be there for another purpose,' continued the lawyer. 'When that nothing had been asked, you would be handed over to the other side, in order that the object of the proceedings might be attained.'

'What object?'

'How the barrister employed might put it I cannot say, but he would examine you as to any knowledge you may have as to that missing will.'

Mr. Apjohn, as he said this, paused for a full minute, looking his client full in the face. It was as though he himself were carrying on a cross-examination. 'He would ask you whether you have such knowledge.' Then again he paused, but Cousin Henry said nothing. 'If you have no such knowledge, if you have no sin in that matter on your conscience, nothing to make you grow pale before the eyes of a judge, nothing to make you fear the verdict of a jury, no fault heavy on your own soul,—then you may answer him with frank courage, then you may look him in the face, and tell him with a clear voice that as far as you are aware your property is your own by as fair a title as any in the country.'

In every word of this there had been con-demnation. It was as though Mr. Apjohn were devoting him to infernal torture, telling him that his only escape would be by the exercise of some herculean power which was notoriously beyond his reach. It was evident to him that Mr. Apjohn was alluring him on with the object of ensuring, not his escape, but most calamitous defeat. Mr.

Apjohn had come there under the guise of his adviser and friend, but was in fact leagued with all the others around him to drive him to his ruin. Of that he felt quite sure. The voice, the eyes, the face, every gesture of his unwelcome visitor had told him that it was so. And yet he could not rise in indignation and expel the visitor from his house. There was a cruelty, an in-humanity, in this which to his thinking was in-finitely worse than any guilt of his own. 'Well?' said Mr. Apjohn.

'I suppose it must be so.'

'I have your instructions, then?'

'Don't you hear me say that I suppose it must be so?'

'Very well. The matter shall be brought in proper course before the magistrates to-morrow, and if, as I do not doubt, an injunction be granted, I will proceed with the matter at once. I will tell you whom we select as our counsel at the assizes, and, as soon as I have learnt, will let you know whom they employ. Let me only implore you not only to tell the truth as to what you know, but to tell all the truth. If you attempt to conceal anything, it will certainly be dragged out of you.'

Having thus comforted his client, Mr. Apjohn took his leave.

CHAPTER XV

COUSIN HENRY MAKES ANOTHER ATTEMPT

WHEN Mr. Apjohn had gone, Cousin Henry sat for an hour, not thinking,—men so afflicted have generally lost the power to think, —but paralysed by the weight of his sorrow, simply repeating to himself assertions that said no man had ever been used so cruelly. Had he been as other men are, he would have turned that lawyer out of the house at the first expression of an injurious suspicion, but his strength had not sufficed for such action. He confessed to himself his own weakness, though he could not bring himself to confess his own guilt. Why did they not find it and have done with it? Feeling at last how incapable he was of collecting his thoughts while he sat there in the book-room, and aware, at the same time, that he must determine on some course of action, he took his hat and strolled out towards the cliffs.

There was a month remaining to him, just a month before the day named on which he was to put himself into the witness-box. That, at any rate, must be avoided. He did after some fashion resolve that, let the result be what it might, he would not submit himself to a cross-examination. They could not drag him from his bed were he to say that he was ill. They could not send policemen to find him, were he to hide himself in London. Unless he gave evidence against himself as to his own guilty knowledge, they could bring no open charge against him; or if he could but summon courage to throw himself from off the rocks, then, at any rate, he would escape from their hands.

What was it all about? This he asked himself as he sat some way down the cliff, looking out over the sea. What was it all about? If they wanted the property for his Cousin Isabel, they were welcome to take it. He desired nothing but to be allowed to get away from this accursed country, to escape, and never more to be heard of there or to hear of it. Could he not give up the property with the signing of some sufficient deed, and thus put an end to their cruel clamour? He could do it all without any signing, by a simple act of honesty, by taking down the book with the will and giving it at once to the lawyer! It was possible,—possible as far as the knowledge of any one but himself was concerned,—that such a thing might be done not only with honesty, but with high-minded magnanimity. How would it be if in truth the document were first found by him on this very day? Had it been so, were it so, then his conduct would be honest. And it was still open to him to simulate that it was so. He had taken down the book, let him say, for spiritual comfort in his great trouble, and lo, the will had been found there between the leaves!

No one would believe him. He declared to himself that such was already his character in the county that no one would believe him. But what though they disbelieved him? Surely they would accept restitution without further reproach. Then there would be no witness-box, no savage terrier of a barrister to tear him in pieces with his fierce words and fiercer eyes. Whether they believed him or not, they would let him go. It would be told of him, at any rate, that having the will in his hands, he had not destroyed it. Up in London, where men would not know all the details of this last miserable month, some good would be spoken of him. And then there would be time left to him to relieve his conscience by repentance.

But to whom should he deliver up the will, and how should he frame the words? He was conscious of his own impotence in deceit. For such a purpose Mr. Apjohn, no doubt, would be the proper person, but there was no one of whom he stood so much in dread as of Mr. Apjohn. Were he to carry the book and the paper to the lawyer and attempt to tell his story, the real truth would be drawn out from him in the first minute of their interview. The man's eyes looking at him, the man's brow bent against him, would extract from him instantly the one truth which it was his purpose to hold within his own keeping. He would find no thankfulness, no mercy, not even justice in the lawyer. The lawyer would accept restitution, and would crush him afterwards. Would it not be better to go off to Hereford, without saying a word to any one in Carmarthenshire, and give up the deed to his Cousin Isabel? But then she had scorned him. She had treated him with foul contempt. As he feared Mr. Apjohn, so did he hate his Cousin Isabel. The only approach to manliness left in his bosom was a true hatred of his cousin.

The single voice which had been kind to him since he had come to this horrid place had been that of old Farmer Griffith. Even his voice had been stern at last, but yet, with the sternness, there had been something of compassion. He thought that he could tell the tale to Mr. Griffith, if to any one. And so thinking, he resolved at once to go to Coed. There was still before him that other means of escape which the rocks and the sea afforded him. As he had made his way on this morning to the spot on which he was now lying that idea was still present to him. He did not think that he could do a deed of such daring. He was almost sure of himself that the power of doing it would be utterly wanting when the moment came. But still it was present to his mind. The courage might reach him at the instant. Were a sudden impulse to carry him away, he thought the Lord would surely forgive him because of all his sufferings. But now, as he looked at the spot, and saw that he could throw himself only among the rocks, that he could not reach the placid deep water, he considered it again, and remembered that the Lord would not forgive him a sin as to which there would be no moment for repentance. As he could not escape in that way, he must carry out his purpose with Farmer Griffith.

'So you be here again prowling about on father's lands?'

Cousin Henry knew at once the voice of that bitter enemy of his, young Cantor; and, wretched as he was, he felt also something of the spirit of the landlord in being thus rebuked for trespassing on his own ground. 'I suppose I have a right to walk about on my own estate?' said he.

'I know nothin' about your own estate,' replied the farmer's son. 'I say nothin' about that. They do be talking about it, but I say nothin'. I has my own opinions, but I say nothin'. Others do be saying a great deal, as I suppose you hear, Mr. Jones, but I say nothin'.'

'How dare you be so impudent to your landlord?'

'I know nothin' about landlords. I know father has a lease of this land, and pays his rent, whether you get it or another; and you have no more right, it 's my belief, to intrude here nor any other stranger. So, if you please, you'll walk.'

'I shall stay here just as long as it suits me,' said Cousin Henry.

'Oh, very well. Then father will have his action against you for trespass, and so you'll be brought into a court of law. You are bound to go off when you are warned. You ain't no right here because you call yourself landlord. You come up here and I'll thrash you, that 's what I will. You wouldn't dare show yourself before a magistrate, that 's what you wouldn't.'

The young man stood there for a while waiting, and then walked off with a loud laugh.

Any one might insult him, any one might beat him, and he could seek for no redress because he would not dare to submit himself to the ordeal of a witness-box. All those around him knew that it was so. He was beyond the protection of the law because of the misery of his position. It was clear that he must do something, and as he could not drown himself, there was nothing better than that telling of his tale to Mr. Griffith. He would go to Mr. Griffith at once. He had not the book and the document with him, but perhaps he could tell the tale better without their immediate presence.

At Coed he found the farmer in his own farmyard.

'I have come to you in great trouble,' said Cousin Henry, beginning his story.

'Well, squire, what is it?' Then the farmer seated himself on a low, movable bar which protected the entrance into an open barn, and Cousin Henry sat beside him.

'That young man Cantor insulted me grossly just now.'

'He shouldn't have done that. Whatever comes of it all, he shouldn't have done that. He was always a forward young puppy.'

'I do think I have been treated very badly among you.'

'As to that, Mr. Jones, opinion does run very high about the squire's will. I explained to you all that when I was with you yesterday.'

'Something has occurred since that,—something that I was coming on purpose to tell you.'

'What has occurred?' Cousin Henry groaned terribly as the moment for revelation came upon him. And he felt that he had made the moment altogether unfit for revelation by that ill-judged observation as to young Cantor. He should have rushed at his story at once. 'Oh, Mr. Griffith, I have found the will!' It should have been told after that fashion. He felt it now,—felt that he had allowed the opportunity to slip by him.

'What is it that has occurred, Mr. Jones, since I was up at Llanfeare yesterday?'

'I don't think that I could tell you here.'

'Where, then?'

'Nor yet to-day. That young man, Cantor, has so put me out that I hardly know what I am saying.'

'Couldn't you speak it out, sir, if it's just something to be said?'

'It's something to be shown too,' replied Cousin Henry, 'and if you wouldn't mind coming up to the house to-morrow, or next day, then I could explain it all.'

'To-morrow it shall be,' said the farmer. 'On the day after I shall be in Carmarthen to market. If eleven o'clock to-morrow morning won't be too early, I shall be there, sir.'

One, or three, or five o'clock would have been better, or the day following better still, so that the evil hour might have been postponed. But Cousin Henry assented to the proposition and took his departure. Now he had committed himself to some revelation, and the revelation must be made. He felt acutely the folly of his own conduct during the last quarter of an hour. If it might have been possible to make the old man believe that the document had only been that morning found, such belief could only have been achieved by an impulsive telling of the story. He was aware that at every step he took he created fresh difficulties by his own folly and want of foresight. How could he now act the sudden emotion of a man startled by surprise? Nevertheless, he must go on with his scheme. There was now nothing before him but his scheme. The farmer would not believe him; but still he might be able to achieve that purpose which he had in view of escaping from Llanfeare and Carmarthenshire.

He sat up late that night thinking of it. For many days past he had not touched the volume, or allowed his eye to rest upon the document.

He had declared to himself that it might remain there or be taken away, as it might chance to others. It should no longer be anything to him. For aught that he knew, it might already have been removed. Such had been his resolution during the last fortnight, and in accordance with that he had acted. But now his purpose was again changed. Now he intended to reveal the will with his own hands, and it might be well that he should see that it was there.

He took down the book, and there it was. He opened it out, and carefully read through every word of its complicated details. For it had been arranged and drawn out in a lawyer's office, with all the legal want of punctuation and unintelligible phraseology. It had been copied verbatim by the old Squire, and was no doubt a properly binding and effective will. Never before had he dwelt over it so tediously. He had feared lest a finger-mark, a blot, or a spark might betray his acquaintance with the deed. But now he was about to give it up and let all the world know that it had been in his hands. He felt, therefore, that he was entitled to read it, and that there was no longer ground to fear any accident. Though the women in the house should see him reading it, what matter?

Thrice he read it, sitting there late into the night. Thrice he read the deed which had been prepared with such devilish industry to rob him of the estate which had been promised him! If he had been wicked to conceal it,—no, not to conceal it, but only to be silent as to its whereabouts,—how much greater had been the sin of that dying old man who had taken so much trouble in robbing him? Now that the time had come, almost the hour in which he was about to surrender the property which he had lately so truly loathed, there came again upon him a love of money, a feeling of the privilege which attached to him as an owner of broad acres, and a sudden remembrance that with a little courage, with a little perseverance, with a little power of endurance, he might live down the evils of the present day. When he thought of what it might be to be Squire of Llanfeare in perhaps five years' time, with the rents in his pocket, he became angry at his own feebleness. Let them ask him what questions they would, there could be no evidence against him. If he were to burn the will, there could certainly be no evidence against him. If the will were still hidden, they might, perhaps, extract that secret from him; but no lawyer would be strong enough to make him own that he had thrust the paper between the bars of the fire.

He sat looking at it, gnashing his teeth together, and clenching his fists. If only he dared to do it! If only he could do it! He did during a moment, make up his mind; but had no sooner done so than there rose clearly before his mind's eye the judge and the jury, the paraphernalia of the court, and all the long horrors of a prison life. Even now those prying women might have their eyes turned upon what he was doing. And should there be no women prying, no trial, no conviction, still there would be the damning guilt on his own soul,—a guilt which would admit of no repentance except by giving himself up to the hands of the law! No sooner had he resolved to destroy the will than he was unable to destroy it. No sooner had he felt his inability than again he longed to do the deed. When at three o'clock he dragged himself up wearily to his bed, the will was again within the sermon, and the book was at rest upon its old ground.

Punctually at eleven Mr. Griffith was with him, and it was evident from his manner that he had thought the matter over, and was determined to be kind and gracious.

'Now, squire,' said he, 'let us hear it; and I do hope it may be something that may make your mind quiet at last. You've had, I fear, a bad time of it since the old squire died.'

'Indeed I have, Mr. Griffith.'

'What is it now? Whatever it be, you may be sure of this, I will take it charitable like. I won't take nothing amiss; and if so be I can help you, I will.'

Cousin Henry, as the door had been opened, and as the man's footstep had been heard, had made up his mind that on this occasion he could

not reveal the secret. He had disabled himself
by that unfortunate manner of his yesterday.
He would not even turn his eyes upon the book,
but sat looking into the empty grate. 'What is
it, Mr. Jones?' asked the farmer.

'My uncle did make a will,' said Cousin Henry
feebly.

'Of course he made a will. He made a many,
—one or two more than was wise, I am thinking.'

'He made a will after the last one.'

'After that in your favour?'

'Yes; after that. I know that he did, by what
I saw him doing; and so I thought I'd tell you.'

'Is that all?'

'I thought I'd let you know that I was sure of
it. What became of it after it was made, that,
you know, is quite another question. I do think
it must be in the house, and if so, search ought
to be made. If they believe there is such a will,
why don't they come and search more regularly?
I shouldn't hinder them.'

'Is that all you've got to say?'

'As I have been thinking about it so much and
as you are so kind to me, I thought I had better
tell you.'

'But there was something you were to show
me.'

'Oh, yes; I did say so. If you will come upstairs, I'll point out the very spot where the old
man sat when he was writing it.'

'There is nothing more than that?'

'Nothing more than that, Mr. Griffith.'

'Then good morning, Mr. Jones. I am afraid we have not got to the end of the matter yet.'

CHAPTER XVI

AGAIN AT HEREFORD

SOME of the people at Carmarthen were taking a great deal of trouble about the matter. One copy of the *Herald* was sent regularly to Mr. Brodrick, another to Isabel, and another to Mr. Owen. It was determined that they should not be kept in ignorance of what was being done. In the first number issued after Mr. Apjohn's last visit to Llanfeare there was a short leading article recapitulating all that was hitherto known of the story. 'Mr. Henry Jones,' said the article in its last paragraph, 'has at length been induced to threaten an action for libel against this newspaper. We doubt much whether he will have the courage to go on with it. But if he does, he will have to put himself into a witness-box, and then probably we may learn something of the truth as to the last will and testament made by Mr. Indefer Jones.' All this reached Hereford, and was of course deeply considered there by persons whom it concerned.

Mr. Owen, for some days after the scene which has been described between him and Isabel, saw her frequently, and generally found means to be alone with her for some moments. She made no effort to avoid him, and would fain have been allowed to treat him simply as her dearest friend. But in all these moments he treated her as though she were engaged to be his wife. There was no embracing, no kiss. Isabel would not permit it. But in all terms of affectionate expression he spoke of her and to her as though she were his own; and would only gently laugh at her when she assured him that it could never be so.

'Of course you can torment me a little,' he said, smiling, 'but the forces arrayed against you are too strong, and you have not a chance on your side. It would be monstrous to suppose that you should go on making me miserable for ever,—and yourself too.'

In answer to this she could only say that she cared but little for her own misery, and did not believe in his. 'The question is,' she said, 'whether it be fitting. As I feel that it is not fitting, I certainly shall not do it.' In answer to this he would again smile, and tell her that a month or two at furthest would see her absolutely conquered.

Then the newspapers reached them. When it became clear to him that there existed in Carmarthenshire so strong a doubt as to the validity of the will under which the property was at present held, then Mr. Owen's visits to the house became rarer and different in their nature. Then he was willing to be simply the friend of the family, and as such he sought no especial interviews with Isabel. Between him and Isabel no word was spoken as to the contents of the newspaper. But between Mr. Brodrick and the clergyman many words were spoken. Mr. Brodrick declared at once to his intended son-in-law his belief in the accusations which were implied,— which were implied at first, but afterwards made in terms so frightfully clear. When such words as those were said and printed there could, he urged, be no doubt as to what was believed in Carmarthen. And why should it be believed without ground that any man had done so hideous a deed as to destroy a will? The lawyer's hair stood almost on end as he spoke of the atrocity; but yet he believed it. Would a respectable newspaper such as the *Carmarthen Herald* commit itself to such a course without the strongest assurance? What was it to the *Carmarthen Herald*? Did not the very continuance of the articles make it clear that the readers of the paper were in accordance with the writer? Would the public of Carmarthen sympathize in such an attack without the strongest ground? He, the attorney, fully believed in Cousin Henry's guilt; but he was not on that account sanguine as to the proof. If, during his sojourn at Llanfeare, either immediately before the old squire's death or after it, but before the funeral, he had been enabled to lay his hand upon the will and destroy it, what hope would there be of evidence of such guilt? As to that idea of forcing the man to tell such a tale against himself by the torment of cross-examination, he did not believe it at all. A man who had been strong enough to destroy a will would be too strong for that. Perhaps he thought that any man would be too strong, not having known Cousin Henry. Among all the possible chances which occurred to his mind,— and his mind at this time was greatly filled with such considerations,—nothing like the truth suggested itself to him. His heart was tormented by the idea that the property had been stolen from his child, that the glory of being father-in-law to Llanfeare had been filched from himself, and that no hope for redress remained. He sympathized altogether with the newspaper. He felt grateful to the newspaper. He declared the editor to be a man specially noble and brave in his calling. But he did not believe that the newspaper would do any good either to him or to Isabel.

Mr. Owen doubted altogether the righteousness of the proceeding as regarded the newspaper. As far as he could see there was no evidence against Cousin Henry. There seemed to him to be an injustice in accusing a man of a great crime, simply because the crime might have been possible, and would, if committed, have been beneficial to the criminal. That plan of frightening the man into self-accusation by

the terrors of cross-examination was distasteful
to him. He would not sympathize with the newspaper. But still he found himself compelled to
retreat from that affectation of certainty in regard to Isabel which he had assumed when he
knew only that the will had been proved, and
that Cousin Henry was in possession of the property. He had regarded Isabel and the property
as altogether separated from each other. Now
he learned that such was not the general opinion
in Carmarthenshire. It was not his desire to
push forward his suit with the heiress of Llanfeare. He had been rejected on what he had
acknowledged to be fitting grounds while that
had been her position. When the matter had
been altogether settled in Cousin Henry's favour,
then he could come forward again.

Isabel was quite sure that the newspaper was
right. Did she not remember the dying words
with which her uncle had told her that he had
again made her his heir? And had she not
always clearly in her mind the hang-dog look
of that wretched man? She was strong-minded,
—but yet a woman, with a woman's propensity
to follow her feelings rather than either facts or
reason. Her lover had told her that her uncle
had been very feeble when those words had been
spoken, with his mind probably vague and his
thoughts wandering. It had, perhaps, been but
a dream. Such words did not suffice as evidence
on which to believe a man guilty of so great a

crime. She knew,—so she declared to herself,—
that the old man's words had not been vague.
And as to those hang-dog looks,—her lover had
told her that she should not allow a man's
countenance to go so far in evidence as that!
In so judging she would trust much too far to
her own power of discernment. She would not
contradict him, but she felt sure of her discernment in that respect. She did not in the least
doubt the truth of the evidence conveyed by the
man's hang-dog face.

She had sworn to herself a thousand times that
she would not covet the house and property.
When her uncle had first declared to her his
purpose of disinheriting her, she had been quite
sure of herself that her love for him should not
be affected by the change. It had been her
pride to think that she could soar above any
consideration of money and be sure of her own
nobility, even though she should be stricken with
absolute poverty. But now she was tempted to
long that the newspaper might be found to be
right. Was there any man so fitted to be exalted
in the world, so sure to fill a high place with
honour, as her lover? Though she might not
want Llanfeare for herself, was she not bound to
want it for his sake? He had told her how certain he was of her heart,—how sure he was that
sooner or later he would win her hand. She had
almost begun to think that it must be so,—that
her strength would not suffice for her to hold

to her purpose. But how sweet would be her
triumph if she could turn to him and tell him
that now the hour had come in which she would
be proud to become his wife! 'I love you well
enough to rejoice in giving you something, but
too well to have been a burden on you when I
could give you nothing.' That would be sweet
to her! Then there should be kisses! As for
Cousin Henry, there was not even pity in her
heart towards him. It would be time to pity him
when he should have been made to give up the
fruits of his wickedness and to confess his faults.

Mrs. Brodrick was not made to understand the
newspapers, nor did she care much about the
work which they had taken in hand. If Isabel
could be made to accept that smaller legacy, so
that Mr. Owen might marry her out of hand and
take her away, that would be enough to satisfy
Mrs. Brodrick. If Isabel were settled somewhere
with Mr. Owen, their joint means being sufficient
to make it certain that no calls would be made
on the paternal resources, that would satisfy
Mrs. Brodrick's craving in regard to the Welsh
property. She was not sure that she was anxious
to see the half-sister of her own children altogether removed from their sphere and exalted
so high. And then this smaller stroke of good
fortune might be so much more easily made
certain! A single word from Isabel herself, a
word which any girl less endowed with wicked
obstinacy would have spoken at once, would

make that sure and immediate. Whereas this great inheritance which was to depend upon some almost impossible confession of the man who enjoyed it, seemed to her to be as distant as ever.

'Bother the newspapers,' she said to her eldest daughter; 'why doesn't she write and sign the receipt, and take her income like any one else? She was getting new boots at Jackson's yesterday, and where is the money to come from? If any of you want new boots, papa is sure to tell me of it!'

Her spirit was embittered too by the severity of certain words which her husband had spoken to her. Isabel had appealed to her father when her stepmother had reproached her with being a burden in the house.

'Papa,' she had said, 'let me leave the house and earn something. I can at any rate earn my bread.'

Then Mr. Brodrick had been very angry. He too had wished to accelerate the marriage between his daughter and her lover, thinking that she would surely accept the money on her lover's behalf. He too had been annoyed at the persistency of her double refusal. But it had been very far from his purpose to drive his girl from his house, or to subject her to the misery of such reproaches as his wife had cast upon her.

'My dear,' he had said, 'there is no necessity for anything of the kind. I and your mother are only anxious for your welfare. I think that you should take your uncle's money, if not for your own sake, then for the sake of him to whom we all hope that you will soon be married. But putting that aside, you are as well entitled to remain here as your sisters, and, until you are married, here will be your home.'

There was comfort in this, some small comfort, but it did not tend to create pleasant intercourse between Isabel and her stepmother. Mrs. Brodrick was a woman who submitted herself habitually to her husband, and intended to obey him, but one who nevertheless would not be deterred from her own little purposes. She felt herself to be ill-used by Isabel's presence in the house. Many years ago Isabel had been taken away, and she had been given to understand that Isabel was removed for ever. There was to be no more expense, no more trouble,— there should be no more jealousies in regard to Isabel. The old uncle had promised to do everything, and that sore had been removed from her life. Now Isabel had come back again, and insisted on remaining there,—so unnecessarily! Now again there were those boots to be bought at Jackson's, and all those other increased expenditures which another back, another head, another mouth, and another pair of feet must create. And then it was so palpable that Hereford thought much of Isabel, but thought little or nothing of her own girls. Such a one as Mrs.

Brodrick was sure to make herself unpleasant in circumstances such as these.

'Isabel,' she said to her one day, 'I didn't say anything about you being turned out of the house.'

'Who has said that you did, mother?'

'You shouldn't have gone to your father and talked about going out as a housemaid.'

'I told papa that if he thought it right, I would endeavour to earn my bread.'

'You told him that I had complained about you being here.'

'So you did. I had to tell him so, or I could not explain my purpose. Of course I am a burden. Every human being who eats and wears clothes and earns nothing is a burden. And I know that this is thought of the more because it had been felt that I had been—been disposed of.'

'You could be disposed of now, as you call it, if you pleased.'

'But I do not please. That is a matter on which I will listen to no dictation. Therefore it is that I wish that I could go away and earn my own bread. I choose to be independent in that matter, and therefore I ought to suffer for it. It is reasonable enough that I should be felt to be a burden.'

Then the other girls came in, and nothing more was said till, after an hour or two, Mrs. Brodrick and Isabel were again alone together.

'I do think it very odd that you cannot take that money; I certainly do,' said Mrs. Brodrick.

'What is the use of going on about it? I shall not be made to take it.'

'And all those people at Carmarthen so sure that you are entitled to ever so much more! I say nothing about burdens, but I cannot conceive how you can reconcile it to your conscience when your poor papa has got so many things to pay, and is so little able to pay them.'

Then she paused, but as Isabel would not be enticed into any further declaration of independence, she continued, 'It certainly is a setting up of your own judgment against people who must know better. As for Mr. Owen, of course it will drive him to look for some one else. The young man wants a wife, and of course he will find one. Then that chance will be lost.'

In this way Isabel did not pass her time comfortably at Hereford.

CHAPTER XVII

MR. CHEEKEY

A MONTH had been left for Cousin Henry to consider what he would do,—a month from the day in which he had been forced to accede to Mr. Apjohn's proposal up to that on which he would have to stand before the barrister at Carmarthen, should he be brave enough at last to undergo the ordeal. He had in truth resolved that he would not undergo the ordeal. He was quite sure of himself that nothing short of cart-ropes or of the police would drag him into the witness-box. But still there was the month. There were various thoughts filling his mind. A great expense was being incurred,—most uselessly, if he intended to retreat before the day came,—and who would pay the money? There was hardly a hope left in his bosom that the property would remain in his hands. His hopes indeed now ran in altogether another direction. In what way might he best get rid of the property? How most readily might he take himself off from Llanfeare and have nothing more to do with the tenants and their rents? But still it was he who would be responsible for this terrible expense. It had been explained to him by the lawyer, that he might either indict the proprietor of the newspaper on a criminal charge or bring a civil action against him for damages. Mr. Apjohn had very strongly recommended the former proceeding. It would be cheaper, he had said, and would show that the man who brought it had simply wished to vindicate his own character. It would be cheaper in the long-run,—because, as the lawyer explained, it would not be so much his object to get a verdict as to show by his presence in the court that he was afraid of no one. Were he to sue for damages, and, as was probable, not to get them, he must then bear the double expense of the prosecution and defence. Such had been the arguments Mr. Apjohn had used; but he had considered also that if he could bind the man to prosecute the newspaper people on a criminal charge, then the poor victim would be less able to retreat. In such case as that, should the victim's courage fail him at the last moment, a policeman could be made to fetch him and force him into the witness-box. But in the conduct of a civil action no such constraint could be put upon him. Knowing all this, Mr. Apjohn had eagerly explained the superior attractions of a criminal prosecution, and Cousin Henry had fallen into the trap. He understood it all now, but had not been ready enough to do so when the choice had been within his power. He had now bound himself to prosecute, and certainly would be dragged into Carmarthen, unless he first made known the truth as to the will. If he did that, then he thought that they would surely spare him the trial. Were he to say to them, 'There; I have at last myself found the will. Here, behold it! Take the will and take Llanfeare, and let me escape from my misery,' then surely they would not force him to appear in reference to a matter which would have been already decided in their own favour. He had lost that opportunity of giving up the will through Mr. Griffith, but he was still resolved that some other mode must be discovered before the month should have run by. Every day was of moment, and yet the days passed on and nothing was done. His last idea was to send the will to Mr. Apjohn with a letter, in which he would simply declare that he had just found it amongst the sermons, and that he was prepared to go away. But as the days flew by the letter was left unwritten, and the will was still among the sermons.

It will be understood that all this was much talked of in Carmarthen. Mr. Henry Jones, of Llanfeare, was known to have indicted Mr. Gregory Evans, of the *Carmarthen Herald*, for the publication of various wicked and malicious libels against himself; and it was known also that Mr. Apjohn was Mr. Jones's attorney in carrying on the prosecution. But not the less was it understood that Mr. Apjohn and Mr. Evans were not hostile to each other in the matter. Mr. Apjohn would be quite honest in what he did. He would do his best to prove the libel,—on condition that his client were the honest owner of the property in question. In truth, however, the great object of them all was to get Henry Jones into a witness-box, so that, if possible, the very truth might be extracted from him.

Day by day and week by week since the funeral the idea had grown and become strong in Carmarthen that some wicked deed had been done. It irked the hearts of them all that such a one as Henry Jones should do such a deed and not be discovered. Old Indefer Jones had been respected by his neighbours. Miss Brodrick, though not personally well known in the county, had been spoken well of by all men. The idea that Llanfeare should belong to her had been received with favour. Then had come that altered intention in the old squire's mind, and the neighbours had disapproved. Mr. Apjohn had disapproved very strongly, and though he was not without that reticence so essentially necessary to the character of an attorney, his opinion had become known. Then the squire's return to his old purpose was whispered abroad. The Cantors had spoken very freely. Everything done and everything not done at Llanfeare was known in Carmarthen. Mr. Griffith had at length spoken, being the last to abandon all hope as to Cousin Henry's honesty.

Every one was convinced that Cousin Henry had simply stolen the property; and was it to be endured that such a deed as that should have been done by such a man and that Carmarthen should not find it out? Mr. Apjohn was very much praised for his energy in having forced the man to take his action against Mr. Evans, and no one was more inclined to praise him than Mr. Evans himself. Those who had seen the man did believe that the truth would be worked out of him; and those who had only heard of him were sure that the trial would be a time of intense interest in the borough. The sale of the

newspaper had risen immensely, and Mr. Evans
was quite the leading man of the hour.

'So you are going to have Mr. Balsam against
me?' said Mr. Evans to Mr. Apjohn one day.
Now Mr. Balsam was a very respectable barrister, who for many years had gone the Welsh
circuit, and was chiefly known for the mildness
of his behaviour and an accurate knowledge of
law,*—two gifts hardly of much value to an advocate in an assize town.

'Yes, Mr. Evans. Mr. Balsam, I have no doubt,
will do all that we want.'

'I suppose you want to get me into prison?'

'Certainly, if it shall be proved that you have
deserved it. The libels are so manifest that it
will be only necessary to read them to a jury.
Unless you can justify them, I think you will
have to go to prison.'

'I suppose so. You will come and see me, I am
quite sure, Mr. Apjohn.'

'I suppose Mr. Cheekey will have something
to say on your behalf before it comes to that.'

Now Mr. John Cheekey was a gentleman
about fifty years of age, who had lately risen to
considerable eminence in our criminal courts of
law. He was generally called in the profession,
—and perhaps sometimes outside it,—'Supercilious Jack', from the manner he had of moving
his eyebrows when he was desirous of intimidat-
ing a witness. He was a strong, young-looking,
and generally good-humoured Irishman, who

had a thousand good points. Under no circumstances would he bully a woman,—nor would he bully a man, unless, according to his own mode of looking at such cases, the man wanted bullying. But when that time did come,—and a reference to the Old Bailey*and assize reports in general would show that it came very often,—Supercilious Jack would make his teeth felt worse than any terrier. He could pause in his cross-examination, look at a man, projecting his face forward by degrees as he did so, in a manner which would crush any false witness who was not armed with triple courage at his breast,—and, alas! not unfrequently a witness who was not false. For unfortunately, though Mr. Cheekey intended to confine the process to those who, as he said, wanted bullying, sometimes he made mistakes. He was possessed also of another precious gift,—which, if he had not invented, he had brought to perfection,—that of bullying the judge also. He had found that by doing so he could lower a judge in the estimation of the jury, and thus diminish the force of a damnatory charge. Mr. Cheekey's services had been especially secured for this trial, and all the circumstances had been accurately explained to him. It was felt that a great day would have arrived in Carmarthen when Mr. Cheekey should stand up in the court to cross-examine Cousin Henry.

'Yes,' said Mr. Evans, chuckling, 'I think that Mr. Cheekey will have something to say to it.

What will be the result, Mr. Apjohn?' he asked abruptly.

'How am I to say? If he can only hold his own like a man, there will, of course, be a verdict of guilty.'

'But can he?' asked he of the newspaper.

'I hope he may with all my heart,—if he have done nothing that he ought not to have done. In this matter, Mr. Evans, I have altogether a divided sympathy. I dislike the man utterly. I don't care who knows it. No one knows it better than he himself. The idea of his coming here over that young lady's head was from the first abhorrent to me. When I saw him, and heard him, and found out what he was,—such a poor, cringing, cowardly wretch,—my feeling was of course exacerbated. It was terrible to me that the old squire, whom I had always respected, should have brought such a man among us. But that was the old squire's doing. He certainly did bring him, and as certainly intended to make him his heir. If he did make him his heir, if that will which I read was in truth the last will, then I hope most sincerely that all that Mr. Cheekey may do may be of no avail against him. If that be the case, I shall be glad to have an opportunity of calling upon you in your new lodgings.'

'But if there was another will, Mr. Apjohn,— a later will?'

'Then, of course, there is the doubt whether this man be aware of it.'

'But if he be aware of it?'

'Then I hope that Mr. Cheekey may tear him limb from limb.'

'But you feel sure that it is so?'

'Ah; I do not know about that. It is very hard to be sure of anything. When I see him I do feel almost sure that he is guilty; but when I think of it afterwards, I again have my doubts. It is not by men of such calibre that great crimes are committed. I can hardly fancy that he should have destroyed a will.'

'Or hidden it?'

'If it were hidden, he would live in agony lest it were discovered. I used to think so when I knew that he passed the whole day sitting in one room. Now he goes out for hours together. Two or three times he has been down with old Griffith at Coed, and twice young Cantor found him lying on the sea cliff. I doubt whether he would have gone so far afield if the will were hidden in the house.'

'Can he have it on his own person?'

'He is not brave enough for that. The presence of it there would reveal itself by the motion of his hands. His fingers would always be on the pocket that contained it. I do not know what to think. And it is because I am in doubt that I have brought him under Mr. Cheekey's thumbscrew. It is a case in which I would, if possible, force a man to confess the truth even against himself. And for this reason I have urged him to prosecute you. But as an honest man myself, I am bound to hope that he may succeed if he be the rightful owner of Llanfeare.'

'No one believes it, Mr. Apjohn. Not one in all Carmarthen believes it.'

'I will not say what I believe myself. Indeed I do not know. But I do hope that by Mr. Cheekey's aid or otherwise we may get at the truth.'

In his own peculiar circle, with Mr. Geary the attorney, with Mr. Jones the auctioneer, and Mr. Powell, the landlord of the Bush Hotel, Mr. Evans was much more triumphant. Among them, and, indeed, with the gentlemen of Carmarthen generally, he was something of a hero. They did believe it probable that the interloper would be extruded from the property which did not belong to him, and that the doing of this would be due to Mr. Evans. 'Apjohn pretends to think that it is very doubtful,' said he to his three friends.

'Apjohn isn't doubtful at all,' said Mr. Geary, 'but he is a little cautious as to expressing himself.'

'Apjohn has behaved very well,' remarked the innkeeper. 'If it wasn't for him we should never have got the rascal to come forward at all. He went out in one of my flies, but I won't let them charge for it on a job like that.'

'I suppose you'll charge for bringing Cousin Henry into the court,' said the auctioneer. They had all got to call him Cousin Henry since the idea had got abroad that he had robbed his Cousin Isabel.

'I'd bring him too for nothing, and stand him his lunch into the bargain, rather than that he shouldn't have the pleasure of meeting Mr. Cheekey.'

'Cheekey will get it out of him, if there is anything to get,' said Mr. Evans.

'My belief is that Mr. Cheekey will about strike him dumb. If he has got anything in his bosom to conceal, he will be so awe-struck that he won't be able to open his mouth. He won't be got to say he did it, but he won't be able to say he didn't.' This was Mr. Geary's opinion.

'What would that amount to?' asked Mr. Powell. 'I'm afraid they couldn't give the place back to the young lady because of that.'

'The jury would acquit Mr. Evans. That's about what it would amount to,' said the attorney.

'And Cousin Henry would go back to Llanfeare, and have all his troubles over,' remarked Mr. Jones. This they deemed to be a disastrous termination to all the trouble which they were taking, but one which seemed by no means improbable.

They all agreed that even Mr. Cheekey would hardly be able to extract from the man an acknowledgment that he had with his own hands destroyed the will. Such a termination as that to a cross-examination had never been known under the hands of the most expert of advocates. That Cousin Henry might be stricken dumb, that he might faint, that he might be committed for contempt of court,—all these events were possible, or perhaps, not impossible; but that he should say, 'Yes, I did it, I burnt the will. Yes, I, with my own hands,'—that they all declared to be impossible. And, if so, Cousin Henry would go back again to Llanfeare confirmed in his possession of the property.

'He will only laugh at us in his sleeve when it is over,' said the auctioneer.

They little knew the torments which the man was enduring, or how unlikely it was that he should laugh in his sleeve at any one. We are too apt to forget when we think of the sins and faults of men how keen may be their conscience in spite of their sins. While they were thus talking of Cousin Henry, he was vainly endeavouring to console himself with the reflection that he had not committed any great crime, that there was still a road open to him for repentance, that if only he might be allowed to escape and repent in London, he would be too glad to resign Llanfeare and all its glories. The reader will hardly suppose that Cousin Henry will return after the trial to laugh in his sleeve in his own library in his own house.

A few days afterwards Mr. Apjohn was up in town and had an interview with Mr. Balsam, the barrister. 'This client of mine does not seem to be a nice sort of country gentleman,' said Mr. Balsam.

'Anything but that. You will understand, Mr. Balsam, that my only object in persuading him to indict the paper has been to put him into a witness-box. I told him so, of course. I explained to him that unless he would appear there, he could never hold up his head.'

'And he took your advice.'

'Very unwillingly. He would have given his right hand to escape. But I gave him no alternative. I so put it before him that he could not refuse to do as I bade him without owning himself to be a rascal. Shall I tell you what I think will come of it?'

'What will come of it?'

'He will not appear. I feel certain that he will not have the courage to show himself in the court. When the day comes, or, perhaps, a day or two before, he will run away.'

'What will you do then?'

'Ah, that's the question. What shall we do then? He is bound to prosecute, and will have to pay the penalty. In such a case as this I think we could have him found and brought into court for the next assizes. But what could we do then? Though we were ever so rough to him in the way of contempt of court and the rest of it, we cannot take the property away. If he has got hold of the will and destroyed it, or hidden it, we can do nothing as to the property as long as he is strong enough to hold his tongue. If he can be made to speak, then I think we shall get at it.'

Mr. Balsam shook his head. He was quite willing to believe that his client was as base as Mr. Apjohn represented him to be; but he was not willing to believe that Mr. Cheekey was as powerful as had been assumed.

CHAPTER XVIII

COUSIN HENRY GOES TO CARMARTHEN

ON his return from London Mr. Apjohn wrote the following letter to his client, and this he sent to Llanfeare by a clerk, who was instructed to wait there for an answer:—

'MY DEAR SIR,—

'I have just returned from London, where I saw Mr. Balsam, who will be employed on your behalf at the assizes. It is necessary that you should come into my office, so that I may complete the instructions which are to be given to counsel. As I could not very well do this at Llanfeare without considerable inconvenience, I must give you this trouble. My clerk who takes this out to you will bring back your answer, saying whether eleven in the morning to-morrow or three in the afternoon will best suit your arrangements. You can tell him also whether you would wish me to send a fly for you. I believe that you still keep your uncle's carriage, in which case it would perhaps be unnecessary. A message sent by the clerk will suffice, so that you may be saved the trouble of writing.

> 'Yours truly,
> 'NICHOLAS APJOHN.'

The clerk had made his way into the book-room in which Cousin Henry was sitting, and stood there over him while he was reading the letter. He felt sure that it had been arranged by Mr. Apjohn that it should be so, in order that he might not have a moment to consider the reply which he would send. Mr. Apjohn had calculated, traitor that he was to the cause of his client,—so thought Cousin Henry,—that the man's presence would rob him of his presence of mind so as to prevent him from sending a refusal.

'I don't see why I should go into Carmarthen at all,' he said.

'Oh, sir, it's quite essential,—altogether essential in a case such as this. You are bound to prosecute, and of course you must give your instructions. If Mr. Apjohn were to bring everything out here for the purpose, the expense would be tremendous. In going there, it will only be the fly, and it will all be done in five minutes.'

'Who will be there?' asked Cousin Henry after a pause.

'I shall be there,' answered the clerk, not unnaturally putting himself first, 'and Mr. Apjohn, and perhaps one of the lads.'

'There won't be any—barrister?' asked Cousin Henry, showing the extent of his fear by his voice and his countenance.

'Oh, dear, no; they won't be here till the assizes. A barrister never sees his own client. You'll go in as a witness, and will have nothing to do with the barristers till you're put up face to face before them in the witness-box. Mr. Balsam is a very mild gentleman.'

'He is employed by me?'

'Oh, yes; he's on our side. His own side never matters much to a witness. It's when the other side tackles you!'

'Who is the other side?' asked Cousin Henry.

'Haven't you heard?' The voice in which this was said struck terror to the poor wretch's soul. There was awe in it and pity, and something almost of advice,—as though the voice were warning him to prepare against the evil which was threatening him. 'They have got Mr. Cheekey!' Here the voice became even more awful. 'I knew they would when I first heard what the case was to be. They've got Mr. Cheekey. They don't care much about money when they're going it like that. There are many of them I have known awful enough, but he's the awfullest.'

'He can't eat a fellow,' said Cousin Henry, trying to look like a man with good average courage.

'No; he can't eat a fellow. It isn't that way

he does it. I've known some of 'em who looked as though they were going to eat a man; but he looks as though he were going to skin you, and leave you bare for the birds to eat you. He's gentle enough at first, is Mr. Cheekey.'

'What is it all to me?' asked Cousin Henry.

'Oh, nothing, sir. To a gentleman like you who knows what he's about it's all nothing. What can Mr. Cheekey do to a gentleman who has got nothing to conceal? But when a witness has something to hide,—and sometimes there will be something,—then it is that Mr. Cheekey comes out strong. He looks into a man and sees that it's there, and then he turns him inside out till he gets at it. That's what I call skinning a witness. I saw a poor fellow once so knocked about by Mr. Cheekey that they had to carry him down speechless out of the witness-box.'

It was a vivid description of all that Cousin Henry had pictured to himself. And he had actually, by his own act, subjected himself to this process! Had he been staunch in refusing to bring any action against the newspaper, Mr. Cheekey would have been powerless in reference to him. And now he was summoned into Carmarthen to prepare himself by minor preliminary pangs for the torture of the auto-da-fé*which was to be made of him.

'I don't see why I should go into Carmarthen at all,' he said, having paused a while after the eloquent description of the barrister's powers.

'Not come into Carmarthen! Why, sir, you must complete the instructions.'

'I don't see it at all.'

'Then do you mean to back out of it altogether, Mr. Jones? I wouldn't be afeared by Mr. Cheekey like that!'

Then it occurred to him that if he did mean to back out of it altogether he could do so better at a later period, when they might hardly be able to catch him by force and bring him as a prisoner before the dreaded tribunal. And as it was his purpose to avoid the trial by giving up the will, which he would pretend to have found at the moment of giving it up, he would ruin his own project,—as he had done so many projects before,—by his imbecility at the present moment. Cheekey would not be there in Mr. Apjohn's office, nor the judge and jury and all the crowd of the court to look at him.

'I don't mean to back out at all,' he said; 'and it's very impertinent of you to say so.'

'I didn't mean impertinence, Mr. Jones;— only it is necessary you should come into Mr. Apjohn's office.'

'Very well; I'll come to-morrow at three.'

'And about the fly, Mr. Jones?'

'I can come in my own carriage.'

'Of course. That's what Mr. Apjohn said. But if I may make so bold, Mr. Jones,—wouldn't all the people in Carmarthen know the old Squire's carriage?'

Here was another trouble. Yes; all the people
in Carmarthen would know the old Squire's
carriage, and after all those passages in the newspapers,—believing, as he knew they did, that he
had stolen the property,—would clamber up on
the very wheels to look at him ! The clerk had
been right in that.

'I don't mean it for any impertinence, Mr.
Jones; but wouldn't it be better just to come in
and to go out quiet in one of Mr. Powell's flies?'

'Very well,' said Cousin Henry. 'Let the fly
come.'

'I thought it would be best,' said the clerk,
taking cowardly advantage of his success over
the prostrate wretch. 'What's the use of a gentleman taking his own carriage through the streets
on such an occasion as this? They are so prying
into everything in Carmarthen. Now, when they
see the Bush fly, they won't think as anybody
particular is in it.' And so it was settled. The
fly should be at Llanfeare by two o'clock on the
following day.

Oh, if he could but die! If the house would
fall upon him and crush him! There had not
been a word spoken by that reptile of a clerk
which he had not understood,—not an arrow
cast at him the sting of which did not enter into
his very marrow! 'Oh, nothing, sir, to a gentleman like you.' The man had looked at him as
he had uttered the words with a full appreciation
of the threat conveyed. 'They've got a rod in

pickle for you;—for you, who have stolen your cousin's estate! Mr. Cheekey is coming for you!' That was what the miscreant of a clerk had said to him. And then, though he had found himself compelled to yield to that hint about the carriage, how terrible was it to have to confess that he was afraid to be driven through Carmarthen in his own carriage!

He must go into Carmarthen and face Mr. Apjohn once again. That was clear. He could not now send the will in lieu of himself. Why had he not possessed the presence of mind to say to the clerk at once that no further steps need be taken? 'No further steps need be taken. I have found the will. Here it is. I found it this very morning among the books. Take it to Mr. Apjohn, and tell him I have done with Llanfeare and all its concerns.' How excellent would have been the opportunity! And it would not have been difficult for him to act his part amidst the confusion to which the clerk would have been brought by the greatness of the revelation made to him. But he had allowed the chance to pass, and now he must go into Carmarthen!

At half-past two the following day he put himself into the fly. During the morning he had taken the will out of the book, determined to carry it with him to Carmarthen in his pocket. But when he attempted to enclose it in an envelope for the purpose, his mind misgave him and he restored it. Hateful as was the property to him, odious as were the house and all things about it, no sooner did the doing of the act by which he was to release himself from them come within the touch of his fingers, than he abandoned the idea. At such moments the estate would again have charms for him, and he would remember that such a deed, when once done, would admit of no recall.

'I am glad to see you, Mr. Jones,' said the attorney as his client entered the inner office. 'There are a few words which must be settled between you and me before the day comes, and no time has to be lost. Sit down, Mr. Ricketts, and write the headings of the questions and answers. Then Mr. Jones can initial them afterwards.'

Mr. Ricketts was the clerk who had come out to Llanfeare. Cousin Henry sat silent as Mr. Ricketts folded his long sheet of folio paper with a double margin. Here was a new terror to him; and as he saw the preparations he almost made up his mind that he would on no account sign his name to anything.

The instructions to be given to Mr. Balsam were in fact very simple, and need not here be recapitulated. His uncle had sent for him to Llanfeare, had told him that he was to be the heir, had informed him that a new will had been made in his favour. After his uncle's death and subsequent to the funeral, he had heard a will read, and under that will had inherited the property. As far as he believed, or at any rate as far as

he knew, that was his uncle's last will and testa-
ment. These were the instructions which, under
Mr. Apjohn's advice, were to be given to Mr.
Balsam as to his (Cousin Henry's) direct evidence.

Then Cousin Henry, remembering his last
communication to Farmer Griffith, remembering also all that the two Cantors could prove,
added something on his own account.

'I saw the old man writing up in his room,'
he said, 'copying something which I knew to be
a will. I was sure then he was going to make
another change and take the property from me.'
'No; I asked him no questions. I thought it very
cruel, but it was of no use for me to say anything.'
'No; he didn't tell me what he was about; but
I knew it was another will. I wouldn't con-
descend to ask a question. When the Cantors
said that they had witnessed a will, I never
doubted them. When you came there to read
the will, I supposed it would be found. Like
enough it's there now, if proper search were
made. I can tell all that to Mr. Balsam if he
wants to know it.'

'Why didn't you tell me all this before?' said
Mr. Apjohn.

'It isn't much to tell. It's only what I thought.
If what the Cantors said and what you all believed yourselves didn't bring you to the will,
nothing I could say would help you. It doesn't
amount to more than thinking after all.'

Then Mr. Apjohn was again confused and

again in doubt. Could it be possible after all
that the conduct on the part of the man which
had been so prejudicial to him in the eyes of all
men had been produced simply by the annoy-
ances to which he had been subjected? It was still
possible that the old man had himself destroyed
the document which he had been tempted to
make, and that they had all of them been most
unjust to this poor fellow. He added, however,
all the details of this new story to the instructions
which were to be given to Mr. Balsam, and to
which Cousin Henry did attach his signature.

Then came some further conversation about
Mr. Cheekey, which, however, did not take an
official form. What questions Mr. Cheekey might
ask would be between Mr. Cheekey and the other
attorney, and formed no part of Mr. Apjohn's
direct business. He had intended to imbue his
client with something of the horror with which his
clerk had been before him in creating, believing
that the cause of truth would be assisted by
reducing the man to the lowest condition of mean
terror. But this new story somewhat changed
his purpose. If the man were innocent,—if there
were but some small probability of his innocence,
—was it not his duty to defend him as a client
from ill-usage on the part of Cheekey? That
Cheekey must have his way with him was a
matter of course,—that is, if Cousin Henry appeared at all; but a word or two of warning
might be of service.

'You will be examined on the other side by Mr. Cheekey,' he said, intending to assume a pleasant voice. At the hearing of the awful name, sweat broke out on Cousin Henry's brow. 'You know what his line will be?'

'I don't know anything about it.'

'He will attempt to prove that another will was made.'

'I do not deny it. Haven't I said that I think another will was made?'

'And that you are either aware of its existence—;' here Mr. Apjohn paused, having resumed that stern tone of his voice which was so disagreeable to Cousin Henry's ears—'or that you have destroyed it.'

'What right has he got to say that I have destroyed it? I have destroyed nothing.'

Mr. Apjohn marked the words well, and was again all but convinced that his client was not innocent. 'He will endeavour to make a jury believe from words coming out of your own mouth, or possibly by your silence, that you have either destroyed the deed,—or have concealed it.'

Cousin Henry thought a moment whether he had concealed the will or not. No! he had not put it within the book. The man who hides a thing is the man who conceals the thing,—not a man who fails to tell that he has found it.

'Or—concealed it,' repeated Mr. Apjohn with that peculiar voice of his.

'I have not concealed it,' said the victim.

'Nor know where it lies hidden?' Ghastly pale he became,—livid, almost blue by degrees. Though he was fully determined to give up the will, he could not yield to the pressure now put upon him. Nor could he withstand it. The question was as terrible to him as though he had entertained no idea of abandoning the property. To acknowledge that he knew all along where it was hidden would be to confess his guilt and to give himself up to the tormentors of the law.

'Nor know where it lies hidden?' repeated Mr. Apjohn, in a low voice. 'Go out of the room, Ricketts,' he said. 'Nor know where it lies hidden?' he asked a third time when the clerk had closed the door behind him.

'I know nothing about it,' gasped the poor man.

'You have nothing beyond that to say to me?'

'Nothing.'

'You would rather that it should be left to Mr. Cheekey? If there be anything further that you can say, I should be more tender with you than he.'

'Nothing.'

'And here, in this room, there is no public to gaze upon you.'

'Nothing,' he gasped again.

'Very well. So be it. Ricketts, see if the fly be there for Mr. Jones.' A few minutes afterwards his confidential clerk was alone with him in the room.

'I have learned so much, Ricketts,' said he. 'The will is still in existence. I am sure of that. And he knows its whereabouts. We shall have Miss Brodrick there before Christmas yet.'

CHAPTER XIX

MR. APJOHN SENDS FOR ASSISTANCE

THE last words in the last chapter were spoken by Mr. Apjohn to his confidential clerk in a tone of triumph. He had picked up something further, and, conscious that he had done so by his own ingenuity, was for a moment triumphant. But when he came to think over it all alone,— and he spent many hours just at present in thinking of this matter,—he was less inclined to be self-satisfied. He felt that a great responsibility rested with him, and that this weighed upon him peculiarly at the present moment. He was quite sure not only that a later will had been made, but that it was in existence. It was concealed somewhere, and Cousin Henry knew the secret of its hiding-place. It had existed, at any rate, that morning; but now came the terrible question whether the man, driven to his last gasp in his misery, would not destroy it. Not only had Mr. Apjohn discovered the secret, but he was well aware that Cousin Henry was conscious that he had done so, and yet not a word had been spoken between them which, should the will now be destroyed, could be taken as evidence that it had ever existed. Let the paper be once burnt, and Cousin Henry would be safe in possession of the property. Mr. Cheekey might torment his victim, but certainly would not extract from him a confession such as that. The hiding of the will, the very place in which it was hidden, might possibly be extracted. It was conceivable that ingenuity on one side and abject terror on the other might lead a poor wretch to betray the secret; but a man who has committed a felony will hardly confess the deed in a court of law. Something of all this would, thought Mr. Apjohn, occur to Cousin Henry himself, and by this very addition to his fears he might be driven to destroy the will. The great object now should be to preserve a document which had lived as it were a charmed life through so many dangers. If anything were to be done with this object,—anything new,—it must be done at once. Even now, while he was thinking of it, Cousin Henry was being taken slowly home in Mr. Powell's fly, and might do the deed as soon as he found himself alone in the book-room. Mr. Apjohn was almost sure that the will was concealed somewhere in the book-room. That long-continued sojourn in the chamber, of which the whole county had heard so much, told him that it was so. He was there always, watching the hiding-place. Would it be well that searchers should again be sent out, and that they should be instructed never to leave that room till after Cousin Henry's examination should be over? If so, it would be right that a man should be sent off instantly on horseback, so as to prevent immediate destruction. But then he had no power to take such a step in reference to another man's house. It was a question whether any magistrate would give him such a warrant, seeing that search had already been made, and that, on the failure of such search, the Squire's will had already been proved. A man's house is his castle, let the suspicion against him be what it may, unless there be evidence to support it. Were he to apply to a magistrate, he could only say that the man's own manner and mode of speech had been evidence of his guilt. And yet how much was there hanging, perhaps, on the decision of the moment! Whether the property should go to the hands of her who was entitled to enjoy it, or remain in the possession of a thief such as this, might so probably depend on the action which should be taken, now, at this very instant!

Mr. Ricketts, his confidential clerk, was the only person with whom he had fully discussed all the details of the case,—the only person to whom he had expressed his own thoughts as they had occurred to him. He had said a word to the clerk in triumph as Cousin Henry left him, but a few minutes afterwards recalled him with an altered tone. 'Ricketts,' he said, 'the man has got that will with him in the book-room at Llanfeare.'

'Or in his pocket, sir,' suggested Ricketts.

'I don't think it. Wherever it be at this moment, he has not placed it there himself. The Squire put it somewhere, and he has found it.'

'The Squire was very weak when he made that will, sir,' said the clerk. 'Just at that time he was only coming down to the dining-room, when the sun shone in just for an hour or two in the day. If he put the will anywhere, it would probably be in his bed-room.'

'The man occupies another chamber?' asked the attorney.

'Yes, sir; the same room he had before his uncle died.'

'It's in the book-room,' repeated Mr. Apjohn.

'Then he must have put it there.'

'But he didn't. From his manner, and from a word or two that he spoke, I feel sure that the paper has been placed where it is by other hands.'

'The old man never went into the book-room. I heard every detail of his latter life from Mrs. Griffith when the search was going on. He hadn't been there for more than a month. If he wanted anything out of the book-room, after the young lady went away, he sent Mrs. Griffith for it.'

'What did he send for?' asked Mr. Apjohn.

'He used to read a little sometimes,' said the clerk.

'Sermons?' suggested Mr. Apjohn. ' For many years past he has read sermons to himself whenever he has failed in going to church. I have seen the volumes there on the table in the parlour when I have been with him. Did they search the books?'

'Had every volume off the shelves, sir.'

'And opened every one of them?'

'That I can't tell. I wasn't there.'

'Every volume should have been shaken,' said Mr. Apjohn.

'It's not too late yet, sir,' said the clerk.

'But how are we to get in and do it? I have no right to go into his house, or any man's, to search it.'

'He wouldn't dare to hinder you, sir.'

Then there was a pause before anything further was said.

'The step is such a strong one to take,' said the lawyer, 'when one is guided only by one's own inner conviction. I have no tittle of evidence in my favour to prove anything beyond the fact that the old Squire in the latter days of his life did make a will which has not been found. For that we have searched, and, not finding it, have been forced to admit to probate the last will which we ourselves made. Since that nothing has come to my knowledge. Guided partly by the man's ways while he has been at Llanfeare, and partly by his own manner and hesitation, I have come to a conclusion in my own mind;

but it is one which I would hardly dare to propose to a magistrate as a ground for action.'

'But if he consented, sir?'

'Still, I should be hardly able to justify myself for such intrusion if nothing were found. We have no right to crush the poor creature because he is so easily crushable. I feel already pricks of conscience because I am bringing down Jack Cheekey upon him. If it all be as I have suggested,—that the will is hidden, let us say in some volume of sermons there,—what probability is there that he will destroy it now?'

'He would before the trial, I think.'

'But not at once? I think not. He will not allow himself to be driven to the great crime till the last moment. It is quite on the cards that his conscience will even at last be too strong for it.'

'We owe him something, sir, for not destroying it when he first found it.'

'Not a doubt! If we are right in all this, we do owe him something,—at any rate, charity enough to suppose that the doing of such a deed must be very distasteful to him. When I think of it I doubt whether he'll do it at all.'

'He asked me why they didn't come and search again.'

'Did he? I shouldn't wonder if the poor devil would be glad enough to be relieved from it all. I'll tell you what I'll do, Ricketts. I'll write to Miss Brodrick's father, and ask him to come over here before the trial. He is much more concerned in the matter than I am, and should know as well what ought to be done.'

The letter was written urging Mr. Brodrick to come at once. 'I have no right to tell you,' Mr. Apjohn said in his letter, 'that there is ground for believing that such a document as that I have described is still existing. I might too probably be raising false hope were I to do so. I can only tell you of my own suspicion, explaining to you at the same time on what ground it is founded. I think it would be well that you should come over and consult with me whether further steps should be taken. If so, come at once. The trial is fixed for Friday the 30th.' This was written on Thursday the 22nd. There was, therefore, not much more than a week's interval.

'You will come with me?' said Mr. Brodrick to the Rev. William Owen, after showing to him the letter from the attorney at Hereford.

'Why should I go with you?'

'I would wish you to do so—on Isabel's behalf.'

'Isabel and I are nothing to each other.'

'I am sorry to hear you say that. It was but the other day that you declared that she should be your wife in spite of herself.'

'So she shall, if Mr. Henry Jones be firmly established at Llanfeare. It was explained to me before why your daughter, as owner of Llanfeare, ought not to marry me, and, as I altogether agreed with the reason given, it would not become me to take any step in this matter. As owner of Llanfeare she will be nothing to me. It cannot therefore be right that I should look after her interests in that direction. On any other subject I would do anything for her.'

The father no doubt felt that the two young people were self-willed, obstinate, and contradictory. His daughter wouldn't marry the clergyman because she had been deprived of her property. The clergyman now refused to marry his daughter because it was presumed that her property might be restored to her. As, however, he could not induce Mr. Owen to go with him to Carmarthen, he determined to go alone. He did not give much weight to this new story. It seemed to him certain that the man would destroy the will,—or would already have destroyed it,—if in the first instance he was wicked enough to conceal it. Still the matter was so great and the question so important to his daughter's interest that he felt himself compelled to do as Mr. Apjohn had proposed. But he did not do it altogether as Mr. Apjohn had proposed. He allowed other matters to interfere, and postponed his journey till Tuesday the 27th of the month. Late on that evening he reached Carmarthen, and at once went to Mr. Apjohn's house.

Cousin Henry's journey into Carmarthen had been made on the previous Thursday, and since that day no new steps had been taken to unravel the mystery,—none at least which had reference to Llanfeare. No further search had been made among the books. All that was known in Carmarthen of Cousin Henry during these days was that he remained altogether within the house. Were he so minded, ample time was allowed to him for the destruction of any document. In the town, preparation went on in the usual way for the assizes, at which the one case of interest was to be the indictment of Mr. Evans for defamation of character. It was now supposed by the world at large that Cousin Henry would come into court; and because this was believed of him there was something of a slight turn of public opinion in his favour. It would hardly be the case that the man, if really guilty, would encounter Mr. Cheekey.

During the days that had elapsed, even Mr. Apjohn himself had lost something of his confidence. If any further step was to be taken, why did not the young lady's father himself come and take it? Why had he been so dilatory in a matter which was of so much greater importance to himself than to any one else? But now the two attorneys were together, and it was necessary that they should decide upon doing something,—or nothing.

'I hoped you would have been here last week,' said Mr. Apjohn.

'I couldn't get away. There were things I couldn't possibly leave.'

'It is so important,' said Mr. Apjohn.

'Of course it is important,—of most vital importance,—if there be any hope.'

'I have told you exactly what I think and feel.'

'Yes, yes. I know how much more than kind, how honourable you have been in all this matter. You still think that the will is hidden?'

'I did think so.'

'Something has changed your opinion?'

'I can hardly say that either,' said Mr. Apjohn. 'There was ground on which to form my opinion, and I do not know that there is any ground for changing it. But in such a matter the mind will vacillate. I did think that he had found the will shut up in a volume of sermons, in a volume which his uncle had been reading during his illness, and that he had left the book in its place upon the shelf. That, you will say, is a conclusion too exact for man to reach without anything in the shape of absolute evidence.'

'I do not say so; but then as yet I hardly know the process by which that belief has been reached.'

'But I say so;—I say that is too exact. There is more of imagination in it than of true deduction. I certainly should not recommend another person to proceed far on such reasoning. You see it has been in this way.' Then he explained to his brother attorney the process of little circumstances by which he had arrived at his own opinion;—the dislike of the man to leave the house, his clinging to one room, his manifest possession of a secret as evinced by his conversations with Farmer Griffith, his continual dread of something, his very clinging to Llanfeare as a residence, which would not have been the case had he destroyed the will, his exaggerated fear of the coming cross-examination, his ready assertion that he had destroyed nothing and hidden nothing,—but his failure to reply when he was asked whether he was aware of any such concealment. Then the fact that the books had not been searched themselves, that the old Squire had never personally used the room, but had used a book or one or two books which had been taken from it; that these books had been volumes which had certainly been close to him in those days when the lost will was being written. All these and other little details known to the reader made the process by which Mr. Apjohn had arrived at the conclusion which he now endeavoured to explain to Mr. Brodrick.

'I grant that the chain is slight,' said Mr. Apjohn, 'so slight that a feather may break it. The strongest point in it all was the look on the man's face when I asked him the last question. Now I have told you everything, and you must decide what we ought to do.'

But Mr. Brodrick was a man endowed with lesser gifts than those of the other attorney. In such a matter Mr. Apjohn was sure to lead. 'What do you think yourself?'

'I would propose that we, you and I, should

go together over to Llanfeare to-morrow and ask
him to allow us to make what further search we
may please about the house. If he permitted
this—'

'But would he?'

'I think he would. I am not at all sure but
what he would wish to have the will found. If
he did, we could begin and go through every
book in the library. We would begin with the
sermons, and soon know whether it be as I have
suggested.'

'But if he refused?'

'Then I think I would make bold to insist on
remaining there while you went to a magistrate.
I have indeed already prepared Mr. Evans of
Llancolly, who is the nearest magistrate. I would
refuse to leave the room, and you would then
return with a search warrant and a policeman.
But as for opening the special book or books, I
could do that with or without his permission.
While you talk to him I will look round the
room and see where they are. I don't think much
of it all, Mr. Brodrick; but when the stake is so
high, it is worth playing for. If we fail in this,
we can then only wait and see what the redoubt-
able Mr. Cheekey may be able to do for us.'

Thus it was settled that Mr. Brodrick and Mr.
Apjohn should go out to Llanfeare on the following morning.

CHAPTER XX

DOUBTS

'I KNOW nothing about it,' Cousin Henry had gasped out when asked by Mr. Apjohn, when Ricketts, the clerk, had left the room, whether he knew where the will was hidden. Then, when he had declared he had nothing further to say, he was allowed to go away.

As he was carried back in the fly he felt certain that Mr. Apjohn knew that there had been a will, knew that the will was still in existence, knew that it had been hidden by some accident, and knew also that he, Henry Jones, was aware of the place of concealment. That the man should have been so expert in reading the secret of his bosom was terrible to him. Had the man suspected him of destroying the will,— a deed the doing of which might have been so naturally suspected,—that would have been less terrible. He had done nothing, had committed no crime, was simply conscious of the existence of a paper which it was a duty, not of him, but of others to find, and this man, by his fearful ingenuity, had discovered it all! Now it was simply necessary that the place should be indicated, and in order that he himself might be forced to indicate it, Mr. Cheekey was to be let loose upon him!

How impossible,—how almost impossible had he found it to produce a word in answer to that one little question from Mr. Apjohn! 'Nor know where it is hidden?' He had so answered it as to make it manifest that he did know. He was conscious that he had been thus weak, though there had been nothing in Mr. Apjohn's manner to appall him. How would it be with him when, hour after hour, question after question should be demanded of him, when that cruel tormentor should stand there glaring at him in presence of all the court? There would be no need of such hour,—no need of that prolonged questioning. All that was wanted of him would be revealed at once. The whole secret would be screwed out of him by the first turn of the tormentor's engine.

There was but one thing quite fixed in his mind. Nothing should induce him to face Mr. Cheekey, unless he should have made himself comparatively safe by destroying the will. In that way he almost thought he might be safe. The suffering would be great. The rack and the thumbscrew, the boots and the wheel, would, to the delight of all those present, be allowed to do their worst upon him for hours. It would be a day to him terrible to anticipate, terrible to endure, terrible afterwards in his memory; but he thought that not even Mr. Cheekey himself would be able to extract from him the admission of such a deed as that.

And then by that deed he would undoubtedly

acquire Llanfeare. The place itself was not dear
to him, but there was rising in his heart so
strong a feeling of hatred against those who were
oppressing him that it seemed to him almost a
duty to punish them by continued possession of
the property. In this way he could triumph over
them all. If once he could come down from Mr.
Cheekey's grasp alive, if he could survive those
fearful hours, he would walk forth from the
court the undoubted owner of Llanfeare. It
would be as though a man should endure some
excruciating operation under the hands of a sur-
geon, with the assured hope that he might enjoy
perfect health afterwards for the remainder of
his life.

To destroy the will was his only chance of
escape. There was nothing else left to him, knowing, as he did, that it was impossible for him to
put an end to his own life with his own hands.
These little plots of his, which he had planned
for the revelation of his secret without the acknowledgment of guilt, had all fallen to pieces
as he attempted to execute them. He began to
be aware of himself that anything that required
skill in the execution was impossible to him.
But to burn the will he was capable. He could
surely take the paper from its hiding-place and
hold it down with the poker when he had thrust
it between the bars. Or, as there was no fire
provided in these summer months, he could con-
sume it by the light of his candle when the dead

hours of the night had come upon him. He had already resolved that, when he had done so, he would swallow the tell-tale ashes. He believed of himself that all that would be within his power, if only he could determine upon the doing of it.

And he thought that the deed when done would give him a new courage. The very danger to which he would have exposed himself would make him brave to avoid it. Having destroyed the will, and certain that no eye had seen him, conscious that his safety depended on his own reticence, he was sure that he would keep his secret even before Mr. Cheekey.

'I know nothing of the will,' he would say; 'I have neither seen it, nor hidden it, nor found it, nor destroyed it.'

Knowing what would be the consequences were he to depart from that assertion, he would assuredly cling to it. He would be safer then, much safer than in his present vacillating, half-innocent position.

As he was carried home in the fly, his mind was so intent upon this, he was so anxious to resolve to bring himself to do the deed, that he hardly knew where he was when the fly stopped at his hall door. As he entered his house, he stared about him as though doubtful of his whereabouts, and then, without speaking a word, made his way into the book-room, and seated himself on his accustomed chair. The woman came to him

and asked him whether money should not be
given to the driver.

'What driver?' said he. 'Let him go to Mr.
Apjohn. It is Mr. Apjohn's business, not mine.'
Then he got up and shut the door violently as
the woman retreated.

Yes; it was Mr. Apjohn's business; and he
thought that he could put a spoke into the wheel
of Mr. Apjohn's business. Mr. Apjohn was not
only anxious to criminate him now, but had
been anxious when such anxiety on his part had
been intrusive and impertinent. Mr. Apjohn
had, from first to last, been his enemy, and by
his enmity had created that fatal dislike which
his uncle had felt for him. Mr. Apjohn was now
determined to ruin him. Mr. Apjohn had come
out to him at Llanfeare, pretending to be his
lawyer, his friend, his adviser, and had recommended this treacherous indictment merely that
he might be able to subject him to the torments
of Mr. Cheekey's persecution. Cousin Henry
could see it all now! So, at least, Cousin Henry
told himself.

'He is a clever fellow, and he thinks that I am
a fool. Perhaps he is right, but he will find that
the fool has been too many for him.'

It was thus that he communed with himself.

He had his dinner and sat by himself during
the whole evening, as had been his practice
every day since his uncle's death. But yet this
peculiar night seemed to him to be eventful.

He felt himself to be lifted into some unwonted eagerness of life, something approaching to activity. There was a deed to be done, and though he was not as yet doing it, though he did not think that he intended to do it that very night, yet the fact that he had made up his mind made him in some sort aware that the dumb spirit which would not speak had been exorcised, and that the crushing dulness of the latter days had passed away from him. No; he could not do it that night; but he was sure that he would do it. He had looked about for a way of escape, and had been as though a dead man while he could not find it. He had lived in terror of Mrs. Griffith the housekeeper, of Farmer Griffith, of the two Cantors, of Mr. Apjohn, of that tyrant Cheekey, of his own shadow,—while he and that will were existing together in the same room. But it should be so no longer. There was one way of escape, and he would take it!

Then he went on thinking of what good things might be in store for him. His spirit had hitherto been so quenched by the vicinity of the will that he had never dared to soar into thoughts of the enjoyment of money. There had been so black a pall over everything that he had not as yet realized what it was that Llanfeare might do for him. Of course he could not live there. Though he should have to leave the house untenanted altogether, it would matter but little. There was no law to make a man live on his own estate.

He calculated that he would be able to draw
1500*l.* a year from the property;—1500*l.* a year!
That would be clearly his own; on which no one
could lay a finger; and what enjoyment could
he not buy with 1500*l.* a year?

With a great resolve to destroy the will he
went to bed, and slept through the night as best
he could. In the dark of his chamber, when the
candle was out, and he was not yet protected by
his bed, there came a qualm upon him. But the
deed was not yet done, and the qualm was kept
under, and he slept. He even repeated the
Lord's Prayer to himself when he was under the
clothes, struggling, however, as he did so, not to
bring home to himself that petition as to the
leading into temptation and the deliverance
from evil.

The next day, the Friday, and the Saturday
were passed in the same way. The resolution
was still there, but the qualms came every night.
And the salve to the qualm was always the same
remembrance that the deed had not been done
yet. And the prayer was always said, morning
and night, with the same persistent rejection of
those words which, in his present condition, were
so damning to him,—rejection from the intelligence though with the whispering voice the
words were spoken. But still there was the resolve the same as ever. There was no other way
of escape. A stag, when brought to bay, will
trample upon the hounds. He would trample

upon them. Llanfeare should all be his own. He would not return to his clerk's desk to be the scorn of all men,—to have it known that he had fraudulently kept the will hidden, and then revealed it, not of grace, but because he was afraid of Mr. Cheekey. His mind was quite made up. But the deed need not be yet done. The fewer nights that he would have to pass in that house, after the doing of the deed, the better.

The trial was to be on the Friday. He would not postpone the deed till the last day, as it might be then that emissaries might come to him, watching him to see that he did not escape. And yet it would be well for him to keep his hands clean from the doing of it up to the last moment. He was quite resolved. There was no other escape. And yet,—yet,—yet, who would say what might not happen? Till the deed should have been done, there would yet be a path open to the sweet easiness of innocence. When it should have been done, there would be a final adieu to innocence. There would be no return to the white way, no possibility of repentance! How could a man repent while he was still holding the guilty prize which he had won? Or how could he give up the prize without delivering himself as a criminal to the law? But, nevertheless, he was resolved, and he determined that the deed should be done on the Tuesday night.

During the whole Tuesday he was thinking of

it. Could he bring himself to believe that all
that story of a soul tormented for its wickedness
in everlasting fire was but an old woman's tale?
If he could but bring himself to believe that!
If he could do that, then could he master his
qualms. And why not? Religious thoughts had
hitherto but little troubled his life. The Church
and her services had been nothing to him. He
had lived neither with the fear nor with the love
of God at his heart. He knew that, and was but
little disposed to think that a line of conduct
which had never been hitherto adopted by him
would be embraced in his later life. He could
not think of himself as being even desirous to be
religious. Why, then, should qualms afflict him?

That prayer which he was accustomed to repeat to himself as he went to rest was but a trick
of his youth. It had come down to him from old,
innocent days; and though it was seldom omitted
without a shiver, nevertheless it was repeated
with contempt. In broad daylight, or when boon
companions had been with him round the candles,
blasphemy had never frightened him. But now,
—now in his troubles, he remembered that there
was a hell. He could not shake from himself the
idea. For unrepented sin there was an eternity
of torment which would last for ever! Such sin
as this which he premeditated must remain unrepented, and there would be torment for him
for ever. Nevertheless, he must do it. And, after
all, did not many of the wise ones of the earth

justify him in thinking that that threat was but an old woman's tale?

Tuesday night came,—the late hours of Tuesday night,—the midnight hour at which he was sure that the women were in bed, and the will was taken out from its hiding-place. He had already trimmed the wick and placed the candle on an outspread newspaper, so that no fragment of the ash should fall where it might not be collected. He had walked round the room to make himself sure that no aperture might possibly be open. He put out the candle so as to see that no gleam of light from any source was making its way into the room, and then relighted it. The moment had come for the destruction of the document.

He read it all through yet again;—why he knew not, but in truth craving some excuse for further delay. With what care the dying old man had written every word and completed every letter! He sat there contemplating the old man's work, telling himself that it was for him to destroy it utterly by just a motion of his wrist. He turned round and trimmed the candle again, and still sat there with the paper in his hand. Could it be that so great a result could come from so short an act? The damning of his own soul! Would it in truth be the giving up of his own soul to eternal punishment? God would know that he had not meant to steal the property! God would know that he did not wish to steal it now! God would know that he was doing this as the only means of escape from misery which others were plotting for him! God would know how cruelly he had been used! God would know the injustice with which the old man had treated him! Then came moments in which he almost taught himself to believe that in destroying the will he would be doing no more than an act of rough justice, and that God would certainly condemn no one to eternal punishment for a just act. But still, whenever he would turn round to the candle, his hand would refuse to raise the paper to the flame. When done, it could not be undone! And whether those eternal flames should or should not get possession of him, there would be before him a life agonized by the dread of them. What could Mr. Cheekey do worse for him than that?

The Wednesday would at any rate do as well. Why rob himself of the comfort of one day during which his soul would not be irretrievably condemned? Now he might sleep. For this night, at any rate, he might sleep. He doubted whether he would ever sleep again after the doing of the deed. To be commonly wicked was nothing to him,—nothing to break through all those ordinary rules of life which parents teach their children and pastors their flocks, but as to which the world is so careless. To covet other men's goods, to speak evil of his neighbours, to run after his neighbour's wife if she came in his path, to steal a little in the ordinary way,—such as selling a lame horse or looking over an adversary's hand at whist, to swear to a lie, or to ridicule the memory of his parents,—these peccadillos had never oppressed his soul. That not telling of the will had been burdensome to him only because of the danger of discovery. But to burn a will, and thereby clearly to steal 1500*l.* a year from his cousin! To commit felony! To do that for which he might be confined at Dartmoor all his life, with his hair cut, and dirty prison clothes, and hard food, and work to do! He thought it would be well to have another day of life in which he had not done the deed. He therefore put the will back into the book and went to his bed.

CHAPTER XXI

MR. APJOHN'S SUCCESS

EARLY on the Wednesday morning Mr. Apjohn and Mr. Brodrick were on foot, and preparing for the performance of their very disagreeable day's work. Mr. Brodrick did not believe at all in the day's work, and in discussing the matter with Mr. Apjohn, after they had determined upon their line of action, made his mind known very clearly. To him it was simply apparent that if the will had fallen into the power of a dishonest person, and if the dishonest man could achieve his purpose by destroying it, the will would be destroyed. Of Cousin Henry he knew nothing. Cousin Henry might or might not be ordinarily honest, as are other ordinary people. There might be no such will as that spoken of, or there might be a will accidentally hidden,—or the will might have been found and destroyed. But that they should be able to find a will, the hiding-place of which should be known to Cousin Henry, was to his thinking out of the question. The subtler intellect of the other lawyer appreciating the intricacies of a weak man's mind saw more than his companion. When he found that Mr. Brodrick did not agree with him, and perceived that the other attorney's mind was not speculative in such a matter as this, he ceased to try to persuade, and simply said that it was the duty of both of them to leave no stone unturned. And so they started.

'I'll take you about half a mile out of our way to show you Mr. Evans's gate,' Mr. Apjohn said, after they had started. 'His house is not above twenty minutes from Llanfeare, and should it be necessary to ask his assistance, he will know all about it. You will find a policeman there ready to come back with you. But my impression is that Cousin Henry will not attempt to prevent any search which we may endeavour to make.'

It was about ten when they reached the house, and, on being shown into the book-room, they found Cousin Henry at his breakfast. The front door was opened for them by Mrs. Griffith, the housekeeper; and when Mr. Apjohn expressed his desire to see Mr. Jones, she made no difficulty in admitting him at once. It was a part of the misery of Cousin Henry's position that everybody around him and near to him was against him. Mrs. Griffith was aware that it was the purpose of Mr. Apjohn to turn her present master out of Llanfeare if possible, and she was quite willing to aid him by any means in her power. Therefore, she gave her master no notice of the arrival of the two strangers, but ushered them into the room at once.

Cousin Henry's breakfast was frugal. All his meals had been frugal since he had become owner of Llanfeare. It was not that he did not like nice eating as well as another, but that he was too much afraid of his own servants to make known his own tastes. And then the general discomforts of his position had been too great to admit of relief from delicate dishes. There was the tea-pot on the table, and the solitary cup, and the bread and butter, and the nearly naked bone of a cold joint of mutton. And the things were not set after the fashion of a well-to-do gentleman's table, but were put on as they might be in a third-rate London lodging, with a tumbled tablecloth, and dishes, plates, and cups all unlike each other.

'Mr. Jones,' said the attorney from Carmarthen, 'this is your uncle, Mr. Brodrick, from Hereford.' Then the two men who were so nearly connected, but had never known each other, shook hands. 'Of course, this matter,' continued Mr. Apjohn, 'is of great moment, and Mr. Brodrick has come over to look after his daughter's interests.'

'I am very glad to see my uncle,' said Cousin Henry, turning his eye involuntarily towards the shelf on which the volume of sermons was resting. 'I am afraid I can't offer you much in the way of breakfast.'

'We breakfasted before we left Carmarthen,' said Mr. Apjohn. 'If you do not mind going on, we will talk to you whilst you are eating.' Cousin Henry said that he did not mind going on, but found it impossible to eat a morsel. That which he did, and that which he endured during that interview, he had to do and had to endure fasting. 'I had better tell you at once,' continued Mr. Apjohn, 'what we want to do now.'

'What is it you want to do now? I suppose I have got to go into the assizes all the same on Friday?'

'That depends. It is just possible that it should turn out to be unnecessary.'

As he said this, he looked into Cousin Henry's face, and thought that he discerned something of satisfaction. When he made the suggestion, he understood well how great was the temptation offered in the prospect of not having to encounter Mr. Cheekey.

'Both Mr. Brodrick and I think it probable

that your uncle's last will may yet be concealed somewhere in the house.' Cousin Henry's eye, as this was said, again glanced up at the fatal shelf.

'When Mr. Apjohn says that in my name,' said Mr. Brodrick, opening his mouth for the first time, 'you must understand that I personally know nothing of the circumstances. I am guided in my opinion only by what he tells me.'

'Exactly,' said Mr. Apjohn. 'As the father of the young lady who would be the heiress of Llanfeare if you were not the heir, I have of course told him everything,—even down to the most secret surmises of my mind.'

'All right,' said Cousin Henry.

'My position,' continued Mr. Apjohn, 'is painful and very peculiar; but I find myself specially bound to act as the lawyer of the deceased, and to carry out whatever was in truth his last will and testament.'

'I thought that was proved at Carmarthen,' said Cousin Henry.

'No doubt. A will was proved,—a will that was very genuine if no subsequent will be found. But, as you have been told repeatedly, the proving of that will amounts to nothing if a subsequent one be forthcoming. The great question is this; Does a subsequent will exist?'

'How am I to know anything about it?'

'Nobody says you do.'

'I suppose you wouldn't come here and bring

my uncle Brodrick down on me,—giving me no notice, but coming into my house just when I am at breakfast, without saying a word to any one, —unless you thought so. I don't see what right you have to be here at all!'

He was trying to pluck up his spirit in order that he might get rid of them. Why, oh! why had he not destroyed that document when, on the previous night, it had been brought out from its hiding-place, purposely in order that it might be burned?

'It is common, Mr. Jones, for one gentleman to call upon another when there is business to be done,' said Mr. Apjohn.

'But not common to come to a gentleman's house and accuse him of making away with a will.'

'Nobody has done that,' said Mr. Brodrick.

'It is very like it.'

'Will you allow us to search again? Two of my clerks will be here just now, and will go through the house with us, if you will permit it.'

Cousin Henry sat staring at them. Not long ago he had himself asked one of Mr. Apjohn's clerks why they did not search again. But then the framing of his thoughts had been different. At that moment he had been desirous of surrendering Llanfeare altogether, so that he might also get rid of Mr. Cheekey. Now he had reached a bolder purpose. Now he was resolved to destroy the will, enjoy the property, and face the barrister. An idea came across his mind that they would hardly insist upon searching instantly if he refused. A petition to that effect had already been made, and a petition implies the power of refusal on the part of him petitioned.

'Where do you want to look?' he asked.

Upon this Mr. Brodrick allowed his eyes to wander round the room. And Cousin Henry's eyes followed those of his uncle, which seemed to settle themselves exactly upon the one shelf.

'To search the house generally; your uncle's bed-room, for instance,' said Mr. Apjohn.

'Oh, yes; you can go there.' This he said with an ill-formed, crude idea which sprang to his mind at the moment. If they would ascend to the bed-room, then he could seize the will when left alone and destroy it instantly,—eat it bit by bit if it were necessary,—go with it out of the house and reduce it utterly to nothing before he returned. He was still a free agent, and could go and come as he pleased. 'Oh, yes; you can go there.'

But this was not at all the scheme which had really formed itself in Mr. Apjohn's brain. 'Or perhaps we might begin here,' he said. 'There are my two clerks just arrived in the fly.'

Cousin Henry became first red and then pale, and he endeavoured to see in what direction Mr. Brodrick had fixed his eye. Mr Apjohn himself had not as yet looked anywhere round the books. He had sat close at the table, with his

gaze fixed on Cousin Henry's face, as Cousin
Henry had been well aware. If they began to
search in the room, they would certainly find
the document. Of that he was quite sure. Not
a book would be left without having been made
to disclose all that it might contain between its
leaves. If there was any chance left to him, it
must be seized now,—now at this very moment.
Suddenly the possession of Llanfeare was endeared to him by a thousand charms. Suddenly
all fear of eternal punishment passed away from
his thoughts. Suddenly he was permeated by a
feeling of contrition for his own weakness in
having left the document unharmed. Suddenly
he was brave against Mr. Cheekey, as would be
a tiger against a lion. Suddenly there arose in
his breast a great desire to save the will even yet
from the hands of these Philistines.

'This is my private room,' he said. 'When I
am eating my breakfast I cannot let you disturb
me like that.'

'In a matter such as this you wouldn't think of
your own comfort!' said Mr. Apjohn severely.
'Comfort, indeed! What comfort can you have
while the idea is present to you that this house
in which you live may possibly be the property
of your cousin?'

'It's very little comfort you've left me among
you.'

'Face it out, then, like a man; and when you
have allowed us to do all that we can on her be-

half, then enjoy your own, and talk of comfort.
Shall I have the men in and go on with the
search as I propose?'

If they were to find it,—as certainly they
would,—then surely they would not accuse him
of having hidden it! He would be enabled to act
some show of surprise, and they would not dare
to contradict him, even should they feel sure in
their hearts that he had been aware of the concealment! There would be great relief! There
would be an end of so many troubles! But then
how weak he would have been,—to have had the
prize altogether within his grasp and to have lost
it! A burst of foul courage swelled in his heart,
changing the very colour of his character for a
time as he resolved that it should not be so. The
men could not search there,—so he told himself,
—without further authority than that which
Mr. Apjohn could give them. 'I won't be treated
in this way!' he said.

'In what way do you mean, Mr. Jones?'

'I won't have my house searched as though I
were a swindler and a thief. Can you go into
any man's house and search it just as you please,
merely because you are an attorney?'

'You told my man the other day,' said Mr.
Apjohn, 'that we might renew the search if we
pleased.'

'So you may; but you must get an order first
from somebody. You are nobody.'

'You are quite right,' said Mr. Apjohn, who

was not at all disposed to be angry in regard to any observation offered personally to himself. 'But surely it would be better for you that this should be done privately. Of course we can have a search-warrant if it be necessary; but then there must be a policeman to carry it out.'

'What do I care for policemen?' said Cousin Henry. 'It is you who have treated me badly from first to last. I will do nothing further at your bidding.'

Mr. Apjohn looked at Mr. Brodrick, and Mr. Brodrick looked at Mr. Apjohn. The strange attorney would do nothing without directions from the other, and the attorney who was more at home was for a few moments a little in doubt. He got up from his chair, and walked about the room, while Cousin Henry, standing also, watched every movement which he made. Cousin Henry took his place at the further end of the table from the fire, about six feet from the spot on which all his thoughts were intent. There he stood, ready for action while the attorney walked up and down the room meditating what it would be best that he should do next. As he walked he seemed to carry his nose in the air, with a gait different from what was usual to him. Cousin Henry had already learned something of the man's ways, and was aware that his manner was at present strange. Mr. Apjohn was in truth looking along the rows of the books. In old days he had often been in that room, and had read many of the titles as given on the backs. He knew the nature of many of the books collected there, and was aware that but very few of them had ever been moved from their places in the old Squire's time for any purpose of use. He did not wish to stand and inspect them,—not as yet. He walked on as though collecting his thoughts, and as he walked he endeavoured to fix on some long set of sermons. He had in his mind some glimmering of a remembrance that there was such a set of books in the room. 'You might as well let us do as we propose,' he said.

'Certainly not. To tell you the truth, I wish you would go away, and leave me.'

'Mr. Cheekey will hear all about it, and how will you be able to answer Mr. Cheekey?'

'I don't care about Mr. Cheekey. Who is to tell Mr. Cheekey? Will you tell him?'

'I cannot take your part, you know, if you behave like this.'

As he spoke, Mr. Apjohn had stopped his walk, and was standing with his back close to the bookshelves, with the back of his head almost touching the set of Jeremy Taylor's works. There were ten volumes of them, and he was standing exactly in front of them. Cousin Henry was just in front of him, doubting whether his enemy's position had not been chosen altogether by accident, but still trembling at the near approach. He was prepared for a spring if it was necessary. Anything should be hazarded now, so that discovery might be avoided. Mr. Brodrick was still seated in the chair which he had at first occupied, waiting till that order should be given to him to go for the magistrate's warrant.

Mr. Apjohn's eye had caught the author's name on the back of the book, and he remembered at once that he had seen the volume,—a volume with Jeremy Taylor's name on the back of it,—lying on the old man's table. 'Jeremy Taylor's Works. Sermons.' He remembered the volume. That had been a long time ago,—six months ago; but the old man might probably take a long time over so heavy a book. 'You will let me look at some of these,' he said, pointing with his thumb over his back.

'You shall not touch a book without a regular order,' said Cousin Henry.

Mr. Apjohn fixed the man's eye for a moment. He was the smaller man of the two, and much the elder; but he was wiry, well set, and strong. The other was soft, and unused to much bodily exercise. There could be no doubt as to which would have the best of it in a personal struggle. Very quickly he turned round and got his hand on one of the set, but not on the right one. Cousin Henry dashed at him, and in the struggle the book fell to the ground. Then the attorney seized him by the throat, and dragged him forcibly back to the table. 'Take them all out one by one, and shake them,' he said to the other

attorney,—'that set like the one on the floor.
I'll hold him while you do it.'

Mr. Brodrick did as he was told, and, one by
one, beginning from the last volume, he shook
them all till he came to volume 4. Out of that
fell the document.

'Is it the will?' shouted Mr. Apjohn, with
hardly breath enough to utter the words.

Mr. Brodrick, with a lawyer's cautious hands,
undid the folds, and examined the document.
'It certainly is a will,' he said,—'and is signed
by my brother-in-law.'

CHAPTER XXII

HOW COUSIN HENRY WAS LET OFF EASILY

IT was a moment of great triumph and of utter
dismay,—of triumph to Mr. Apjohn, and of
dismay to Cousin Henry. The two men at this
moment,—as Mr. Brodrick was looking at the
papers,—were struggling together upon the
ground. Cousin Henry, in his last frantic efforts,
had striven to escape from the grasp of his enemy
so as to seize the will, not remembering that by
seizing it now he could retrieve nothing. Mr.
Apjohn had been equally determined that ample
time should be allowed to Mr. Brodrick to secure
any document that might be found, and, with
the pugnacity which the state of fighting always

produces, had held on to his prey with a firm grip. Now for the one man there remained nothing but dismay; for the other was the full enjoyment of the triumph produced by his own sagacity. 'Here is the date,' said Mr. Brodrick, who had retreated with the paper to the furthest corner of the room. 'It is undoubtedly my brother-in-law's last will and testament, and, as far as I can see at a glance, it is altogether regular.'

'You dog!' exclaimed Mr. Apjohn, spurning Cousin Henry away from him. 'You wretched, thieving miscreant!' Then he got up on to his legs and began to adjust himself, setting his cravat right, and smoothing his hair with his hands. 'The brute has knocked the breath out of me,' he said. 'But only to think that we should catch him after such a fashion as this!' There was a note of triumph in his voice which he found it impossible to repress. He was thoroughly proud of his achievement. It was a grand thing to him that Isabel Brodrick should at last get the property which he had so long been anxious to secure for her; but at the present moment it was a grander thing to have hit the exact spot in which the document had been hidden by sheer force of intelligence.

What little power of fighting there had ever been in Cousin Henry had now been altogether knocked out of him He attempted no further struggle, uttered no denial, nor did he make any answer to the words of abuse which Mr. Apjohn had heaped on his head. He too raised himself from the floor, slowly collecting his limbs together, and seated himself in the chair nearest at hand, hiding his face with his hand.

'That is the most wonderful thing that ever came within my experience,' said Mr. Brodrick.

'That the man should have hidden the will?' asked Mr. Apjohn.

'Why do you say I hid it?' moaned Cousin Henry.

'You reptile!' exclaimed Mr. Apjohn.

'Not that he should have hidden it,' said the Hereford attorney, 'but that you should have found it, and found it without any search;—that you should have traced it down to the very book in which the old man must have left it!'

'Yes,' said Cousin Henry. 'He left it there. I did not hide it.'

'Do you mean,' said Mr. Apjohn, turning upon him with all the severity of which he was capable, 'do you mean to say that during all this time you have not known that the will was there?' The wretched man opened his mouth and essayed to speak, but not a word came. 'Do you mean to tell us that when you refused us just now permission to search this room, though you were willing enough that we should search elsewhere, you were not acquainted with the hiding-place? When I asked you in my office the other day whether you knew where the will was hidden, and you wouldn't answer me for very fear, though

you were glib enough in swearing that you had
not hidden it yourself, then you knew nothing
about the book and its enclosure? When you
told Mr. Griffith down at Coed that you had
something to divulge, were you not then almost
driven to tell the truth by your dastardly
cowardice as to this threatened trial? And did
you not fail again because you were afraid?
You mean poltroon! Will you dare to say before
us, now, that when we entered the room this
morning you did not know what that book contained?' Cousin Henry once more opened his
mouth, but no word came. 'Answer me, sir, if
you wish to escape any part of the punishment
which you have deserved.'

'You should not ask him to criminate himself,'
said Mr. Brodrick.

'No!' shrieked Cousin Henry; 'no! he shouldn't
ask a fellow to tell against himself. It isn't fair;
is it, Uncle Brodrick?'

'If I hadn't made you tell against yourself one
way or another,' said Mr. Apjohn, 'the will
would have been there still, and we should all
have been in the dark. There are occasions in
which the truth must be screwed out of a man.
We have screwed it out of you, you miserable
creature! Brodrick, let us look at the paper. I
suppose it is all right.' He was so elated by the
ecstasy of his success that he hardly knew how
to contain himself. There was no prospect to
him of any profit in all this. It might, indeed,

well be that all the expenses incurred, including the handsome honorarium which would still have to be paid to Mr. Cheekey, must come out of his own pocket. But the glory of the thing was too great to admit of any considerations such as those. For the last month his mind had been exercised with the question of this will, whether there was such a will or not, and, if so, where was its hiding-place? Now he had brought his month's labour, his month's speculation, and his month's anxiety to a supreme success. In his present frame of mind it was nothing to him who might pay the bill. 'As far as I can see,' said Mr. Brodrick, 'it is altogether in order.'

'Let us look at it.' Then Mr. Apjohn, stretching out his hand, took the document, and, seating himself in Cousin Henry's own chair at the breakfast-table, read it through carefully from beginning to end. It was wonderful,—the exactness with which the old Squire had copied, not only every word, but every stop and every want of a stop in the preceding will. 'It is my own work, every morsel of it,' said Mr. Apjohn, with thorough satisfaction. 'Why on earth did he not burn the intermediate one which he made in this rascal's favour,'—then he indicated the rascal by a motion of his head—'and make it all straight in that way?'

'There are men who think that a will once made should never be destroyed,' suggested Mr. Brodrick.

'I suppose it was something of that kind. He was a fine old fellow, but as obstinate as a mule. Well, what are we to do now?'

'My nephew will have to consult his lawyer whether he will wish to dispute this document or not.'

'I do not want to dispute anything,' said Cousin Henry, whining.

'Of course he will be allowed time to think of it,' said Mr. Apjohn. 'He is in possession now, and will have plenty of time. He will have to answer some rather difficult questions from Mr. Cheekey on Friday.'

'Oh, no!' shouted the victim.

'I am afraid it must be "oh, yes", Mr. Jones! How are you to get out of it; eh? You are bound over to prosecute Mr. Evans, of the *Herald*, for defamation of character. Of course it will come out at the trial that we have found this document. Indeed, I shall be at no trouble to conceal the fact,—nor, I suppose, will be Mr. Brodrick. Why should we?'

'I thought you were acting as my lawyer.'

'So I was,—and so I am,—and so I will. While you were supposed to be an honest man,—or, rather, while it was possible that it might be so supposed,—I told you what, as an honest man, you were bound to do. The *Carmarthen Herald* knew that you were not honest,—and said so. If you are prepared to go into the court and swear that you knew nothing of the existence of this document, that you were not aware that it was concealed in that book, that you did nothing to prevent us from looking for it this morning, I will carry on the case for you. If I am called into the witness-box against you, of course I must give my evidence for what it is worth;— and Mr. Brodrick must do the same.'

'But it won't go on?' he asked.

'Not if you are prepared to admit that there was no libel in all that the newspaper said. If you agree that it was all true, then you will have to pay the costs on both sides, and the indictment can be quashed. It will be a serious admission to make, but perhaps that won't signify, seeing what your position as to character will be.'

'I think you are almost too hard upon him,' said Mr. Brodrick.

'Am I? Can one be too hard on a man who has acted as he has done?'

'He is hard,—isn't he, Mr. Brodrick?'

'Hard! Why, yes;—I should think I am. I mean to be hard. I mean to go on trampling you to pieces till I see your cousin, Miss Brodrick, put into full possession of this estate. I don't mean to leave you a loop-hole of escape by any mercy. At the present moment you are Henry Jones, Esq., of Llanfeare, and will be so till you are put out by the hard hand of the law. You may turn round for anything I know, and say that this document is a forgery.'

'No, no!'

'That Mr. Brodrick and I brought it here with us and put it in the book.'

'I sha'n't say anything of the kind.'

'Who did put it there?' Cousin Henry sobbed and groaned, but said nothing. 'Who did put it there? If you want to soften our hearts to you in any degree, if you wish us to contrive some mode of escape for you, tell the truth. Who put the will into that book?'

'How am I to know?'

'You do know! Who put it there?'

'I suppose it was Uncle Indefer.'

'And you had seen it there?' Again Cousin Henry sobbed and groaned.

'You should hardly ask him that,' said Mr. Brodrick.

'Yes! If any good can be done for him, it must be by making him feel that he must help us by making our case easy for us. You had seen it there? Speak the word, and we will do all we can to let you off easily.'

'Just by an accident,' said he.

'You did see it, then?'

'Yes;—I chanced to see it.'

'Yes; of course you did. And then the Devil went to work with you and prompted you to destroy it?' He paused as though asking a question, but to this question Cousin Henry found it impossible to make any answer. 'But the Devil had not quite hold enough over you to make you do that? It was so;—was it not? There was a conscience with you?'

'Oh, yes.'

'But the conscience was not strong enough to force you to give it up when you found it?' Cousin Henry now burst out into open tears. 'That was about it, I suppose? If you can bring yourself to make a clean breast of it, it will be easier for you.'

'May I go back to London at once?' he asked.

'Well; as to that, I think we had better take some little time for consideration. But I think I may say that, if you will make our way easy for us, we will endeavour to make yours easy for you. You acknowledge this to be your uncle's will as far as you know?'

'Oh, yes.'

'You acknowledge that Mr. Brodrick found it in this book which I now hold in my hand?'

'I acknowledge that.'

'This is all that I will ask you to sign your name to. As for the rest, it is sufficient that you have confessed the truth to your uncle and to me. I will just write a few lines that you shall sign, and then we will go back to Carmarthen and do the best we can to prevent the trial for next Friday.' Thereupon Mr. Apjohn rang the bell, and asked Mrs. Griffith to bring him paper and ink. With these he wrote a letter addressed to himself, which he invited Cousin Henry to sign as soon as he had read it aloud to him and to

Mr. Brodrick. The letter contained simply the two admissions above stated, and then went on to authorize Mr. Apjohn, as the writer's attorney, to withdraw the indictment against the proprietor of the *Carmarthen Herald*, 'in consequence,' as the letter said, 'of the question as to the possession of Llanfeare having been settled now in an unexpected manner.'

When the letter was completed, the two lawyers went away, and Cousin Henry was left to his own meditation. He sat there for a while, so astounded by the transaction of the morning as to be unable to collect his thoughts. All this that had agitated him so profoundly for the last month had been set at rest by the finding of the will. There was no longer any question as to what must be done. Everything had been done. He was again a London clerk, with a small sum of money besides his clerkship, and the security of lowliness into which to fall back! If only they would be silent;—if only it might be thought by his fellow-clerks in London that the will had been found by them without any knowledge on his part,—then he would be satisfied. A terrible catastrophe had fallen upon him, but one which would not be without consolation if with the estate might be made to pass away from him all responsibilities and all accusations as to the estate. That terrible man had almost promised him that a way of retreat should be made easy to him. At any rate, he would not be cross-examined by Mr. Cheekey. At any rate, he would not be brought to trial. There was almost a promise, too, that as little should be said as possible. There must, he supposed, be some legal form of abdication on his part, but he was willing to execute that as quickly as possible on the simple condition that he should be allowed to depart without being forced to speak further on the matter to any one in Wales. Not to have to see the tenants, not to have to say even a word of farewell to the servants, not to be carried into Carmarthen,—above all, not to face Mr. Cheekey and the Court,—this was all he asked now from a kind Fate.

At about two Mrs. Griffith came into the room, ostensibly to take away the breakfast things. She had seen the triumphant face of Mr. Apjohn, and knew that some victory had been gained. But when she saw that the breakfast had not been touched, her heart became soft. The way to melt the heart of a Mrs. Griffith is to eat nothing. 'Laws, Mr. Jones, you have not had a mouthful. Shall I do you a broil?' He assented to the broil, and ate it, when it was cooked, with a better appetite than he had enjoyed since his uncle's death. Gradually he came to feel that a great load had been taken from off his shoulders. The will was no longer hidden in the book. Nothing had been done of which he could not repent. There was no prospect of a life before him made horrid by one great sin. He could not be Squire of Llanfeare; nor would he be a felon,—a felon always in his own esteem. Upon the whole, though he hardly admitted as much to himself, the man's condition had been improved by the transactions of the morning.

'You don't quite agree with all that I have done this morning,' said Mr. Apjohn, as soon as the two lawyers were in the fly together.

'I am lost in admiration at the clearness of your insight.'

'Ah! that comes of giving one's undivided thoughts to a matter. I have been turning it over in my mind till I have been able to see it all. It was odd, wasn't it, that I should have foretold to you all that happened, almost to the volume?'

'Quite to the volume!'

'Well, yes; to the volume of sermons. Your brother-in-law read nothing but sermons. But you thought I shouldn't have asked those questions.'

'I don't like making a man criminate himself,' said Mr. Brodrick.

'Nor do I,—if I mean to criminate him too. My object is to let him off. But to enable us to do that we must know exactly what he knew and what he had done. Shall I tell you what occurred to me when you shook the will out of the book? How would it be if he declared that we had brought it with us? If he had been sharp enough for that, the very fact of our having gone to the book at once would have been evidence against us.'

'He was not up to it.'

'No, poor devil! I am inclined to think that he has got as bad as he deserves. He might have been so much worse. We owe him ever so much for not destroying the will. His cousin will have to give him the 4000*l*. which he was to have given her.'

'Certainly, certainly.'

'He has been hardly used, you know, by his uncle; and, upon my word, he has had a bad time of it for the last month. I wouldn't have been hated and insulted as he has been by those people up there,—not for all Llanfeare twice over. I think we've quenched him now, so that he'll run smooth. If so, we'll let him off easily. If I had treated him less hardly just now, he might have gathered courage and turned upon us. Then it would have been necessary to crush him altogether. I was thinking all through how we might let him off easiest.'

CHAPTER XXIII

ISABEL'S PETITION

THE news was soon all about Carmarthen. A new will had been found, in accordance with which Miss Brodrick was to become owner of Llanfeare, and,—which was of more importance to Carmarthen at the present moment,—

there was to be no trial! The story, as told publicly, was as follows;—Mr. Apjohn, by his sagacity, had found the will. It had been concealed in a volume of sermons, and Mr. Apjohn, remembering suddenly that the old man had been reading these sermons shortly before his death, had gone at once to the book. There the will had been discovered, which had at once been admitted to be a true and formal document by the unhappy pseudo-proprietor. Henry Jones had acknowledged his cousin to be the heiress, and under these circumstances had conceived it to be useless to go on with the trial. Such was the story told, and Mr. Apjohn, fully aware that the story went very lame on one leg, did his best to remedy the default by explaining that it would be unreasonable to expect that a man should come into court and undergo an examination by Mr. Cheekey just when he had lost a fine property.

'Of course I know all that,' said Mr. Apjohn, when the editor of the paper remarked to him that the libel, if a libel, would be just as much a libel whether Mr. Henry Jones were or were not the owner of Llanfeare. 'Of course I know all that; but you are hardly to expect that a man is to come and assert himself amidst a cloud of difficulties when he has just undergone such a misfortune as that! You have had your fling, and are not to be punished for it. That ought to satisfy you.'

'And who'll pay all the expenses?' asked Mr. Evans.

'Well,' said Mr. Apjohn, scratching his head; 'you, of course, will have to pay nothing. Geary will settle all that with me. That poor devil at Llanfeare ought to pay.'

'He won't have the money.'

'I, at any rate, will make it all right with Geary; so that needn't trouble you.'

This question as to the expense was much discussed by others in Carmarthen. Who in truth would pay the complicated lawyers' bill which must have been occasioned, including all these flys out to Llanfeare? In spite of Mr. Apjohn's good-natured explanations, the public of Carmarthen was quite convinced that Henry Jones had in truth hidden the will. If so, he ought not only to be made to pay for everything, but be sent to prison also and tried for felony. The opinion concerning Cousin Henry in Carmarthen on the Thursday and Friday was very severe indeed. Had he shown himself in the town, he would almost have been pulled in pieces. To kill him and to sell his carcase for what it might fetch towards lessening the expenses which he had incurred would not be too bad for him. Mr. Apjohn was, of course, the hero of the hour, and, as far as Carmarthen could see, Mr. Apjohn would have to pay the bill. All this, spoken as it was by many mouths, reached Mr. Brodrick's ears, and induced him to say a word or two to Mr. Apjohn.

'This affair,' said he, 'will of course become a charge upon the property?'

'What affair?'

'This trial which is not to take place, and the rest of it.'

'The trial will have nothing to do with the estate,' said Mr. Apjohn.

'It has everything to do with it. I only mention it now to let you know that, as Isabel's father, I shall make it my business to look after that.'

'The truth is, Brodrick,' said the Carmarthen attorney, with that gleam of triumph in his eye which had been so often seen there since the will had tumbled out of the volume of sermons in the book-room, 'the whole of this matter has been such a pleasure to me that I don't care a straw about the costs. If I paid for it all from beginning to end out of my own pocket, I should have had my whack for my money. Perhaps Miss Isabel will recompense me by letting me make her will some day.'

Such were the feelings and such were the words spoken at Carmarthen; and it need only be said further, in regard to Carmarthen, that the operations necessary for proving the later will and annulling the former one, for dispossessing Cousin Henry and for putting Isabel into the full fruition of all her honours, went on as quickly as it could be effected by the concentrated energy of Mr. Apjohn and all his clerks.

Cousin Henry, to whom we may be now

allowed to bid farewell, was permitted to remain within the seclusion of the house at Llanfeare till his signature had been obtained to the last necessary document. No one spoke a word to him; no one came to see him. If there were intruders about the place anxious to catch a glimpse of the pseudo-Squire, they were disappointed.

Mrs. Griffith, under the attorney's instructions, was more courteous to him than she had been when he was her master. She endeavoured to get him things nice to eat, trying to console him by titbits. None of the tenants appeared before him, nor was there a rough word spoken to him, even by young Cantor.

In all this Cousin Henry did feel some consolation, and was greatly comforted when he heard from the office in London that his stool at the desk was still kept open for him.

The *Carmarthen Herald,* in its final allusion to the state of things at Llanfeare, simply declared that the proper will had been found at last, and that Miss Isabel Brodrick was to be restored to her rights. Guided by this statement, the directors in London were contented to regard their clerk as having been unfortunate rather than guilty.

For the man himself, the reader, it is hoped, will feel some compassion. He had been dragged away from London by false hopes. After so great an injury as that inflicted on him by the last change in the Squire's purpose it was hardly unnatural that the idea of retaliation should present itself to him when the opportunity came in his way. Not to do that which justice demands is so much easier to the conscience than to commit a deed which is palpably fraudulent! At the last his conscience saved him, and Mr. Apjohn will perhaps be thought to have been right in declaring that much was due to him in that he had not destroyed the will. His forbearance was recompensed fully.

As soon as the money could be raised on the property, the full sum of 4000*l.* was paid to him, that having been the amount with which the Squire had intended to burden the property on behalf of his niece when he was minded to put her out of the inheritance.

It may be added that, notorious as the whole affair was at Carmarthen, but little of Cousin Henry's wicked doings were known up in London.

We must now go back to Hereford. By agreement between the two lawyers, no tidings of her good fortune were at once sent to Isabel. 'There is so many a slip 'twixt the cup and the lip,' said Mr. Apjohn to her father. But early in the following week Mr. Brodrick himself took the news home with him.

'My dear,' he said to her as soon as he found himself alone with her,—having given her intimation that an announcement of great importance was to be made to her,—'it turns out that after all your Uncle Indefer did make another will.'

'I was always quite sure of that, papa.'

'How were you sure?'

'He told me so, papa.'

'He told you so! I never heard that before.'

'He did,—when he was dying. What was the use of talking of it? But has it been found?'

'It was concealed within a book in the library. As soon as the necessary deeds can be executed Llanfeare will be your own. It is precisely word for word the same as that which he had made before he sent for your Cousin Henry.'

'Then Henry has not destroyed it?'

'No, he did not destroy it.'

'Nor hid it where we could not find it?'

'Nor did he hide it.'

'Oh, how I have wronged him;—how I have injured him!'

'About that we need say nothing, Isabel. You have not injured him. But we may let all that pass away. The fact remains that you are the heiress of Llanfeare.'

Of course he did by degrees explain to her all the circumstances,—how the will had been found and not revealed, and how far Cousin Henry had sinned in the matter; but it was agreed between them that no further evil should be said in the family as to their unfortunate relative. The great injury which he might have done to them he had abstained from doing.

'Papa,' she said to her father when they were again together alone that same evening, 'you must tell all this to Mr. Owen. You must tell him everything, just as you have told me.'

'Certainly, my dear, if you wish it.'

'I do wish it.'

'Why should you not have the pleasure of telling him yourself?'

'It would not be a pleasure, and therefore I will get you to do it. My pleasure, if there be any pleasure in it, must come afterwards. I want him to know it before I see him myself.'

'He will be sure to have some stupid notion,' said her father, smiling.

'I want him to have his notion, whether it be stupid or otherwise, before I see him. If you do not mind, papa, going to him as soon as possible, I shall be obliged to you.'

Isabel, when she found herself alone, had her triumph also. She was far from being dead to the delights of her inheritance. There had been a period in her life in which she had regarded it as her certain destiny to be the possessor of Llanfeare, and she had been proud of the promised position. The tenants had known her as the future owner of the acres which they cultivated, and had entertained for her and shown to her much genuine love. She had made herself acquainted with every homestead, landmark, and field about the place. She had learnt the wants of the poor, and the requirements of the little school. Everything at Llanfeare had had an interest for her. Then had come that sudden change in her uncle's feelings,—that new idea of duty,—and she had borne it like a heroine. Not only had she never said a word of reproach to him, but she had sworn to herself that even in her own heart she would throw no blame upon him. A great blow had come upon her, but she had taken it as though it had come from the hand of the Almighty,—as it might have been had she lost her eyesight, or been struck with palsy. She promised herself that it should be so, and she had had strength to be as good as her word. She had roused herself instantly from the effect of the blow, and, after a day of consideration, had been as capable as ever to do the work of her life. Then had come her uncle's last sickness, those spoken but doubtful words, her uncle's death, and that conviction that her cousin was a felon. Then she had been unhappy, and had found it difficult to stand up bravely against misfortune. Added to this had been her stepmother's taunts and her father's distress at the resolution she had taken. The home to which she had returned had been thoroughly unhappy to her. And there had been her stern purpose not to give her hand to the man who loved her and whom she so dearly loved! She was sure of her purpose, and yet she was altogether discontented with herself. She was sure that she would hold by her purpose, and yet she feared that her purpose was wrong. She had refused the man when she was rich, and her pride would not let her go to him now that she was poor. She was sure of her purpose,—but yet she almost knew that her pride was wrong.

But now there would be a triumph. Her eyes gleamed brightly as she thought of the way in which she would achieve her triumph. Her eyes gleamed very brightly as she felt sure within her own bosom that she would succeed. Yes: he would, no doubt, have some stupid notion, as her father said. But she would overcome his stupidity. She, as a woman, could be stronger than he as a man. He had almost ridiculed her obstinacy, swearing that he would certainly overcome it. There should be no ridicule on her part, but she would certainly overcome his obstinacy.

For a day or two Mr. Owen was not seen. She heard from her father that the tidings had been told to her lover, but she heard no more. Mr. Owen did not show himself at the house; and she, indeed, hardly expected that he should do so. Her stepmother suddenly became gracious, —having no difficulty in explaining that she did so because of the altered position of things.

'My dearest Isabel, it does make such a difference!' she said; 'you will be a rich lady, and will never have to think about the price of shoes.' The sisters were equally plain-spoken, and were almost awe-struck in their admiration.

Three or four days after the return of Mr.

Brodrick, Isabel took her bonnet and shawl, and walked away all alone to Mr. Owen's lodgings. She knew his habits, and was aware that he was generally to be found at home for an hour before his dinner. It was no time, she said to herself, to stand upon little punctilios. There had been too much between them to let there be any question of a girl going after her lover. She was going after her lover, and she didn't care who knew it. Nevertheless, there was a blush beneath her veil as she asked at the door whether Mr. Owen was at home. Mr. Owen was at home, and she was shown at once into his parlour.

'William,' she said;—throughout their intimacy she had never called him William before;—'you have heard my news?'

'Yes,' he said, 'I have heard it;'—very seriously, with none of that provoking smile with which he had hitherto responded to all her assertions.

'And you have not come to congratulate me?'

'I should have done so. I do own that I have been wrong.'

'Wrong;—very wrong! How was I to have any of the enjoyment of my restored rights unless you came to enjoy them with me?'

'They can be nothing to me, Isabel.'

'They shall be everything to you, sir.'

'No, my dear.'

'They are to be everything to me, and they can be nothing to me without you. You know that, I suppose?' Then she waited for his reply.

'You know that, do you not? You know what I feel about that, I say. Why do you not tell me? Have you any doubt?'

'Things have been unkind to us, Isabel, and have separated us.'

'Nothing shall separate us.' Then she paused for a moment. She had thought of it all, and now had to pause before she could execute her purpose. She had got her plan ready, but it required some courage, some steadying of herself to the work before she could do it. Then she came close to him,—close up to him, looking into his face as he stood over her, not moving his feet, but almost retreating with his body from her close presence. 'William,' she said, 'take me in your arms and kiss me. How often have you asked me during the last month! Now I have come for it.'

He paused a moment as though it were possible to refuse, as though his collected thoughts and settled courage might enable him so to outrage her in her petition. Then he broke down, and took her in his arms, and pressed her to his bosom, and kissed her lips, and her forehead, and her cheeks,—while she, having once achieved her purpose, attempted in vain to escape from his long embrace.

'Now I shall be your wife,' she said at last, when her breath had returned to her.

'It should not be so.'

'Not after that? Will you dare to say so to

me,—after that? You could never hold up your head again. Say that you are happy. Tell me that you are happy. Do you think that I can be happy unless you are happy with me?' Of course he gave her all the assurances that were needed, and made it quite unnecessary that she should renew her prayer.

'And I beg, Mr. Owen, that for the future you will come to me, and not make me come to you.' This she said as she was taking her leave. 'It was very disagreeable, and very wrong, and will be talked about ever so much. Nothing but my determination to have my own way could have made me do it.' Of course he promised her that there should be no occasion for her again to put herself to the same inconvenience.

CHAPTER XXIV

CONCLUSION

ISABEL spent one pleasant week with her lover at Hereford, and then was summoned into Carmarthenshire. Mr. Apjohn came over at her father's invitation, and insisted on taking her back to Llanfeare.

'There are a thousand things to be done,' he said, 'and the sooner you begin to do them the better. Of course you must live at the old house, and you had better take up your habitation there

for a while before this other change is made.'
The other change was of course the coming
marriage, with the circumstances of which the
lawyer had been made acquainted.

Then there arose other questions. Should her
father go with her or should her lover? It was,
however, at last decided that she should go alone
as regarded her family, but under the care of Mr.
Apjohn. It was she who had been known in the
house, and she who had better now be seen there
as her uncle's representative.

'You will have to be called Miss Jones,' said
the lawyer, 'Miss Indefer Jones. There will be
a form, for which we shall have to pay, I am
afraid; but we had better take the name at once.
You will have to undergo a variety of changes
in signing your name. You will become first
Miss Isabel Brodrick Indefer Jones, then Mrs.
William Owen, then, when he shall have gone
through the proper changes, Mrs. William Owen
Indefer Jones. As such I hope you may remain
till you shall be known as the oldest inhabitant
of Carmarthenshire.'

Mr. Apjohn took her to Carmarthen, and
hence on to Llanfeare. At the station there
were many to meet her, so that her triumph, as
she got into the carriage, was almost painful to
her. When she heard the bells ring from the
towers of the parish churches, she could hardly
believe that the peals were intended to welcome
her back to her old home. She was taken some-

what out of her way round by the creek and Coed, so that the little tinkling of her own parish church might not be lost upon her. If this return of hers to the estate was so important to others as to justify these signs, what must it be to her and how deep must be the convictions as to her own duties?

At the gate of Coed farmyard the carriage stopped, and the old farmer came out to say a few words to her.

'God bless you, Miss Isabel; this is a happy sight to see.'

'That is so kind of you, Mr. Griffith.'

'We've had a bad time of it, Miss Isabel;—not that we wished to quarrel with your dear uncle's judgment, or that we had a right to say much against the poor gentleman who has gone;—but we expected you, and it went against the grain with us to have our expectations disappointed. We shall always look up to you, miss; but, at the same time, I wish you joy with all my heart of the new landlord you're going to set over us. Of course that was to be expected, but you'll be here with us all the time.' Isabel, while the tears ran down her cheeks, could only press the old man's hand at parting.

'Now, my dear,' said Mr. Apjohn, as they went on to the house, 'he has only said just what we've all been feeling. Of course it has been stronger with the tenants and servants than with others. But all round the country it has been the same. A man, if an estate belong to himself personally, can do what he likes with it, as he can with the half-crowns in his pocket; but where land is concerned, feelings grow up which should not be treated rudely. In one sense Llanfeare belonged to your uncle to do what he liked with it, but in another sense he shared it only with those around him; and when he was induced by a theory which he did not himself quite understand to bring your cousin Henry down among these people, he outraged their best convictions.'

'He meant to do his duty, Mr. Apjohn.'

'Certainly; but he mistook it. He did not understand the root of that idea of a male heir. The object has been to keep the old family, and the old adherences, and the old acres together. England owes much to the manner in which this has been done, and the custom as to a male heir has availed much in the doing of it. But in this case, in sticking to the custom, he would have lost the spirit, and, as far as he was concerned, would have gone against the practice which he wished to perpetuate. There, my dear, is a sermon for you, of which, I dare say, you do not understand a word.'

'I understand every syllable of it, Mr. Apjohn,' she answered.

They soon arrived at the house, and there they found not only Mrs. Griffith and the old cook, who had never left the premises, but the old butler also, who had taken himself off in disgust at Cousin Henry's character, but had now returned as though there had been no break in his continuous service. They received her with triumphant clamours of welcome. To them the coming of Cousin Henry, and the death of the old Squire, and then the departure of their young mistress, had been as though the whole world had come to an end for them. To serve was their only ambition,—to serve and to be made comfortable while they were serving; but to serve Cousin Henry was to them altogether ignominious. The old Squire had done something which, though they acknowledged it to be no worse on his part than a mistake, had to them been cruelly severe. Suddenly to be told that they were servants to such a one as Cousin Henry, —servants to such a man without any contract or agreement on their part;—to be handed over like the chairs and tables to a disreputable clerk from London, whom in their hearts they regarded as very much inferior to themselves! And they, too, like Mr. Griffith and the tenants, had been taught to look for the future reign of Queen Isabel as a thing of course. In that there would have been an implied contract,—an understanding on their part that they had been consulted and had agreed to this destination of themselves. But Cousin Henry! Now this gross evil to themselves and to all around them had been remedied, and justice was done. They had all been strongly convinced that the Squire had made and had left behind him another will. The butler had been quite certain that this had been destroyed by Cousin Henry, and had sworn that he would not stand behind the chair of a felon. The gardener had been equally violent, and· had declined even to cut a cabbage for Cousin Henry's use. The women in the house had only suspected. They had felt sure that something was wrong, but had doubted between various theories. But now everything was right; now the proper owner had come; now the great troubles had been vanquished, and Llanfeare would once again be a fitting home for them.

'Oh, Miss Isabel! oh, Miss Isabel!' said Mrs. Griffith, absolutely sobbing at her young mistress's feet up in her bed-room; 'I did say that it could never go on like that. I did use to think that the Lord Almighty would never let it go on like that! It couldn't be that Mr. Henry Jones was to remain always landlord of Llanfeare.'

When she came downstairs and took her seat, as she did by chance, in the old arm-chair which her uncle had been used to occupy, Mr. Apjohn preached to her another sermon, or rather sang a loud pæan of irrepressible delight.

'Now, my dear, I must go and leave you,— happily in your own house. You can hardly realize how great a joy this has been to me,— how great a joy it is.'

'I know well how much we owe to you.'

'From the first moment in which he intimated

to me his wish to make a change in his will, I became so unhappy about it as almost to lose my rest. I knew that I went beyond what I ought to have done in the things that I said to him, and he bore it kindly.'

'He was always kind.'

'But I couldn't turn him. I told him what I told you to-day on the road, but it had no effect on him. Well, I had nothing to do but to obey his orders. This I did most grudgingly. It was a heart-break to me, not only because of you, my dear, but for the sake of the property, and because I had heard something of your cousin. Then came the rumour of this last will. He must have set about it as soon as you had left the house.'

'He never told me that he was going to do it.'

'He never told any one; that is quite certain. But it shows how his mind must have been at work. Perhaps what I said may have had some effect at last. Then I heard from the Cantors what they had been asked to do. I need not tell you all that I felt then. It would have been better for him to send for me.'

'Oh, yes.'

'So much better for that poor young man's sake.' The poor young man was of course Cousin Henry. 'But I could not interfere. I could only hear what I did hear,—and wait. Then the dear old man died!'

'I knew then that he had made it.'

'You knew that he had thought that he had done it; but how is one to be sure of the vacillating mind of an old dying man? When we searched for the one will and read the other, I was very sure that the Cantors had been called upon to witness his signature. Who could doubt as to that? But he who had so privately drawn out the deed might as privately destroy it. By degrees there grew upon me the conviction that he had not destroyed it; that it still existed,—or that your cousin had destroyed it. The latter I never quite believed. He was not the man to do it,— neither brave enough nor bad enough.'

'I think not bad enough.'

'Too small in his way altogether. And yet it was clear as the sun at noonday that he was troubled in his conscience. He shut himself up in his misery, not knowing how strong a tale his own unhappiness told against him. Why did he not rejoice in the glory of his position? Then I said to myself that he was conscious of insecurity.'

'His condition must have been pitiable.'

'Indeed, yes. I pitied him from the bottom of my heart. The contumely with which he was treated by all went to my heart even after I knew that he was misbehaving. I knew that he was misbehaving;—but how? It could only be by hiding the will, or by being conscious that it was hidden. Though he was a knave, he was not cunning. He failed utterly before the slightest cunning on the part of others. When I asked him whether he knew where it was hidden, he told a weak lie, but told the truth openly by the look of his eyes. He was like a little girl who pauses and blushes and confesses all the truth before she half murmurs her naughty fib. Who can be really angry with the child who lies after that unwilling fashion? I had to be severe upon him till all was made clear; but I pitied him from the bottom of my heart.'

'You have been good to all of us.'

'At last it became clear to me that your uncle had put it somewhere himself. Then came a chance remembrance of the sermons he used to read, and by degrees the hiding-place was suggested to me. When at last he welcomed us to go and search in his uncle's bed-room, but forbade us to touch anything in the book-room,— then I was convinced. I had but to look along the shelves till I found the set, and I almost knew that we had got the prize. Your father has told you how he flew at me when I attempted to lift my hand to the books. The agony of the last chance gave him a moment of courage. Then your father shook the document out from among the leaves.'

'That must have been a moment of triumph to you.'

'Yes;—it was. I did feel a little proud of my success. And I am proud as I see you sitting there, and feel that justice has been done.'

'By your means!'

'That justice has been done, and that every one has his own again. I own to all the litigious pugnacity of a lawyer. I live by such fighting, and I like it. But a case in which I do not believe crushes me. To have an injustice to get the better of, and then to trample it well under foot,—that is the triumph that I desire. It does not often happen to a lawyer to have had such a chance as this, and I fancy that it could not have come in the way of a man who would have enjoyed it more than I do.' Then at last, after lingering about the house, he bade her farewell. 'God bless you, and make you happy here,—you and your husband. If you will take my advice you will entail the property. You, no doubt, will have children, and will take care that in due course it shall go to the eldest boy. There can be no doubt as to the wisdom of that. But you see what terrible misery may be occasioned by not allowing those who are to come after you to know what it is they are to expect.'

For a few weeks Isabel remained alone at Llanfeare, during which all the tenants came to call upon her, as did many of the neighbouring gentry.

'I know'd it,' said young Cantor, clenching his fist almost in her face. 'I was that sure of it I couldn't hardly hold myself. To think of his leaving it in a book of sermons!'

Then, after the days were past during which

it was thought well that she should remain at Llanfeare to give orders, and sign papers, and make herself by very contact with her own property its mistress and owner, her father came for her and took her back to Hereford. Then she had incumbent upon her the other duty of surrendering herself and all that she possessed to another. As any little interest which this tale may possess has come rather from the heroine's material interests than from her love,—as it has not been, so to say, a love story,—the reader need not follow the happy pair absolutely to the altar. But it may be said, in anticipation of the future, that in due time an eldest son was born, that Llanfeare was entailed upon him and his son, and that he was so christened as to have his somewhat grandiloquent name inscribed as William Apjohn Owen Indefer Jones.

THE END

EXPLANATORY NOTES

1 '*I have a conscience, my dear, on this matter,*': Trollope rarely begins a chapter, let alone a novel, *in medias res*; in both *The Duke's Children* (Ch. IX) and the opening pages of *Is He Popenjoy?* (quoted here) he discusses the pitfalls of the method:

The plan of jumping at once into the middle has been often tried, and sometimes seductively enough for a chapter or two; but the writer still has to hark back, and to begin again from the beginning—not always very comfortably after the abnormal brightness of his few opening pages; and the reader who is then involved in some ancient family history, or long local explanation, feels himself to have been defrauded. (*Is He Popenjoy?*, World's Classics, pp. 1–2)

Presumably Trollope felt the narrative of Cousin Henry sufficiently compact to avoid excessive backtracking.

4 *as though the old place were entailed*: Trollope's contemporary readership would take such a brief reference to an entail as referring to some variant of a 'strict settlement'. The Llanfeare estate was probably settled when the father of the current Indefer Jones was married, in consultation with his own father, who then possessed the estate in fee simple. Under this settlement, the grandfather retained for himself a life estate; Indefer Jones's father got a life estate 'in remainder'—to take effect in possession upon his grandfather's death; a fee tail in remainder was created, so as to vest

in the eldest male child of the father by his new bride. The present Indefer Jones is that person, and if this settlement were still in force, which it is not, the estate could only go from him to the next in a sequence of named persons, in effect the eldest surviving legitimate male child of his eldest brother with issue, who is his nephew Henry Jones. Uncle Indefer, like Henry Jones a habitual vacillator, would thus be freed from the responsibility of making up his mind as to who should be his heir.

7 *the entail had not been carried on*: entails could be 'barred', that is, prematurely ended. The only person who could do this was the tenant in tail, in this case Indefer Jones himself. It was usual for this to be done by agreement between the life tenant and the tenant in tail, who would usually be father and son, the initiative, as in this case, often coming from the father. The purpose of barring the entail in this way was to enable father and son to deal more freely with the land. In this case Indefer Jones assisted his father to sell off part of the estate to finance the father's extravagant lifestyle, and the acres thus lost had only recently been repurchased (see p. 10). After the Settled Land Act of 1882 there was less need to bar entails in this way, as tenants in tail were thus enabled to sell the land, free from interests arising under the settlement. On such a sale the purchase money replaced the land as the subject of the settlement, but the ancestral link with the land ended. In Trollope's novel *Ralph the Heir* (1871), Ralph Newton, the legitimate heir to the estate of Newton Priory, attempts to sell the

reversion of his interest in the estate to his uncle, the current squire, thus circumventing the entail. The old squire is killed in a hunting accident, however, before the transaction can be completed. (I am indebted to Mr Stuart Anderson of Hertford College, Oxford, for assistance with this note and the previous one.)

8 *sent away from Oxford for some offence not altogether trivial*: Trollope focuses so thoroughly on Cousin Henry's predicament at Llanfeare that the hints given here about his escapades at University, and the suggestions of Metropolitan dissipation on pp. 233–4, are not really capitalized upon dramatically. It is left for the reader to judge whether so craven a man as Cousin Henry could really have contrived to get himself sent down from Oxford, or would dare to 'run after his neighbour's wife if she came in his path' (p. 234).

9 *It was a religion to him that a landed estate in Britain should go from father to eldest son*: other characters in Trollope who adhere to the same religion of 'heirland' include such rural conservatives as the Thornes of the Barchester Novels, Roger Carbury in *The Way We Live Now*, and the Whartons of *The Prime Minister*. All, like Indefer Jones, are presented sympathetically but not uncritically. Trollope's interest in the vagaries of wills and the precariousness of inheritance under the law of primogeniture will be familiar to readers of *Orley Farm* (1862), *Ralph the Heir* (1871), *Is He Popenjoy?* (1878), and *Mr Scarborough's Family* (1883). It may have had a particular cause: Trollope's brother Tom was at first brought up as heir to the family

estate, only to be disappointed when the great-
uncle in possession of it married and had a son in
comparative old age.

12 *'I have put a charge on the estate for four thousand
pounds'*: in the event, Indefer Jones leaves the four
thousand pounds 'as a sum of money, and not as
a charge on the property' (p. 62). On the first
morning of composition of the novel Trollope
wrote to his barrister friend Charles Hall (an
authority on real property law), asking for an
'opinion' on this matter: 'If A. leave to B. by will
an estate X; and also leave to C a sum of £1,000,
will C be able to get out of X his legacy, if on A's
death there be no other property beside or beyond
the estate X?' (N. John Hall, ed., *The Letters of
Anthony Trollope*, ii. 799).

13 *a weekly copy of the Guardian*: The *Guardian* referred
to was a weekly newspaper founded in 1846 by
young Tractarians such as Church and Rogers, as
an organ for 'intelligent and moderate' High
Churchmen. Owen Chadwick in *The Victorian
Church* notes its generous and scholarly reception
of the theories of Darwin, and judges it 'the most
intelligent weekly' among the Victorian churches
(ii. 125) and 'among the best of the weeklies for
intelligent men' (ii. 426).

14 *some half-dozen worn-out old labourers . . . no return
from the land was ever forthcoming*: agrarian
historians continue to debate the nature and
extent of the 'Great Depression' that struck rural
Britain in the 1870s and 1880s, Trollope also
depicts the sympathetic landlord protecting the
livelihood of farmworkers on land that cannot

possible pay in *The Prime Minister*, Ch. XVI, where Sir Alured Wharton farms a few acres to keep the 'older people' in work.

17 *a minor canon attached to the cathedral*: a minor canon is an Anglican clergyman attached to a cathedral, who assists in performing the daily service but is not a member of the chapter. Despite his 'moderate professional income' of £250 a year, as an official at Hereford, Owen carries sufficient social kudos to attract the attention of a girl like Isabel, who thinks much of rank.

19 *'his grandfather kept the inn at Pembroke!'*: compare Owen's lowly birth with the 'very humble origin' of the Dean of Brotherton in *Is He Popenjoy?* Trollope frequently points out in his fiction and non-fiction that the backgrounds of even relatively senior clergy are less distinguished than was once the case. In 'The Parson of the Parish' in *Clergymen of the Church of England* he declares that the typical product of the new theological colleges is 'a man less attractive, less urbane, less genial—in one significant word, less of a gentleman' than were his clerical forebears.

23 *a sea of troubles*: *Hamlet* III. i. 59.

24 *Chapter Three: Cousin Henry*: Trollope's working diary for the novel (now kept in the Bodleian Library, Oxford) shows that this chapter was originally entitled 'I Do Not Love You in the Least'.

28 *of the world worldly*: cf. 1 Corinthians 15: 47.

45 *In the course of the afternoon she did leave Hereford, and at about ten o'clock that night she was at Carmarthen*:

Trollope has obviously consulted his Bradshaw with some care. The 1880 summer timetable shows two possibilities for Isabel's journey. She could have left Barrs Court station at Hereford on the Great Western Railway train that had a through carriage or carriages to Swansea, leaving Hereford at 16.00 hours (to use present-day nomenclature). This went via Hirwaun, and she would have needed to change at Landore, just outside Swansea. The train arrived there at approximately 20.25, and the onward train left at 20.30, arriving at Carmarthen at 21.55. The whole route, with the exception of a short length of line just south of Hereford, was over the Great Western Railway. Alternatively, she could have taken a Midland Railway train from Barton station in Hereford, leaving at 15.40, which would have taken her to St. Thomas's station in Swansea, where she would have arrived at 19.40. From St. Thomas's it is not a very long walk to Swansea High Street station, where she could have caught the train out at 20.15 to Landore to pick up the 20.30 departure for Carmarthen. I am indebted to Mr John Edgington and Mr P. W. B. Semmens of the National Railway Museum, York, for this information.

a fly ready to take her to Llanfeare: a 'fly' was the name given to a one-horse covered carriage let out on hire from a livery stable rather than hailed in the street (*OED*).

77 *a volume of Jeremy Taylor's works*: Trollope has carefully selected vol. iv of Taylor's *Works* (see p. 246) as the book especially close to the old

squire's heart. As Robert Tracy has pointed out:

When we turn to Bishop Heber's edition of 1822 [of Jeremy Taylor's *Works*] (reissued 1847–54), the only edition available at the time Trollope was writing, we find in Volume IV a course of sermons written at Golden Grove, in Carmarthenshire, only a few miles from the imaginary estate of Llanfeare, and from its book room where Henry broods for so long. (*Trollope's Later Novels*, p. 258)

99 *a sword of Damocles*: Damocles was a member of the court of Dionysius I, tyrant of Syracuse. According to Cicero, Dionysius invited him to eat his dinner with a sword suspended by a hair over his head, to illustrate the tyrant's life of luxury at the cost of insecurity. 'A sword of Damocles' became proverbial (Betty Radice, *Who's Who in the Ancient World*).

103 *There is a pleasant game . . . till one is enabled to touch it*: Trollope is probably thinking of the parlour game variously entitled 'Animal, Vegetable, or Mineral' or 'Yes and No'. Trollope's prowess at parlour games is not recorded, but Dickens' zest for them is well known (see Edgar Johnson, *Charles Dickens: His Tragedy and Triumph* (revised ed., Penguin, 1977), p. 192, etc.), and a game similar to the one Trollope describes forms the climax of Scrooge's visit to his nephew's Christmas party in *A Christmas Carol* (1843), Stave Three.

123 *Philistine*: the word was frequently applied in Victorian times to persons regarded as the enemy, after the Biblical Philistines who continually harassed the Israelites. The more usual modern

sense of 'without liberal culture or enlightenment' (*OED*) is not present here; cf. p. 241.

135 *She was standing about six feet from him*: Trollope seems unnecessarily precise in giving the distance between Isabel Brodrick and her lover in this scene. Yet, as Stephen Wall has pointed out, such precision is usually an indication that his imagination is fully involved, and that he is visualizing events in considerable detail as he writes them down. See Wall's discussion of the scene in *Can You Forgive Her?* (Ch. L) in which Palliser confesses his love to Lady Glencora:

> Not only is it intensely dramatised . . . but the registration of gesture is extremely attentive. When Glencora goes up to Palliser and takes him by the coat, he, being much taller, looks down on her and 'very gradually, *as though he were afraid of what he was doing*, he put his arm round her waist'; she shakes her head, '*touching his breast with her hair as she did so.*' These physical tentativenesses are not only, in their context, deeply touching: they mark the real beginning of the Palliser marriage, whose superficial instability but essential durability is studied further in the later Palliser novels. (Stephen Wall, Introduction to *Can You Forgive Her?* (Penguin English Library, 1972), 21).

136 *The Prayer-Book tells the young wife that she should love her husband till death shall part them*: the well-known form of words from 'The Form of Solemnization of Matrimony' in the 1662 Anglican *Book of Common Prayer*, where the bride promises 'to love, cherish, and to obey' her husband 'till death us do part, according to God's holy ordinance'.

142 *The Carmarthen Herald*: compare Trollope's

treatment of the local press in *Miss Mackenzie*, when the curate Mr Maguire, disappointed in his suit for the hand of the heroine, inserts in a respectable evangelical newspaper a series of dark hints as to the influence of her family. The gutter pressman Quintus Slide's persecution of Phineas Finn in *Phineas Finn* and *Phineas Redux* is not strictly comparable, as *The People's Banner*, Slide's newspaper, could hardly be said to bear a 'high character'.

148 *incubus on his bosom*: originally an evil spirit seeking sexual intercourse with women in their sleep, it has come to refer to a person or thing that weighs upon or oppresses like a nightmare (*OED*).

191 *the mildness of his behaviour and an accurate knowledge of law, —two gifts hardly of much value to an advocate in an assize town*: Trollope suggests that the talents of Mr Balsam's adversary, 'Supercilious Jack' Cheekey, who 'browbeats' his witnesses with the finesse of a sportsman, are more likely to tell with a Carmarthen jury. Trollope had criticized the class of barrister to which Cheekey belongs in the satirical portrait of Mr Allewinde in his first novel, *The Macdermots of Ballycloran* (1847), and even more outspokenly in his overview of mid-Victorian society, *The New Zealander* (1856). Trollope's strongest objection to the British barrister was of the often brutal way in which he handled his witnesses. In *The Three Clerks* he shows Mr Chaffanbrass 'getting to work' on a bank-clerk who has simply come to bear witness to a transaction formally recorded in the bank-book:

To one clerk it was suggested that he might now and then, once in three months or so, make an error in a figure; and, having acknowledged this, he was driven about until he admitted that it was very possible that every entry he made in the bank books in the course of the year was false. (*The Three Clerks*, Ch. XL)

Cousin Henry obviously fears that a similar catechism, repeated many times over, awaits him at Carmarthen. Apart from Chaffanbrass, who appears in *The Three Clerks* (1858), *Orley Farm* (1862), and *Phineas Redux* (1874), and Cheekey, similar barristers in Trollope's works include the London advocate at Scrobby's trial in *The American Senator* (Ch. XV) who runs rings around the provincial bench; the barrister who deals with Lizzie Eustace when she is called as a witness in *The Eustace Diamonds* (Ch. LXXIV); and, most sharply treated of all, the ambitious and materialistic Sir Henry Harcourt, whose mercurial career in *The Bertrams* ends in financial ruin and suicide.

192 *the Old Bailey*: in early and mid-Victorian times the Old Bailey barrister in particular was noted for his disrespect for truth and unsavoury intimidation of witnesses. See Raymond Cocks, *Foundations of the Modern Bar* (London: Sweet and Maxwell, 1983), 21–2, who quotes the *Law Times* in 1844: 'Practices unrecognised by the Bar have existed and do exist to a great extent at the Old Bailey'. 'The world also knows, and long has known, that "An Old Bailey Practitioner" is a byword for disgrace and infamy.' Old Bailey advocates putting themselves forward for admis-

sion to London clubs were invariably blackballed (see J. R. Lewis, *The Victorian Bar* (London: Robert Hale, 1982), 241). Trollope created the literary embodiment of the type in Mr Chaffanbrass. By 1874, however, when *Phineas Redux*, the last novel featuring Mr Chaffanbrass, appeared, the days of the advocate of his type were numbered, and Mr Cheekey, a younger man, is sketched as a somewhat milder figure.

202 *auto-da-fé*: Portuguese phrase meaning 'act of (the) faith' and referring to the execution of a sentence of the Inquisition, especially judicial torture or the burning to death of a heretic.